Hillary Potter has produced a groundbreaking volume that synthesizes, complicates, and thrusts forward research in intersectional criminology. Race, class, gender, sexuality, and other social forces are decompartmentalized in order to gain a systematic understanding of crime, criminalization, the law, in/justice, and the research process. The discipline of Criminology has long marginalized intersectional approaches to research. This volume places intersectional research at front and center, establishing it as a key paradigm in the discipline and beyond; a must-read for every student trained in criminology.

Victor M. Rios, *Department of Sociology, University of California Santa Barbara, USA*

Hillary Potter makes a reflective, cogent, and compelling case for the value – in fact, necessity – of an interdisciplinary approach across criminology. An important read.

Katheryn Russell-Brown, *Chesterfield Smith Professor of Law, and Director, Center for the Study of Race and Race Relations, University of Florida, USA*

Potter has made a critically important contribution to feminist criminology and critical race theory. *Intersectionality and Criminology* fills a major gap in the literature and will leave readers better prepared to take up the issues of racism, gender oppression, class exploitation, transphobia, and other manifestations of structural inequality in our study of crime and work for justice.

Beth E. Richie, *Professor, University of Illinois at Chicago, USA*

INTERSECTIONALITY AND CRIMINOLOGY

The use of intersectionality theory in the social sciences has proliferated in the past several years, putting forward the argument that the interconnected identities of individuals, and the way these identities are perceived and responded to by others, must be a necessary part of any analysis. Fundamentally, intersectionality claims that not only are people's lived experiences affected by their racial identity and by their gender identity, but these identities, and others, continually operate together and affect each other.

With "official" statistical data that indicate people of Color have higher offending and victimization rates than White people, and with the overrepresentation of men and people of Color in the criminal legal system, new theories are required that address these phenomena and that are devoid of stereotypical or debasing underpinnings.

Intersectionality and Criminology provides a comprehensive review of the need for, and use of, intersectionality in the study of crime, criminality, and the criminal legal system. This is essential reading for academics and students researching and studying in the fields of crime, criminal justice, theoretical criminology, and gender, race, and socioeconomic class.

Hillary Potter is Associate Professor of Ethnic Studies at the University of Colorado at Boulder. She holds a B.A. and a Ph.D. in sociology from the University of Colorado at Boulder and an M.A. in criminal justice from the John Jay College of Criminal Justice, New York. Dr. Potter's research has focused on the intersections of race, gender, and class as they relate to crime and violence, and she is currently researching Black women's use of violence in response to abusive intimate partners; men's use of violence; and antiviolence activism in Black and Latina/o communities. Dr. Potter is the author of *Battle Cries: Black Women and Intimate Partner Abuse* (2008) and the editor of *Racing the Storm: Racial Implications and Lessons Learned from Hurricane Katrina* (2007).

New Directions in Critical Criminology
Edited by Walter S. DeKeseredy,
West Virginia University, USA

This series presents new cutting-edge critical criminological empirical, theoretical, and policy work on a broad range of social problems, including drug policy, rural crime and social control, policing and the media, ecocide, intersectionality, and the gendered nature of crime. It aims to highlight the most up-to-date authoritative essays written by new and established scholars in the field. Rather than offering a survey of the literature, each book takes a strong position on topics of major concern to those interested in seeking new ways of thinking critically about crime.

1. **Contemporary Drug Policy**
   Henry Brownstein
2. **The Treadmill of Crime**
   Political economy and green criminology
   Paul B. Stretesky, Michael A. Long and Michael J. Lynch
3. **Rural Criminology**
   Walter S. DeKeseredy and Joseph F. Donnermeyer
4. **Policing and Media**
   Public relations, simulations and communications
   Murray Lee and Alyce McGovern
5. **Green Cultural Criminology**
   Constructions of environmental harm, consumerism and resistance to ecocide
   Avi Brisman and Nigel South
6. **Crimes of Globalization**
   Dawn L. Rothe and David O. Friedrichs
7. **Contradictions of Terrorism**
   Security, risk and resilience
   Sandra Walklate and Gabe Mythen

8. **Feminism and Global Justice**
   Kerry Carrington
9. **Power and Crime**
   Vincenzo Ruggiero
10. **Youth Street Gangs**
    A critical appraisal
    David C. Brotherton
11. **Revitalizing Criminological Theory**
    Towards a new ultra-realism
    Steve Hall and Simon Winlow
12. **Intersectionality and Criminology**
    Disrupting and revolutionizing studies of crime
    Hillary Potter

INTERSECTIONALITY AND CRIMINOLOGY

Disrupting and revolutionizing studies of crime

Hillary Potter

LONDON AND NEW YORK

First published 2015
by Routledge
2 Park Square, Milton Park, Abingdon, Oxon, OX14 4RN

and by Routledge
711 Third Avenue, New York, NY 10017

Routledge is an imprint of the Taylor & Francis Group, an informa business

British Library Cataloguing in Publication Data
A catalogue record for this book is available from the British Library

Library of Congress Cataloguing in Publication data
Potter, Hillary, 1969–
Intersectionality and criminology : disrupting and revolutionizing studies of crime / Hillary Potter.
pages cm. – (New directions in criminology ; 12)
1. Criminology–Study and teaching. 2. Crime–Sociological aspects. I. Title.
HV6024.P68 2015
364.01–dc23 2014042677

ISBN: 978-0-415-63439-7 (hbk)
ISBN: 978-0-415-63440-3 (pbk)
ISBN: 978-0-203-09449-5 (ebk)

Typeset in Bembo
by Out of House Publishing

MIX
Paper from responsible sources
FSC® C013604

Printed and bound in Great Britain by
CPI Group (UK) Ltd, Croydon, CR0 4YY

I dedicate this book to two of the fiercest and most fearless criminologists in the game, Joanne Belknap and Ruth Peterson

CONTENTS

ACKNOWLEDGMENTS

My journey to completing this book has not been an easy one. I was faced with personal and professional dilemmas that continually interrupted my mental and temporal ability to complete this piece. While this book does not serve as the definitive or ultimate treatise on intersectionality within the field of criminology, the tribulations I endured during the composition of the book proved to be good fodder for my conceptualization of intersectional criminology.

I am especially grateful to Walt DeKeseredy (Routledge series editor for New Directions in Critical Criminology) and Tom Sutton (Routledge commissioning editor) for identifying me as a scholar who could write a book on a gendered approach to race and crime. *Walt* and *Tom*, thank you for providing me with a space to have my say. I also thank the *anonymous reviewers* of the proposal for this book – your insights aided me in better organizing my thoughts on the subject. Routledge editorial assistant Heidi Lee receives a very special acknowledgment. Without a doubt, I tested Heidi's patience throughout this entire process with my multiple delays and those periods when I "disappeared." *Heidi*, I owe you much gratitude for putting up with me. Thank you!

I am grateful for the support I have received from folks at my academic post, the University of Colorado at Boulder. In particular, I thank the members of my new unit, the Department of Ethnic

Studies. Department chair, Daryl Maeda, was there when I landed on his doorstep seeking refuge in a healthy, non-toxic environment – something we *all* deserve. *Daryl*, thank you for "having my back" and for your leadership and your support in my research, teaching, and service endeavors. In addition, *Dean Stephen Leigh* and *Associate Dean Ann Carlos*, thank you for supporting this request to switch departments – my days as an academic would have been numbered but for your attentiveness and swiftness to my relocation.

While writing this book, I continued with teaching my classes and serving on thesis and dissertation committees. I was inspired by some of these students, as well as by a few others I have met through other avenues in recent years – some of whom have since completed their doctoral education. I was motivated by their eagerness for knowledge, their talents in producing knowledge, and their tenacity when faced with a variety of undertakings and challenges. I witnessed them do great things and, simply, *being* great individuals. Thank you, *Nishaun Battle, CheyOnna Sewell, Jason Williams, Erin Kerrison, Vanessa Roberts, Kenly Brown, Cassy Gonzalez, Patrina Duhaney, Deanne Grant, Jenn Roark, Beth Whalley*!

My parents, other family members, and friends remain my system of support and my sources of inspiration to press on with my work. They have continued to supply me the nourishment I need to balance my research, writing, teaching, academic service work, community service work, and activist activities. Over the course of 14 years, Joanne Belknap has moved from being my advisor/mentor to friendtor to friend for life. *Jo*, I thank you for your commitment to students and victims of crime, and for "taking a bullet" for all of us.

1

DISRUPTING CRIMINOLOGY

The need to integrate intersectionality into criminological research and theory

Black feminist[1] legal scholar Kimberlé Crenshaw is acknowledged as originating the term *intersectionality*. Crenshaw has indicated that her conceptualization of intersectionality is based in Black feminist theory and critical race theory. Critical race theory, developed by legal scholars, lawyers, and activists, was built on critical legal studies and "radical feminism" and maintains that race is socially constructed, racism is ordinary in society and cannot be easily resolved with law, and that the legal system privileges some races over others (Delgado and Stefancic 2012). Critical race theory also promotes a "voice-of-Color thesis," which maintains that because of their experiences of oppression, people of Color "may be able to communicate to their white counterparts matters that the whites are unlikely to know" and encourages "black and brown writers to recount their experiences with racism and the legal system and to apply their own unique perspectives to assess law's master narratives" (Delgado and Stefancic 2012:10). Similar doctrine is found in Black feminist theory, which preceded critical race theory. In Crenshaw's (1991) article "Mapping the Margins: Intersectionality, Identity, Politics, and Violence Against Women of Color," she specified that she unequivocally utilized a Black feminist perspective in her appraisal of violence experienced by women of Color. Black feminist theory is the theoretical perspective that places the lived experiences, including any forms of resistance to their situations, of Black women at the center of the analysis, considering her as an individual encompassing numerous and interwoven identities including, but not limited to, race, ethnicity, gender, sexuality, nationality, and socioeconomic class. The standpoint is that Black women are typically oppressed within both the Black community and society-at-large based on subordinated statuses within each of these areas of classification, and that research on Black women should be conducted based on this perspective. But *all* women of Color fit within this definition; for instance, feminist theorizing and activism engaged in by and about Latina and Indigenous women unveils intersectional views like those proffered by Black feminists. While there may be some variations in the foci among the groups of women of Color feminists, their subordination by race, ethnicity, sex, and gender yields a shared philosophy. The enduring effects of colonialism, patriarchy, racism and gendered racism, and sexism or genderism are clearly evident among women of Color feminisms and activism. Although Black feminists have produced the greatest amount of published works and are, arguably, the most visible among feminists of Color in the United States, the long overdue recognition of the work of Asian, Indigenous (North America), and Latina feminists is now occurring to a greater extent, and other feminisms are emerging, such as Arab and Arab American feminism (Jarmakani 2011; Naber 2006).

Thus, contrary to indications by some scholars and academic references that an intersectional ideology only surfaced three to four decades ago, the *conceptual foundations* of intersectionality had been in development long before Crenshaw's seminal articles. Intersectionality was particularized in Crenshaw's articles and, essentially, was a retooling and special application of Black feminist thought and critical race theory. Consequently, to understand intersectionality, it is important to understand on what it is based. In Chapter 2, I trace the history and development of activism and theory by Black women feminists and other women of Color feminists before describing what intersectionality is and what it does and its use (or potential use) by academics. In Chapters 3 and 4, I describe the use of intersectionality in criminology specifically. For now, I provide a brief definition here. I use the terms intersectionality and intersectional to mean the same thing, referring to *the concept or conceptualization that each person has an assortment of coalesced socially constructed identities that are ordered into an inequitable social stratum.* The interchangeable use of intersectionality and intersectional is seen in many other academic publications addressing the concept delineated in my definition, thus only further complicating the "what is" question regarding intersectionality.

In its entirety, this book offers an explication of and a justification for *intersectional criminology*. Intersectional criminology is a perspective that incorporates the intersectional or intersectionality concept into criminological research and theory and into the evaluation of crime or crime-related policies and laws and the governmental administration of "justice." Because girls and women of Color experience life differently from boys and men and White girls and women, scholars argue that male- and White-oriented criminological theories may be inadequate for explaining criminal behavior by women of Color and the responses of women of Color to victimization (Joseph 2006; Potter 2008; Russell-Brown 2004). Likewise, criminological theories on White boys and men may not provide the most adequate explanations for the criminal activities of boys and men of Color, or vice versa. Further, scholars who include in their research a diverse sample population by race and gender often fail to conduct comparisons between the distinct groups (Joseph 2006; Russell-Brown 2004). Criminologist Ruth Peterson (2012:319) admonished, "When a society is organized along race/ethnic lines, we cannot assume that the sources and responses to crime, or the application of criminal justice, are race neutral in their effects and consequences." The same can be said for sex or gender and for the *interaction* of race/ethnicity *and* sex/gender *and* other identities and statuses. These identities and statuses, as well as the designation of acts as crimes and the practices in "criminal justice" systems, are social constructs. The remainder of this chapter is devoted to making some sense of these social constructs, and serves as a foundation for the overarching theme of *Intersectionality and Criminology*.

When and where we enter[2]

Sociologist Joe R. Feagin (2010) has established that throughout North America and Europe, a White racial frame is what we are all expected to follow. Since the 1600s, a White racial frame "has provided the vantage point from which whites and others have regularly viewed and interpreted [US] society.... [T]his strong framing has had a very positive orientation to whites and whiteness and a negative orientation to the racial 'others' who are oppressed" (Feagin 2010:25). Within a White racial frame, White and Whiteness is the default identity; for example, if race is not identified in the description of a protagonist in a novel, we are typically expected to assume that, naturally, the subject is a White person. This assumption is solidified when "non-White" characters in the novel are described with a race label. Sociologist Elijah Anderson (2011:258) exemplified the labeling of those who are racialized (people of Color) in his assessment of the Black experience: "A person with black skin is viewed as black long before he or she is viewed as a doctor, lawyer, or professor. Blackness is a 'master status' that supersedes whatever else a person may claim to be; he or she is viewed as a black doctor, a black lawyer, or a black professor, whatever that adjective might mean." Arguably, as globalization has flourished, a White racial frame has been indoctrinated throughout the world. The popular use of skin lightening products in India and parts of Africa illustrates the breadth and power of the White racial frame. Feagin (2010) paid minimal attention to gender within the context of race, but, clearly, the White racial frame also prioritizes male perspectives above other sexes or genders, so the White racial frame is more aptly referenced as the White *male* racial frame. This White male racial frame also bleeds into the production of theory and research and into the determination of who is considered a valid practitioner and producer of academic enterprise.

In the academic discipline of criminology,[3] not only do the factors related to crime-related transgressions committed by and against subjugated populations need to be brought to the center, so too do the scholars who are marginalized and who utilize "alternative" theoretical perspectives and propositions. This is an issue of old and of new, as evidenced in an examination of the life and works of William E. Burghardt Du Bois. Du Bois was born in 1868 in Massachusetts, received undergraduate degrees at Fisk University and Harvard University and a doctorate degree at Harvard (as the first Black person to receive a Ph.D. from Harvard), and, after several rejections from

White colleges not wishing to hire him because of his denounced racial classification, began his first faculty position at Wilberforce University, an historically all-Black student institution in Ohio (for extensive Du Bois biographies see Gabbidon 2007; Horne 2010). After a brief stint at Wilberforce, Du Bois accepted a temporary position as a researcher at the University of Pennsylvania. His studies at his new post led to his book *The Philadelphia Negro* (1899), in which he expounded on the unique social conditions and problems of Blacks living in northern US urban settings, including their experiences with crime and the criminal legal system. He concluded, "Crime is a phenomenon of organized social life, and is the open rebellion of an individual against its social environment" (p. 235). One of Du Bois's earliest statements on crime and justice, however, appeared in his 1892 report on the rarely or poorly enforced US slave trade act of 1807 that made it illegal for individuals to traffic into the United States "any negro, mulatto, or person of colour, with intent to hold, sell, or dispose of such negro, mulatto, or person of colour, as a slave, or to be held to service or labour" (2 Stat. 426). Throughout his career, Du Bois continued to consider the perplexing intersected subject of race, crime, and justice, including the convict-lease system as an extension of slavery, the impact of racial segregation on Blacks participating in criminal activity, and the unevenly distributed "justice" by race in criminal courts. Undoubtedly, few scholars and students are aware of the contribution Du Bois could have made to the academic field of criminology. I use "could have" because, but for his being marginalized (Gabbidon 2007; Hanson 2010), we might have been at least decades ahead of where we are now in the social-scientific study and theorization of crime, and because Du Bois's criminological research and theory continues to go widely unrecognized.

Race theorist and criminologist Shaun L. Gabbidon's (2007) thorough evaluation of the criminology-related works of Du Bois supports an argument for changing the way the history of criminological theory is presented. As Gabbidon underscores, findings of the Chicago School of criminology – specifically, the work of Clifford R. Shaw and Henry D. McKay (1931, 1942) – were not an especially novel concept. In the 1920s, Shaw and McKay were heralded as the leaders of a new way of considering criminal behavior; a way that was not focused on biological or psychological determinism, but on the influences of the social or environmental setting on the commission of crime. Granted, Shaw and McKay should be lauded for their achievements and for advancing sociological theories of crime causation. But Gabbidon's substantiation of Du Bois's research and findings in criminology necessitate that we not continue to disregard the contributions Du Bois made at the time of his research and the contributions that can still be made to criminology based in a Du Boisian conceptualization. Du Bois's work made a widespread reappearance in the late 1990s around the time of the first centurial anniversary of *The Philadelphia Negro*, particularly in the field of sociology, and some sociologists now consider him as a "founding father" of US sociology (Anderson 1996; Jones 2009). Regrettably, Du Bois's criminological scholarship is still overwhelmingly ignored in criminological research and in criminology program curricula and textbooks. Still, Black feminist criminologist Nikki Jones (2009:246) foretold, "Embracing Du Bois as a founding father of American criminological thought will allow future criminologists to inherit a scholarship committed to the study of crime as a social problem and not a biological or genetic deficiency."[4]

Nearly 125 years after Du Bois's first publication that laid the foundation for his criminological research and conceptualization, feminist, critical, and progressive race[5] criminologists continue to stress the importance of addressing race, gender, socioeconomics, inequality, and oppression in the study of crime. Criminologists Kathleen Daly and Lisa Maher (1998) and James W. Messerschmidt (2013) have challenged the dominant views in criminology for the way the White male racial frame affects knowledge production within the discipline. Even though most individuals who participate in criminal activity in the United States are White, Messerschmidt (2013:123) has observed that Whiteness "is an invisible variable throughout criminological theory and research." And Daly and Maher (1998:5) declared, "White criminology avoids 'the race issue' because of racism both in the discipline and the wider society, a lack of theoretical grounding in what racial-ethnic relations and identities are, and too few scholars of color in criminology who are in a position to take on white criminology." Although, worldwide, people of Color outnumber Whites

(US Census Bureau 2004) and it is projected for the year 2060 that people of Color in the United States, with Latinas and Latinos comprising the largest proportion, will represent 57 percent of the US population (US Census Bureau 2012), some race scholars believe that White dominance (Haney López 2006) or the White male racial frame will persevere. Hence, what incentive is there for members of "White criminology" to become more attuned to the significance of power and identity in our social worlds? Unlike legal race scholar Ian Haney López (2006), but consistent with Feagin (2010), I have an outlook (perhaps utopian) that a critical mass of critical scholars can cause a paradigm shift and that a critical mass of consciousness-raising can work toward dismantling *Whitemaleness* as the default and the standard on which we measure all people. One of the paths that will aid in disrupting the norm is the incorporation of intersectionality into criminological theory and research.

Overwhelmingly, feminist criminologists working on women's and girls' experiences with crime, victimization, and the criminal legal system have been the enthusiasts to take up the project of incorporating an intersectional approach in criminological research. Feminist criminology originated during the 1960s (Daly and Chesney-Lind 1988), and Daly and Maher (1998) referred to the intersectional incorporation as the *second phase* of feminist criminology, which began in the late 1980s and resulted in the start of the shift away from essentialist and singular views of women within feminist criminology. Advocating for an intersectional approach to consider race, gender, and class, feminist criminologist Dana M. Britton (2000:72–73) argued, "The challenge for feminist criminology in the years to come will lie in formulating theory and carrying out empirical studies that prioritize all of these dimensions rather than relegating one or more of them to the background for the sake of methodological convenience." Critical criminologists[6] (Barak *et al.* 2010; DeKeseredy 2011; Schwartz and Milovanovic 1996) and progressive race criminologists (Gabbidon 2010; Russell-Brown 2004) have also advocated for an intersectional approach. Utilizing intersectionality in criminological research has focused mainly on the experiences of women of Color; however, the concept has been applied to men of Color, White women, and White men. In this book, I review the debate surrounding extended applications of intersectionality or an intersectional perspective, and provide relevant examples of where it has been and how it could be used with these other populations.

In any diverse society – or, arguably, in all societies – the effect of one's identity/ies must be considered to understand individuals' participation in crime, individuals' responses to being a victim of crime, and the processes of the criminal legal system. Variations in identity and levels of privilege can lead to variations in the treatment of certain groups within a society, particularly for those identities deemed deviant or subordinate. Because of the overrepresentation of subordinated people of Color and the poor in many criminal legal systems in racially or ethnically diverse societies throughout the world, it is imperative that people of Color are centered in the analysis. Intersectional criminology will assure this centering, as the concept necessitates that social identities and social power and privilege be given top billing.

Defining identities

Because the concept of intersectionality is a practice of interrogating and understanding the role of identities, we must understand the social construction of the major identities categorized within our societies. The defining, and naming, of identities is a slippery task because of the ever-changing perceptions and self-perceptions of identities. Thus, the following summary serves to chronicle contemporary context on the major identities attended to in the social sciences and throughout this book. A contemporary context shows that a commonly used term such as "non-White" (which I am guilty of using previously) upholds the continued subordination of people of Color. We would be less inclined to use counterpart terms like non-male, non-man, non-heterosexual, non-straight – which demonstrates the devaluing also embedded in the non-White identifier. As illuminated by intersectionality and women of Color feminist thought, it is inevitable that social definitions of race and ethnicity are impacted by gender and sexuality, and that social definitions of gender and sexuality are impacted by race and ethnicity. Social class, nationality, and any multitude of other identities further compound a race/gender/sexuality identity. This is evidenced in the overview to follow, which is separated into sections on race and ethnicity, gender and sexuality, and socioeconomic class for the purposes of defining the social aspects of each category. While these are often treated as social elements that can be independently assessed, intersectional scholarship insists that doing so is incomplete. The identity attributes given the most attention in this book are race, ethnicity, gender, sexuality, and socioeconomic class; but it is important to remember that *any* identity/ies an individual holds and believes to be significant in the lived experience should be considered for analysis in criminological research. Other prominent identities would include religion, nationality, political affiliation and ideology, occupation, physical ability, body shape, and age.

Defining race and ethnicity

Some public commentary, often from Whites, questions why we still need to categorize by race. Progressive race scholars would answer that studying race and race relations remains necessary because of the inequities and subordination that continue to thrive. Other public commentary demonstrates the need to continue raising awareness of the workings of race, such as comments made by North Carolina politician Thom Tillis, North Carolina Republican Party's 2014 nominee for the US Senate, and eventual winner of the election. During an appearance in 2012 on a local television news program, Tillis spoke of the need for the Republican Party to better communicate with the North Carolina Black and Latina/o population to demonstrate that the party's politics are able to service these populations. In discussing the Black and Latina/o populations, which he referred to as "growing sectors" of North Carolina, Tillis concluded, "The *traditional* population of North Carolina and the United States is more or less stable. It's not growing. The African American population is roughly growing but the Hispanic population and the other immigrant populations are growing in significant numbers. We've got to resonate with those future voters" (Maloy 2014; emphasis added). This is a seemingly inclusive and welcoming statement, but Tillis *others* Blacks and Latinas/os by juxtaposing them with an ideal White population, assumes that all Latinas/os are immigrants, and appears to view Blacks and Latinas/os as unstable and in a state of flux. Additionally, Tillis indicated a move toward "limited government," which contradicts his US Senate election website that he "and his House colleagues have pushed a ban on gay marriage, pro-life protection laws, and required drug testing for welfare recipients" (thomtillis.com) – legislation that does not represent cultural inclusiveness and which disproportionately affects those already marginalized. In response to Tillis's comments, his communications director stated that Tillis's use of the term "traditional" referred to North Carolinians who had lived in the state for a few generations, citing, "the state's recent population growth is from people who move from other states live, work, and settle down in North Carolina. Thom Tillis for example" (Bump 2014).

Sociologist Tukufu Zuberi (2001:12) recounted that in the geographical region that was to become the United States, racialization began with debasing the Indigenous population and summarized, "The settlers considered Africans to be natural slaves, indigenous Americans to be noble natives, and other Europeans as potential citizens. The problem of race was born." Race and ethnicity are often used interchangeably; however, social scientists identify *race* as the socially constructed categorization of the presumed varying forms of the human body, and *ethnicity* as the culture, customs, religion, language, dialect, and national identity of a group (Davis 1991; Feagin 2010; Gallagher 2009; Omi and Winant 1994; Zuberi 2001). Among scholars, it has been common knowledge and an increasingly acceptable idea that race is socially constructed. That is, members within the society determine what race is, and relationships between the defined racial groups are stratified into superior and subordinate classifications (Bonilla-Silva 2010; Feagin 2010; Haney López 2006; Zuberi 2001). Regardless of the few physical scientists who believe that inferior intelligence among a high proportion of people of Color is due to genetic variations by race – based on measurements such as the IQ (intelligence quotient) test – most social scientists solidly maintain that race is a social artifact (Feagin 2010). The way in which one's race is identified in a particular society is typically based on phenotypical characteristics, but race is not simply defined by physical differences between people. As imparted by journalist Francie Latour (2012), "The African-American grandmother of a friend of mine once summed up the laws that govern black identity in this country. 'If you ever want to know if someone's black or not,' she would say, 'go ask their white neighbor.'" For someone like the infamous entertainer Michael Jackson, his numerous facial reconstruction surgeries, which included slimming his nose, and the lightening of his skin (either by use of chemicals or due to a reported skin condition) raised many discussions on racial identification. Although a number of Blacks felt alienated by Jackson because of his physical transformation and many people hurled prurient comments about his gender and sexual identities (Braxton 2009), Jackson was still viewed by general society as a Black man.

Clearly, members of a society typically attempt to place others into a race category (as well as make attempts to identify one's sexuality and gender or sex). We often attempt to locate a person's race by focusing on the shape of the eyes, the contours of the nose, the texture and color of the hair, the tone of the skin. If a person is not easily identifiable with a presumptive race (and a presumptive sex), the question becomes "What are you?" Many onlookers are disturbed if a person is not easily identifiable by race (and sex), thereby rendering the "subject" as some exotic or unsettling creature. Individuals whose biological parents are identified as two distinct races (that is, interracial couples) have long been the subjects of much curiosity in many societies. We often hear the phrase "mixed kids are so beautiful" in conversations about biracial or multiracial persons (such as actors Halle Berry and Thandie Newton, actor and athlete Duane "The Rock" Johnson, and singer Mariah Carey). Interestingly, multiraciality is a complex racial typing since most, if not all, individuals are of multiple races (Davis 1991). Nevertheless, in the case and history of the United States, the "one-drop rule" designated anyone with any Black African blood as Black, and, to the present era, many Indigenous individuals must meet a minimum blood quorum to claim "Native American" status. In the case of Mexico, race theorist and ethnographer Christina A. Sue (2013) investigated that country's denial of its Black and African history and its attempts to minimize or erase Blackness from its national image. In current times, some individuals will identify with or claim a race not believed to be part of their lineage. In the United States, this is often the case when claiming an Indigenous identity or heritage; conversely, few people admit to being Black if they do not believe they have any indigenous African stock.[7] In some countries, such as several of those in Latin America, racial categorization is more about actual skin color than about lineage (Sue 2009; Telles 2004).

Regarding the mutability of race identity, Zuberi (2001:124) observed, "Racial classification typically occurs at birth but in some societies can change during a person's lifetime. When an individual's race can change, race is not an attribute but a dynamic characteristic dependent on other social circumstances." For instance, groups in the United States identified as *White* significantly changed between 1790 and 1923, with Greeks and Italians not originally classified as White, but deemed racially inferior to western and northern Europeans (Haney López 2006). Feagin (2010) administered a survey to 151 White US college students to determine which ethnic groups are viewed as White and which are not. A large majority (86–100 percent) of the respondents identified English, German, Irish, and Italian Americans as White. Most of the respondents did not classify Chinese and Japanese Americans and other Asian Americans as White and none of the Latina/o groups or "African Americans" were identified as White. That Latinas/os in Feagin's study were not identified as White is not in contrast to the way some Latinas/os see themselves; some surveys indicate that most Latinas/os do not identify as White (Taylor *et al.* 2012). In sociologist Jessica M. Vasquez's (2010) interviews with third-generation Mexican Americans living in California, the informants were able to practice a "flexible ethnicity" depending on their skin tone, hair color, facial features, and surname. As would be expected, lighter Mexican Americans with non-Spanish surnames were more able to "deftly and effectively navigate different racial terrains and be considered an 'insider' in more than one racial or ethnic group" (p. 46). Vasquez found that gender mattered in the racialized experiences of the research participants, in that the women were better able to be accepted into a White identity (by Whites), likely due to the "softer" controlling images of Latinas (exotic, sexual) in comparison with the "harder" more threatening controlling images of Latinos (gang member). Undoubtedly, passing as White garners many benefits. In Fannie Hurst's 1933 novel *Imitation of Life* (and in the two film adaptations released in 1934 and 1959), the fair-skinned daughter of a Black woman housekeeper rejects a Black racial identity and leaves her mother to live as a White woman in order to escape the stigma of Black identity. Although a fictional account, this narrative is indeed an imitation of life; many people of Color who phenotypically resemble Whites have opted to pass as White to reap the many privileges afforded Whites in countless settings worldwide. For those who are unwilling or unable to pass as White, there still exists the pressure to perform Whiteness or conform to the White male racial frame when interacting with Whites. Du Bois (1903:3) used the concepts of the "veil" and a "double-consciousness" to describe these experiences for Black people:

> It is a peculiar sensation, this double-consciousness, this sense of always looking at one's self through the eyes of others, of measuring one's soul by the tape of a world that looks on in amused contempt and pity. One ever feels his two-ness – an American, a Negro; two souls, two thoughts, two unreconciled strivings; two warring ideals in one dark body, whose dogged strength alone keeps it from being torn asunder.

Colorism is another social dynamic that positions individuals on a social ladder. Colorism involves the evaluation of the skin tone of a person of Color by others within their racial or ethnic group and by members of an out-group. Eye color and, for Blacks specifically, hair texture are also assessed in this discriminatory ordering. Individuals with the lightest skin tones are often privileged within Black, Latina/o, and certain Asian groups, and having eye color that is not brown is esteemed. Among Blacks, hair texture that more closely resembles White hair textures is praised. These predilections tend to be gendered; throughout the world and among many racial groups, skin tone and hair texture are typically used as measurements of attractiveness for women, not men (Glenn 2008; Hill 2002; Hunter 2005, 2013). Colorism within groups is perpetuated at different levels and, of course, not every dark-skinned and thick-haired person (as relative to their racial group) is debased. In fact, resembling the Afro hairstyle movement in the 1960s and 1970s, there is currently a movement among a critical mass of Black women to reject conforming to the White-woman ideal by rebuffing the use of chemical hair "relaxers" and returning to their natural hair texture. Furthermore, the origins of colorism cannot be assessed separate from the grander social structure. The White racial frame provided the foundation for colorism to form and flourish. Out-group members also exhibit preferential treatment of individuals with physical features more similar to Whites. This is manifested in research that has found that in comparison with lighter-skinned people of Color, darker-skinned people of Color have fewer years of education (Monk 2014), are in less prestigious occupations (Monk 2014), obtain lower employment wages (Goldsmith *et al.* 2007), have lower household incomes (Monk 2014), have higher school suspension rates (Hannon *et al.* 2013), experience disadvantages in securing legitimate opportunities that "induce a transition into criminal activity" (Gyimah-Brempong and Price 2006:248), and receive longer prison sentences (Gyimah-Brempong and Price 2006; Viglione *et al.* 2011).

It is clear to most observers that Whites in the United States occupy the top of the racial hierarchy, above people of Color, where there exists an additional ordering, such as Japanese Americans, Chinese Americans, or light-skinned Latinas/os elevated with an "honorary White" status (Bonilla-Silva 2010),[8] or certain Asian American ethnic groups attributed with a "model minority" status. Even if people of Color thrive or attempt to thrive in heterogeneous societies such as those in the United States, the United Kingdom, and many other countries and regions, they are often reminded, either explicitly or implicitly, of their "place" in society. Stories abound from women and men of Color and White women about being reminded of their place and then put back in their place. Anderson (2011) shared a common experience among Blacks, in which we are often reminded of our place when we are confronted with a *nigger moment*. Anderson relayed an example of this racial injury as intertwined with socioeconomic class and occupation status:

> Emotions flood over the victim as this middle-class, cosmopolitan-oriented black person is humiliated and shown that he or she is, before anything else, a racially circumscribed black

> person after all. No matter what she has achieved, or how decent and law-abiding she is, there is no protection, no sanctuary, no escaping from this fact ... Whatever the educated and often professionally successful person previously thought her position in society was, now she is challenged, as random white persons casually but powerfully degrade her. This moment is always insulting, and even a relatively minor incident can have a significant impact.
>
> (p. 253)

Anderson iterated that, in reality, *any* marginalized person can have a *nigger moment*. The subtlety of many of these moments is commonly referred to as a *racial microaggression*, as opposed to *racism*, which generally includes two standard forms. *Interpersonal racism* engaged in by individuals is an overt, intentional, and conscious behavior, motivated by hatred of a particular racial group, that explicitly disparages a member of a racial group to which the actor does not belong; *systemic racism* (Feagin 2010) or *institutional racism* (Sue 2010) occurs at the macrostructural level, where practices, procedures, policies, and law that operate within the social institutions of economy, government, schools, housing, healthcare, and religion place or keep people of Color in subordinate and disadvantaged positions to Whites who are then able to maintain a position at the apex of social ordering.[9] Regarding the many ways that racial abhorrence and bigotry is exhibited, psychiatrist Chester M. Pierce (1974:516) is credited with coining the term microaggression and warned, "one must not look for the gross and obvious. The subtle, cumulative miniassault is the substance of today's racism." Racial microaggressions[10] pose a greater threat to people of Color than explicit interpersonal racism, according to race theorist Derald Wing Sue (2010:xv), because microaggressions are engaged in by "well-intentioned people, who are strongly motivated by egalitarian values, believe in their own morality, and experience themselves as fair-minded and decent people who would never consciously discriminate." Sue defined microaggressions as "brief and commonplace daily verbal, behavioral, and environmental indignities, whether intentional or unintentional that communicate hostile, derogatory, or negative racial, gender, sexual-orientation, and religious slights and insults to the target person or group" (p. 5). While naysayers – both academic and general public – deny any significant harm from these affronts (Bonilla-Silva 2010; Feagin 2010; Sue 2010), research has found that microaggressions "assail the self-esteem of recipients, produce anger and frustration, deplete psychic energy, lower feelings of subjective well-being and worthiness, produce physical health problems, shorten life expectancy, and deny minority populations equal access and opportunity in education, employment, and health care" (Sue 2010:6).

Just as racial identities are fluid, so are the names used to label the various identities. As the twenty-first century approached, the United Kingdom and United States governments recognized the changing ways in which individuals wish to racially identify themselves. Although the US census guidelines continue to force individuals who identify with Latin American heritage (for example, Brazilian, Cuban American, Hispanic, Latina/o, Mexican American, Dominican) to identify with the "race" of Asian, Black, White, Native American, or Pacific Islander, a category was added that allowed respondents who identify as multiracial to choose more than one race. Similarly, in the United Kingdom, census respondents can select "mixed race." Movements are currently being made to have the 2020 US census reclassify Latin American lineage as a race instead of an ethnicity and to add a Middle East/North Africa category that would allow Arab Americans and others indigenous to that region a more precise description of their identity instead of being classified as White or "other" (Krogstad 2014; Lopez and Krogstad 2014).

Evolving into a more democratic world (at least in certain societies) has increased the ability for subordinated or marginalized racial groups to make their own determinations on how they wish to be referred to. *People of Color* is becoming the more preferable term to describe individuals who do not identify as White. Although use of "people of Color" seems to infer that Whites are devoid of color, use of the term does not translate to Whites being devoid of race and racial identity. White is obviously a color in the context of hue, but White as a racial identifier is not contrasted with "people of Color" to (necessarily) differentiate individuals by skin tone. White and people of Color are terms utilized to designate *social* categorization. Within certain US locales, ethnicities among Whites, such as Italian or Irish, are sometimes differentiated, but the White racial group is not customarily partitioned. However, the pan-ethnic group of people of Color encompasses a wide variety of individuals who are specially marginalized in Western societies and at the global level since White-dominated Western societies hold much power within the global setting. The grouping of peoples of Color serves to identify heterogeneous experiences and the imbalance of power between people of Color as a group and Whites. But among people of Color, there exist a large variety of groups, including other pan-ethnic appellations, such as Asians, Latinas/os, and Blacks.

In the United States, "colored" and "Negro" were replaced with "Black" and then "African American," while "mulatto," "quadroon," and "octoroon" were replaced with "biracial" or "multiracial" – of course, the earlier terms, along with other racial epithets, continue to be inflicted on racially marginalized persons as a form of abuse or insult. Confusion about race-group labeling prevails among out-group members since even in-group members may argue among themselves as to the most suitable designation. And for some groups there is less consensus for the labeling – such as "Hispanic" versus "Latina/Latino," "Native American" versus "American Indian," and "minorities" versus "people of Color." Naming is further complicated within these larger categories, when groups or individuals rightfully wish to be more specifically identified. For instance, a US resident of Mexican descent may prefer to be identified as Chicano, while others, because of the politicized connotation of *Chicana/o* that began during the 1960s with *El Moviemiento* (the Brown Power or Chicano movement), shun the label and prefer Mexican American, Hispanic, or Latina/o (Comas-Díaz 2001). Regarding new immigrants, although government policies or laws may classify immigrants based on phenotype and the country of origin, some immigrants reject being placed into a country's existing racial categories. An Ethiopian immigrant to the United States, for example, may not identify as Black or African American, preferring to be identified as Habasha in an effort to maintain cultural identity and to distance her from the racism and exclusion that often comes with being African American (Habecker 2012). Likewise, the term "mulattos" used in the United States to describe

Black/White biracial individuals is usually a derogatory term, while in Brazil the term is one of the accepted categorizations. And though "colored" is an insulting term to use to describe Blacks in the United States, "coloured" is an acceptable identifier in South Africa for individuals who comprise a race mixture of any of the three majority races: Indigenous (Black/African), White (European descent), and Indian (Finchilescu and Tredoux 2010).

A final issue of race labeling is the debate of capitalization for the racial categorizations Black and White. In some cases, within one composition, Black is capitalized but White is not (such as the author guidelines of the academic journal *Gender and Society*; see also Harris 1993). I prefer to capitalize both terms because race is a strong social determinant and a matter of identity, and other race labels are capitalized, such as Asian and Latina. I also choose to capitalize the word Color when referencing racial identity (as in women of Color, persons of Color) and the term Indigenous for the same reason.[11] (I use Indigenous to signify a lineage that traces to the peoples indigenous to an area. Hence, I would not use the racial/ethnic identifier for a White/European person born in the United States.)

Although there has been some level of self-empowerment among marginalized groups (especially people of Color) in regulating how they wish to be identified, Latina/o studies scholar Suzanne Oboler (1995: xvi) noted that "ethnic labels" can become "stigmatizing labels." In speaking specifically about the conflated label of "Hispanics" in the United States, Oboler wrote that the designation

> obscures rather than clarifies the varied social and political experiences in US society of more than 23 million citizens, residents, refugees, and immigrants with ties to Caribbean and Central and South American countries. It reduces their distinct relations among themselves and with US society to an ethnic label that in fact fails to do justice to the variety of backgrounds and conditions of the populations to whom it has been applied.
>
> (p. 2)

According to the 2010 US census, individuals identifying with Mexican heritage comprise the large majority of Latinas/os at

64.6 percent (33.5 million). Individuals identifying a Puerto Rican heritage comprised 9.5 percent (almost 5 million), followed by Salvadoran (nearly 2 million; 3.8 percent), Cuban (1.9 million; 3.6 percent), and Dominican (1.5 million; 2.9 percent) origins. Although the US government continues to use the term Hispanic, as do many individuals who self-identify this way, the adoption of Latina/o has become more widely accepted by individuals fitting within this category (Oboler 1995; Sáenz and Murga 2011).

In sum, the notion that race/ethnicity is a complex social condition is a gross understatement. Perhaps it is the complexity and messiness that comes with assessing race effects that routes criminologists and other researchers down the uncomplicated avenue, where attempts at conceptualizing how race may be operating in their studies is avoided. Considering other identities that are intertwined with and cannot be divorced from race and ethnicity only further muddles an analysis.

Defining sex, gender, and sexuality

Just as race is a social construct, so is gender. The term *gender* has grown to become a common term in public discourse; but depending on the context, *sex* (or *biological sex*) may be the appropriate term. Additionally, *sexuality* (or *sexual orientation, sexual desire*) is often commingled with the contrivance of gender or sex. There is also a close relationship between the ways in which gender and sexuality are socially organized (Weeks 2010). Like race and ethnicity, the complexity of sex, gender, and sexuality can be evaluated with highly publicized cases. Gender and sex questions have been raised about athletes Caster Semenya, a South African runner, and Brittney Griner, a player on the Phoenix Mercury professional US basketball team and formerly a member of a Baylor University basketball team. For both women, since they do not present as *cisgender* females because of the athletic build of their bodies, their facial features, and the deeper timbre of their voices, speculations arose about their biological sex categorization and if it is fair for them to "play with the girls." That both of these women are Black should also be taken into account in the public commentary about their sex categorization and gender identity. Black women's bodies have been subject to inspection and scrutiny since the degradation and exploitation of the "Hottentot Venus" and of African women enslaved by North American colonists (Collins 2005; Roberts 1997). The exploitation of Sarah Bartmann, who originally hailed from what later became South Africa, is one of the first infamous and publicized instances of exploitation of the Black female's body and sexuality (Collins 2000a, 2005). White men regularly placed Bartmann on display in carnival-like settings in early nineteenth-century London and Paris, subjecting the misnamed "Hottentot Venus" to curious White Europeans who believed Africans possessed deviant sexual behaviors and bodies (Collins 2000a; Fausto-Sterling 1995). Even Serena Williams, the professional tennis player with a conventionally "acceptable" female body and higher-pitched voice, is subject to questions about her biological sex categorization, with public comments questioning if she is a man because of her physical strength that surpasses the feats of many top male-identified tennis players. As should be evident from this overview of a few Black women athletes, the gendered, sexed, and sexualized characterizations are entwined with other identities. Feminist scholars of Color have a sustained record of connecting sex, gender, and sexuality with race and racism, including consideration of how White European colonists feared and were threatened by a so-called Black sexuality (Collins 2005). Black women's sexuality has long been demonized, whether as oversexed, unchaste "freaks" or as emasculating, masculine, nonsexual "bitches." So when generalizations are made regarding biological sex, social gender, and sexual desire, "they should be drawn carefully, by always asking the questions '*which* women?' and '*which* men?'" (Baca Zinn *et al.* 2005:2; emphases in original text).

In the social sciences, biological sex refers to a socially established agreement of physiological characteristics that identify an individual as female or male (Kessler and McKenna 1978; West and Zimmerman 1987). This categorization is becoming problematic in present times, however, because this binary does not acknowledge intersex individuals who have ambiguous genitalia or both male-identified and female-identified genitalia, which can be evident at birth or revealed during puberty (Andersen and Hysock 2011; Dreger and Herndon 2009; Fausto-Sterling 2012). While sex is categorized based on chromosomal makeup or genitalia, a *sex category* is a better description of what we *do* in society in assigning an individual to a particular sex. Thus, the conventional sex categorization of some individuals does not always match with general society's definitions of sex (West and Zimmerman 1987). In the past, intersex individuals were usually reassigned to either a definitive male or female sex categorization at the urging of doctors or parents, which sometimes involved reconstructive surgery during infancy or later in childhood. Presently, many doctors and biologists do not agree with this practice, opting to allow intersex individuals to determine their sex (and gender) identity, whether in youth or later in life (Fausto-Sterling 2012).

The normative – or, more appropriately, *hetero*normative – performances that members of a society deem appropriate for a particular sex categorization are what social scientists refer to as *gender*. That is, gender is the personal traits and social position that members of a society attach to being female or male. In Candace West and Don H. Zimmerman's (1987) seminal article "Doing Gender," they explain that doing gender in a societally acceptable manner involves participating in correct feminine and masculine performances that match one's female or male sex assignment, respectively. But "to 'do' gender is not always to live up to normative conceptions of femininity or masculinity; it is to engage in behavior *at the risk of gender assessment*" (p. 136; emphases in original text). This means that others either approve of the way in which we are performing gender or reject our choices ("She has a haircut like a dude!" "He's wearing lipstick!"). Individuals' understanding of their gender is often referred to as gender *identity*, and the presentation of this identity is referred to as gender *expression* or gender *roles*. These expressions or roles are developed through the process of socialization by a variety of social institutions and people throughout a person's life (Andersen and Hysock 2011). While some individuals are *trans*gender because of their divergence from the conventional teachings of how sex and gender are to be expressed, other individuals, those doing gender "correctly," can be referred to as *cis*gender. Cisgender signifies "individuals who have a match between the gender they were assigned at birth, their bodies, and their personal identity" (Schilt and Westbrook 2009:461).

Gender expression includes the performance of femininity and masculinity. Like sex, gender, and sexuality, the terms femininity and masculinity are commonly used, but locating explicit definitions of femininity and masculinity is rare (Spence and Buckner 1995). Dictionary definitions typically refer to masculine as qualities or behaviors associated with men, and have a complementary definition for feminine. The inability to locate precise definitions of femininity and masculinity demonstrate the extent to which they are social constructs. What is feminine and what is masculine will vary across societies and cultures and change across time. Over three decades ago, Raewyn (formerly R.W.) Connell (1983, 1987; Carrigan *et al.* 1985; Connell and Messerschmidt 2005) introduced an array of masculinities, emphasizing the importance of diversity among men – and women – in their gendered performances. Using the term "hegemonic masculinity," Connell and colleagues (Carrigan *et al.* 1985:592) indicated that this form of masculinity interrogates "how particular groups of men inhabit positions of power and wealth, and how they legitimate and reproduce the social relationships that generate their dominance." Hegemonic masculinity is housed at the top of the masculinities hierarchy and is not understood without considering its relationship to "emphasized femininity" and nonhegemonic masculinities (Connell 1987; Connell and Messerschmidt 2005). Emphasized femininity is an embodiment of women and, as expected, a subordinated position to men that involves accommodating men. Nonhegemonic masculinities include subordinate masculinities of gay men and marginalized masculinities of men of Color. A recently reformulated conceptualization of hegemonic masculinity stresses the consideration of women's roles in the "processes of constructing masculinities" (Connell and Messerschmidt 2005:848).

We typically learn that *sex*, as in the erotic or intimate act, is a "natural" desire and behavior occurring between individuals belonging to the "opposite sex" (Seidman *et al.* 2011; Weeks 2010). The term *sexuality* refers to the quality of being sexual and only appeared in the latter half of the nineteenth century (Weeks 2010). Current studies on sexuality challenge the idea that sex between humans is natural. Although certainly not rejecting the biological aspect of sexuality, by the 1970s, social scientists began considering sex as social

(Seidman *et al.* 2011). An explanation of sexuality's social orientation supposes that "it is social forces which determine which organs and orifices become 'sexual,' how such organs and orifices may be used or expressed, their social and moral meaning, which desires and acts become the basis of identities, and what social norms regulate behavior and intimacies" (Seidman *et al.* 2011:xvi; see also Collins 2005). For instance, because of the conflation of sex, gender, and sexuality, there is the expectation that a cisgender woman has sex only with men, and a cisgender man has sex only with women.

Regarding the interconnection of sex, gender, and sexuality, social psychologists Laura E. Kuper, Robin Nussbaum, and Brian Mustanski (2012) raised concerns about the term transgender, questioning whether the diverse set of individuals who fall within the broad definition of the term (Valentine 2007) would *self*-identify as transgender. The researchers also sought to determine variations in identity by age and birth sex (the biological sex categorization determined at birth). Participants for the study were recruited through virtual social networking and were asked to complete an Internet-based survey that asked respondents about the sex, gender, and sexuality identities they used over the course of their lives, and any surgeries and hormonal usage related to these identities (such as genital or breast re/construction, hysterectomy, testosterone use for birth sex females). The final sample included 292 valid participants who identified within the spectrum of gender variance (for example, transgender, intersex, genderqueer, drag). The respondents spanned ages 18 through 73 (mean of 27.88 years) and lived in the United States, Canada, and eight additional countries. Approximately 87 percent of the respondents identified as White. The survey offered an expansive list of gender and sexual orientation identities from which respondents could choose (including options to make multiple choices). Genderqueer was the most common gender identity response endorsed by the respondents; however, this term was not as popular among older respondents. Only 3 percent of participants identified as female and only 2 percent as male. Pansexual and queer were the most common sexual orientation identities among the respondents, followed by the traditional terms lesbian, bisexual, and straight/heterosexual. A majority of the birth sex males (59 percent) were taking hormones or had a desire to do so in the future. This significantly contrasted with birth sex females, a majority (77 percent) of whom did not plan to take hormones in the future or were unsure about doing so. Also, a higher proportion of birth sex males (43 percent) reported a desire to undergo "bottom" sex reassignment surgery (genital re/construction) than birth sex females (4 percent). Though not explicitly addressed by the researchers, these significant differences by birth sex align with the study results that show genderqueer was a more common self-identity among birth sex females, while transsexual was more common among birth sex males. Kuper and her colleagues surmised, "masculinity in those born female is less stigmatized and pathologized than femininity in those born male.... Sociocultural considerations such as these, coupled with the greater difficulty associated with passing as female, may also delay the coming out or transition process for those born male" (p. 251). This detailed account of this study provides a good measure of the ever-changing nature of self-identity, even though, as recognized by the researchers, there is a lack of racial and ethnic diversity among the respondents.

Perspectives on sex, gender, and sexuality identity of genderqueer individuals of Color were considered in another study conducted by Kuper and colleagues (Kuper, Wright, and Mustanski 2014). In extensive personal interviews with four youth of Color born as females, each of the respondents embodied conventional male and masculine presentations and reported sexual attraction or preference for "femme" women. None of the informants wished to have surgery to change their bodies. "Stud," as opposed to transgender or genderqueer, was the common term with which they identified. The researchers acknowledge that identifying as a stud may be specific to the inner-city location where the informants lived, but recognize that the term transgender is one that stemmed from a primarily White, middle- and upper-class contextualization (Valentine 2007) and, therefore, may not be one with which genderqueer individuals of Color can identify.

In a follow-up article to West and Zimmerman's (1987) "Doing Gender" article, West and Sarah Fenstermaker (1995) addressed how race and class interact with doing gender – something they admit was neglected in the earlier article. Likewise, in response to reviews of their hegemonic masculinity concept, Connell and Messerschmidt's (2005:848) reformulation stressed the necessity "to incorporate a more holistic understanding of gender hierarchy" that would better incorporate additional social factors like race and class. Henceforth, common scholarly sentiment now commands an intersectional evaluation in studies of sex, gender, and sexuality – and scholars have been more attentive about making this a regular practice, yet a great need still exists for intersectional analyses. Black feminist social theorist Patricia Hill Collins (2000a, 2005) has been one of the foremost voices in demanding intersectional approaches in social science research. Collins (2005:6) has emphasized the need to consider how race and ethnicity affect gender and sexual expressions, realizing that men and masculinities must be included in these investigations:

> Regardless of race, ethnicity, social class, citizenship status, and sexual orientation, all men and women encounter social norms about gender. These norms influence...perceptions of masculinity and femininity. For African Americans, the relationship between gender and race is intensified, producing a Black gender ideology that shapes ideas about Black masculinity and Black femininity.

Latinas are also confronted with devalued views about their sexuality. An assessment of Latinas' experiences and those of Black women underscore how views, often stereotypical, of Latinas and Black women are measured up against the White-woman ideal (also an essentialized and typecast view). Undoubtedly, gendered and sexual microaggressions are perpetrated against women and genderqueer individuals (as well as against sexually queer individuals) (Sue 2010), but multiplying a subjugated gender identity with a subjugated racial identity often exacerbates the experiences of girls and women of Color. A review of statistics on sexual interactions and pregnancy among adolescents in the United States demonstrates how stereotypes of Black and Latina girls can be fueled. Statistics from the Centers for Disease Control and Prevention (2012) indicate that during 2006 to 2010, 43 percent of young women aged 15 to 19 in the United States had engaged in penile-vaginal sexual intercourse.

Approximately 52 percent of the girls reported using "highly effective" birth control methods (such as an intrauterine device [IUD] or hormonal methods). By race, 66 percent of sexually experienced White teenage girls used "highly effective" methods of contraception, compared with 54 percent of Latina teenagers and 46 percent of Black teenage girls. Nonuse of any contraception was significantly higher among Black girls (25.6 percent) and Latina girls (23.7 percent) than for White girls (14.6 percent). These instances of sexual intercourse result in birth rates among teenage girls of approximately 50 pregnancies for every 1,000 Latinas, 47 among Blacks, 36 among "American Indian and Alaska Natives," 22 among Whites, and 10 among "Asian or Pacific Islander" teenagers (Hamilton *et al.* 2012). Further, there are disparities by race in repeat births among teenage girls, with the highest proportions for 2010 found among "American Indian/Alaska Natives" (21.6 percent), Latinas (20.9 percent), and Blacks (20.4 percent) – all of which are higher than the percentage of repeat births among "Asian and Pacific Islander" teens (17.6 percent) and White teens (14.8 percent) (Centers for Disease Control and Prevention 2013). A variety of intersectional social factors can be used to understand the different rates of teenage sex and pregnancy by race, such as the following three trends that should be considered in concert with each other: (1) the feminization of birth control, where girls and women, not boys or men, are seen as being responsible for assuring contraception is used (Fields 2008; Luker 1996; Weber 2012); (2) the differential views on healthcare access by race and ethnicity, with people of Color (especially *poor* people of Color), in comparison with Whites, having lower rates of access to healthcare and higher rates of distrust in medical professionals (Boulware *et al.* 2003; Santelli *et al.* 2000); and (3) the lower quality of healthcare provided to people of Color compared with Whites (Smedley *et al.* 2009). The impact of an inequitable society on gender and sexuality behaviors and identity can be seen in Lorena Garcia's (2012) ethnographic study that included intensive interviews with US-born daughters of Mexican and Puerto Rican im/migrants and their mothers in Chicago. Garcia explored the simultaneity of invisibility and visibility regarding Latina youth's sexuality and concluded that the girls

> are rendered invisible by the assumption that the experiences of middle- and upper-class white young women are the norm, the yardstick by which we measure all other girls, and yet, they are made quite visible to us by the constant association of teen pregnancy with young Latinas by which teen pregnancy among Latina youth is regularly described as a "normal" and "cultural" phenomenon.
>
> (pp. 150–151)

The girls in Garcia's study were sexually active, identified as lesbian or heterosexual, and had never been pregnant. While fully aware of the widely perpetrated sexualized stereotypes about Latinas, the girls navigated practicing safe sex, and saw taking responsibility for pregnancy and infection prevention as an appropriate form of femininity. However, in their objective to "fashion a gendered sexual subjectivity that was specifically grounded in their identities as Latinas and that affirmed their sexual respectability" (p. 153), they also unintentionally reproduced the stigmatization of Latina adolescents who became pregnant or teen mothers by situating themselves in a counter identity. The informants also distanced themselves from young White women, who they saw as sexually immoral based on popular media representations, as depicted by research participant Isela, who was angry at having been goaded by boys at a dance party to kiss another girl: "They just love to see girls kissing each other, you know, like some white girls be acting, kissing each other, showing their thongs, acting like hos! I ain't no white girl" (p. 102).

Although I have outlined race/ethnicity and sex/gender/sexuality in separate sections, as can be gleaned from some of the examples and research reviewed here, the need to consider the fusion between the two clusters is warranted. As was also seen, the inclusion of socioeconomic class further produces varied experiences.

Defining socioeconomic class

In the study of social and lived experiences, one's socioeconomic class can serve as both a status and an identity. Government agencies, academics, and others often measure economic class standing by income alone (Marable 2000; Oliver and Shapiro 2006), such as the US Census Bureau's measurement of economic status that only includes income and not other measures like the effect of taxes, partial payment of health insurance provided by an employer, or receiving school lunches or housing assistance (DeNavas-Walt *et al.* 2003). Sociologists Melvin L. Oliver and Thomas M. Shapiro (2006:2) argued that *wealth* should be measured when determining class level as opposed to income because "[w]ealth is what people own, while income is what people receive for work, retirement, or social welfare." They elaborated:

> Wealth signifies the command over financial resources that a family has accumulated over its lifetime along with these resources that have been inherited across generations. Such resources, when combined with income, can create the opportunity to secure the "good life" in whatever form is needed – education, business, training, justice, health, comfort, and so on. Wealth is a special form of money not used to purchase milk and shoes and other life necessities. More often, it is used to create opportunities, secure a desired stature and standard of living, or pass class status along to one's children.

Accordingly, many other pecuniary factors aside from work income must be taken into account when categorizing individuals by socioeconomic class. There exist general social science conceptualizations and definitions of the various socioeconomic classes – most commonly, low, middle, and upper classes. While these labels and their specifications provide a general understanding of socioeconomic classes and how they are operationalized in the social sciences and in society generally, there is much variance within these classes. Therefore, scholars have begun to classify beyond three or four socioeconomic levels.

Donna M. Beegle (2007), consultant and trainer for organizations with the capacity to improve the lives of people in poverty, developed a nine-level socioeconomic scale within a US context that offers a better-specified hierarchy, beginning with generational poverty at the bottom and followed by working poor, working class, temporary or situational poverty, low (aspiring) middle class, solidly middle class, upper middle class, owning-class rich, and ruling-class rich.[12] The primary focus of persons in generational poverty is to survive each day. When those in generational poverty do work, it is typically in low-wage and unstable jobs. They experience high mobilization due to migrating for work and getting evicted from their homes, and have never owned land or other major assets. They internalize the societal blame that they are the cause of their own poverty and they often fear or have anger for police and other authority figures. Members of society living in generational poverty are surrounded by immediate family members and acquaintances who endure similar fates and therefore are unable to assist each other with social, cultural, and economic resources that would elevate anyone in their social set out of poverty. Generational poverty is demonstrated in the findings of a 25-year longitudinal study of residents living in high-poverty neighborhoods of west Baltimore, Maryland. In *The Long Shadow: Family Background, Disadvantaged Urban Youth, and the Transition to Adulthood*, sociologists Karl Alexander, Doris Entwisle, and Linda Olson (2014) explained that the study's urban disadvantaged were barred from upward mobility because of multiple factors, including,

> their families are not well positioned to help them advance through schooling; they live in high poverty, and for some violent, neighborhoods; they attend high-poverty schools; their balance of school-based risk and protective factors is heavy on risk and short on protection; their employment in early adulthood is erratic or absent; and their attempts at postsecondary education, when they do enroll, mostly are unsuccessful.
>
> (p. 157)

According to Beegle, the "working poor" differ from the "working class" in that the working class hold jobs that are more stable than those held by the working poor, who regularly fear losing their jobs due to a layoff or often have their work hours reduced. Most in the working class hope at least one of their children will attend college, while working poor do not see graduating from high school as attainable. Also, some members of the working class own property.

The next rung on the socioeconomic scale identified by Beegle is temporary or situational poverty, which is experienced by people who were raised in economically stable environments and have educational accomplishments and good health, but are dropped to poverty from middle class due to a unique crisis, such as divorce or macrostructural economic recessions and depressions. Unlike those at the generational poverty level, individuals encountered with temporary or situational poverty attribute their poverty only to an exceptional situation, do not view their poverty as something they caused, and typically return to middle class. Presumably, Beegle placed members of the temporary or situational poverty class higher in her hierarchy than those in the working poor and working classes because the former can draw on their middle-class cultural competence and would retain cultural capital and, possibly, some measure of social capital (see Bourdieu 1986).

Members of the middle classes tend to work in professional or highly skilled occupations or occupations that require college education. Their jobs often provide a stable environment and include benefits such as health insurance and retirement plans. Home ownership, or the potential to own a home, is an additional salient factor to classify the middle classes, even though this asset was devalued for many in Western countries as a result of the 2008–2009 Great Recession that began in the United States and had global implications. Beegle applied these general aspects of the middle classes in her definitions, but also differentiated the three middle classes by their consumption. According to Beegle, members of the aspiring middle class attempt to "keep up with the Joneses" by imitating the purchasing practices of neighbors and associates in the other middle classes. The aspiring middle class also has less education and/or professional skills compared with the other middle classes. The solidly middle class – who tend to have supplemental income from investments or businesses – have "arrived" in comparison to the aspiring middle class, and its members view their ability to purchase items such as season tickets for sport or other entertainment (such as, season theater tickets) as social capital. The upper middle-class members have all that the solidly middle-class members have, in addition to the likelihood of having children in private schools, using nannies to care for their children, belonging to country clubs, and having homes with security systems. They also view government-operated law enforcement (the police) as protectors of their homes and other property. Finally, at the top of the socioeconomic class hierarchy, Beegle established that the owning-class rich differ from the ruling-class rich because the former group has significant economic power and social capital, while the latter group possesses these aspects in addition to social power and influence by way of holding positions of considerable authority in major social institutions.

In spite of the tired stereotype that the urban disadvantaged are "all poor black women having babies out of wedlock, or predatory black men," poverty traverses race (Alexander *et al.* 2014:185). Data indicate that a greater proportion of women and persons of Color across the globe are situated in the lower socioeconomic statuses than are White men and that there continue to be significant gender and racial gaps in (paid) labor market participation (Alexander *et al.* 2014; International Labour Office 2011). Alexander, Entwisle, and Olson (2014) attested in their Baltimore study that poor Whites, men especially, still maintain some benefits of White privilege, as seen in their greater likelihood of securing employment in comparison with Blacks with similar employment and criminal legal system histories (see also Pager 2007). Further, Black women in the United States tend to do worse financially than White women because there is a greater likelihood that Black women are unpartnered, thus they do not have the advantage of having a second adult earner in the home, and if they do marry or partner, their partners tend to have lower income than the typical partners of White women (Alexander *et al.* 2014). Obviously, people of Color positioned in higher socioeconomic classes also endure discrimination or racism; however, the racism – whether interpersonal or institutional – that solidly and upper middle-class people of Color encounter can be more easily combated (in comparison with the classes lower on the scale) by rallying the support and resources that middle-class professional status has afforded. Even so, I submit that middle-class people of Color, especially *women* of Color because of the multiplication of genderism, are at much greater risk than Whites in the same class and people of Color in the uppermost classes of losing their wealth or access to wealth because of institutional racism. Although interpersonal and institutional racism encountered by women and people of Color in the upper classes is significantly less likely to affect their current financial status or future economic gains, which may not affect their material way of living, extreme wealth is not necessarily able to protect them from the mental toll that racism, genderism, and racism×genderism can take. Ultimately, we are better enlightened about societal machinations of power and partiality when race, gender, and socioeconomics are treated as compounded factors.

Defining crime

Most people, including children, have a general understanding of what constitutes *crime* within their society, and they have common knowledge that the ascription of acts as criminal changes over time (recreational marijuana vending and use is now allowed in the states of Colorado and Washington), and vary by place (sex work allowed in Nevada counties with populations less than 400,000) and age (youth and young adults restricted from drinking alcohol). This widespread comprehension is perhaps the reason many criminologists, in their respective published works, do not provide a definition of what they mean when they use the term crime, although, depending on the subject matter or the research conducted, it may not always be necessary to include an operational definition for crime.

Like social identities, designating certain acts as crimes is also a social construct. Marxist criminologist Richard Quinney (1970:207) summarized that "'criminal behavior' differs from 'noncriminal behavior' only according to the definition that has been created by others." Elite members of many modern societies have traditionally been those who ultimately determine what is criminal. Polity-designated crime is the group of behaviors that "the State" deem to be transgressions committed by individuals or groups against other people or against the morality of the populace. These acts are determined by a consensus of lawmakers within a jurisdiction, some of whom make moral judgments that may not be in keeping with the populace (see the decriminalization of marijuana as determined by a majority of voting Colorado residents). Quinney concluded,

> Criminal definitions are formulated according to the interests of those *segments* (types of social groupings) of a society which have the *power* to translate their interests into *public policy*. The interests – based on desires, values, and norms – which are ultimately incorporated into the criminal law are those which are treasured by the dominant interest groups in the society.
>
> (p. 16; emphases in original text)

There is certainly truth in this declaration, but it is also a complicated notion because the largest proportion of the populace voted many of these elites into office to represent the populace. Further, many acts deemed criminal by the polity are supported by a majority of its citizens, such as sexual and nonsexual assault, murder, and theft.

The majority of the types of crimes that are researched by criminologists, addressed by politicians, and reported by news media outlets are referred to by many criminologists as "ordinary crime," which tends to include violence, theft, and use and selling of "illicit" or "street" drugs (like marijuana, cocaine, methamphetamine, and heroin). In particular, politicians and news media frequently address acts of violence, especially when they occur between parties previously unknown to each other. Of course, these are grave violations that deserve attention. But labeling these as ordinary crimes asserts that such crime is normal or common, and that other crimes, like those committed by individuals in their capacity as employees or executives in corporate or state organizations, are abnormal or special cases (that is, *extra*ordinary). There remains a great need for attention to be paid to infractions that go undetected or unsanctioned because certain individuals and institutions and the egregious acts they commit are not perceived as criminal. Social power is the discrete factor shielding many of these individuals and institutions from a criminal tag. Many criminologists across ideologies have delved into addressing the crimes of the powerful, but it is the critical, feminist, and progressive race criminologists who have more frequently taken up the inclusion of this extraordinary group of criminal offenses and offenders. These offenders are actually committing acts that are quite ordinary, as substantiated by the regularity of some of the acts, the large number of people affected (victimized), and the vast amount of financial and intangible harm caused.

Critical, feminist, and progressive race criminologists widen the definition of crime to include violative acts like irresponsible or disregarded environmental hazards like polluting air, water, food, and land; harmful or violent acts committed during wars between nations (and sometimes war itself); corporate or "white-collar" crime; misuse and overuse of force by police officers, jail and prison officers, and other law enforcement agents against citizens; enactment of legal statutes and policies that more harshly punish the poor and the powerless; and biased sentencing that over-incarcerates people of Color and the poor. Accordingly, some criminologists are not confined by the government definitions of crime and legal or depraved practices of enforcement. Even if the acts are not formally and legally recognized as a crime, these criminologists expand definitions of crime to transgressions by the state and harms to humanity, while simultaneously critiquing the polity's emphasis on activities that cause little or no conceivable harm (such as the over-regulation and over-criminalization of marijuana users and sex workers). Although much of the research I present in this book references interpersonal crimes of violence, theft, and street drug selling and use, readers should remain mindful of the role of intersectionality in criminology from the stance of a broader definition of crime.

Disrupting criminology

Integrating intersectionality into studies of crime ensures that criminologists make attempts at racing gender, gendering race, racing sexuality, gendering class, and so on, as well as (and more importantly) considering the multiplicative effects of *several* identities. The impact of oppression is detrimental in many ways, as demonstrated in research on discrimination, microaggressions, and bigotry. As an example, the resultant detriment can serve as a path to behaviors to alleviate the pain, such as self-medicating with alcohol or other drugs, which can lead to addiction and then involvement in activities offensive to others to continue to support the addiction or because legitimate employment was lost due to the addiction. For individuals who hold multiple intertwined identities at the lowest end of the social hierarchy, discrimination, microaggressions, and bigotry are multiplied. An intersectional approach to criminology therefore provides a more rigorous and relevant interpretation of the overrepresentation in criminal activity of socially marginalized groups.

Feminist sociologist Kathy Davis (2008) identified that intersectionality is now a "buzzword"; referencing the fact that it is the hottest new concept in the feminist theory market. Its *presumed* newness has resulted in much discourse to resolve intersectionality's definition and purpose. To be sure, and as I explicate in this book, we do know that intersectionality was born from the activism, research, feminism, and theory building undertaken by Black women and other women of Color, and from the work in critical race legal studies, and we have been able to gain consensus on a definition for intersectionality. However, some debate has centered on the application of intersectionality. Is the concept only appropriate for interpreting the social experiences of Black women or of all women of Color, or can the experiences of all individuals be considered? Is intersectionality a paradigm, a perspective, a theory, an epistemology, a methodology, or a research method, or some combination of any of these? In Chapter 2, Illuminating Intersectionality, I provide an expansive review of intersectionality's precursors and an assessment of the purposes of intersectionality and where it fits intellectually within criminology.

In determining intersectionality's fit within criminology, in Chapter 3, Reduxing Criminology, I assess how an intersectional approach relates to acclaimed criminological research and theories. I especially focus on the major works of Michael R. Gottfredson and Travis Hirschi (1990), John H. Laub and Robert J. Sampson (1993, 2003), and Peggy C. Giordano (2010). Feminist sociologists Hae Yeon Choo and Myra Marx Ferree (2010) engaged in this form of assessment in their review of four monographs on the study of social inequalities that have received high praise within the field of sociology: *Sidewalk* (Mitchell Duneier 1999), *Promises I Can Keep: Why Poor Women Put Motherhood Before Marriage* (Kathryn Edin and Maria Kefalas 2005), *The Dignity of Working Men: Morality and the Boundaries of Race, Class, and Immigration* (Michèle Lamont 2000), and *Unequal Childhoods: Class, Race, and Family Life* (Annette Lareau 2003). Choo and Ferree demonstrated how the studies could have improved upon their rich findings "if they had emphasized the inclusion of perspectives, not only persons, from the margins of society … problematized relationships of power for unmarked categories, such as whiteness and masculinity; or … treated inequalities as multiply-determined and intertwined rather than assuming one central institutional framework" (p. 131). My analysis of select criminological studies yields similar results. I also identify intersectionality's fit within criminology in Chapter 4, Intersecting Criminology, with exemplar studies. Within the field of criminology, several empirical research projects that incorporate an intersectional analysis are viewed as seminal contributions to feminist criminology, including the research of Beth E. Richie (1996) and Lisa Maher (1997). I detail these works, along with other studies that unequivocally employed a theoretical and analytical framework resembling intersectionality.

Daly and Maher (1998) boldly employed the label of "White criminology" – where most other places this would simply be called "mainstream criminology." This "mainstream criminology" is typically juxtaposed with forms of criminology that, even though gaining support, are still marginalized within the field of criminology. Both its own members and out-group members have thrust the mainstream label upon a certain group of criminologies and criminologists. Continuing to use the term "mainstream" to identify the criminologies put forward by those with the biggest names and most famed theories in criminology only perpetuates the marginalization of other criminologies and those who question the most recognized theories in the field. Instead, I opt for *orthodox* criminology to signify criminologies that are "accepted as true or correct by most people" and "supporting or believing what most people think is true" (definition of orthodox at http://www.merriam-webster.com/). In his book, *Toward a Unified Criminology: Integrating Assumptions about Crime, People, and Society*, criminologist Robert Agnew (2011) contended that these theoretical divisions that exist within criminology only serve to damage the field and, as a result, cannot provide society-at-large with unified solutions to combating crime. While *Intersectionality and Criminology* may seem only to stir the battle between criminologies, I contend that this book works toward the unification Agnew promotes.

I see my exposition as thought-provoking, not hypercritical. By first disrupting orthodox criminological thought and demonstrating how intersectionality can aid in criminological research and conceptualization, the discipline of criminology would be revolutionized and modernized. Part of this revolution involves making better and more effective connections with the practical side of criminology. I address this issue in Chapter 5, Revolutionizing Criminology, focusing on the policy implications for incorporating an intersectional approach in criminology. With the push for making our research relevant in the practical world of the criminal legal system ("public criminology"), it is important that we connect the benefits of utilizing intersectionality in criminological studies with the ways in which this standpoint can improve upon the function and effectiveness of social support and legal systems.

This book is not presented as the concluding or definitive statement on intersectional criminology. Just as intersectionality is considered a traveling theory (Carbado 2013; Carbado *et al.* 2013; Cho *et al.* 2013), still being formulated and trying to decide what she wants to be when she grows up, intersectional criminology will also likely be an evolving concept. This book does, however, serve to demonstrate how intersectional approaches have been used in criminological research and theory, and how other criminological research based in orthodox, colorblind, identity-blind, and power-blind theorizing can benefit from an intersectional approach.

Notes

1 The term "Black feminist" references, all at once, (1) a social, racial, and cultural identity (Black and Blackness), (2) a racial group location and affinity (Black community), and (3) a standpoint. Because individuals who do not identify as female/woman can be feminists, gender is not an assumption or a requirement for a person identifying as a Black feminist; however, individuals usually labeling themselves as Black feminists tend to be Black women (which includes transgender or genderqueer Black women). Upon modifications based on the appropriate racial and cultural experience and identity, Latina feminists, Indigenous feminists, and other women of Color feminists also fit within this description. A White person identifying as a Black feminist (or other feminist of Color) would typically be considered an encroachment, although many Black feminists and women of Color feminists are often open to White allies under certain circumstances.

2 This is a paraphrasing and broader application of a commonly used expression in Black feminism. In the late nineteenth century, Black activist scholar Anna Julia Cooper (1892:31) wrote that she told a group of Black male clergy members, "Only the BLACK WOMAN can say 'when and where I enter, in the quiet, undisputed dignity of my womanhood, without violence and without suing or special patronage, then and there the whole *Negro race enters with me.*'"

3 While there is an abundance of references in print and in conversation among criminologists that criminology is an *academic discipline*, some question this designation: "Our language and methods are borrowed from other disciplines, and we have no uniform theoretical infrastructure, in part because we employ the various theoretical orientations of those several disciplines. We are an area of study, not a discipline, and we use the tools (sometimes especially honed for our particular purposes) of the established areas. We are multidisciplinary always, interdisciplinary at our best" (Clear 2001:711). In this book, however, I have chosen to represent criminology as a discipline.

4 While many criminologists base their work in sociology, others do not; thus my separation of the designations criminology/criminologists and sociology/sociologists throughout the text. See also note 3.

5 I use the terms *progressive race criminology/criminologists* and *race-and-crime scholars* interchangeably to refer to criminologists who study race and crime from a critical stance that impels orthodox criminological views to be conscious of the ways racialized inequities and discrimination are manifested in offending, victimization, and the workings of the criminal legal system.

6 While feminist criminology is considered by some to be one of the schools of thought within critical criminology (see DeKeseredy 2011; Schwartz and Milovanovic 1996), other references have feminist criminology appearing as a stand-alone perspective or paradigm (see Chesney-Lind 2006; Chesney-Lind and Morash 2013; Moore 2008). Chesney-Lind and Morash (2013:288) have discerned, "We know that some scholars see feminist criminology as a subfield of critical criminology. In our view, that is not really an accurate depiction, since not all critical criminologists place gender at the center of theory, and not all feminist criminologists see their work as part of the broader struggle for social justice."

7 For an intriguing exception to this, see Robert Courtney Smith's (2014) study on Mexican Americans who identified themselves as Black during adolescence and while living in predominately Black neighborhoods or attending predominantly Black schools in New York City, but who abandoned their Black identity upon reaching adulthood and living or working in settings with a larger proportion of Whites.

8 Bonilla-Silva (2010:179) suggested that the racial order in the United States is a "triracial stratification system" with Whites on top followed by "honorary Whites" and then the "collective Black" at the bottom. In addition to Whites, the "Whites" group includes "assimilated" White Latinas/os and

Indigenous persons, "a few Asian-origin people," "new" Whites, such as Russian or Albanian immigrants, and some multiracial persons. Honorary Whites include light-skinned Latinas/os, Japanese American, Chinese Americans, Korean Americans, Asian Indians, Middle Eastern Americans, and most multiracial persons. In addition to Blacks, the "Collective Black" includes Filipino Americans, Hmong Americans, Laotian Americans, Vietnamese Americans, dark-skinned Latinas/os, new West Indian and African immigrants, and "reservation-bound Native Americans" (p. 180, Figure 8.1).

9 Because of the oppression of certain racial groups within a society, some argue that the oppressed group (e.g. people of Color in the United States and the United Kingdom) within that society is unable to be racist against the oppressor (e.g. Whites in the United States and the United Kingdom).

10 Concepts similar to Sue's (2010) conceptualization of racial microaggressions – that is, subtle forms of racism – include *colorblind racism* (Bonilla-Silva 2010), *aversive racism* (Dovidio 2001), and *modern racism* (McConahay 1986).

11 The instances where Black, Indigenous, and White (as racial categorizations) are not capitalized in this book are when I quote authors who do not capitalize these terms.

12 Beegle's (2007) categorizations are based on her dissertation research for her doctoral degree in leadership education, *Interrupting Generational Poverty: Factors Influencing Successful Completion of the Bachelor's Degree* (2000, Portland State University).

2

ILLUMINATING INTERSECTIONALITY

Formation of the intersectional standpoint

The concept of intersectionality was developed within the US context and is rooted in US Black feminist theory and in critical race theory. To best understand intersectionality, academics must be engaged with the history of Black women's activism and theory, and with congruent activism and theory of other women of Color. The elements of critical race theory (or progressive race and antiracism perspectives) are found within women of Color feminist theorizing, thus, I argue that intersectionality's base is mainly in Black feminist and women of Color feminist theorizing. To be unaware of, ignore, or not acknowledge this foundation is to risk misunderstanding or misreading intersectionality and similar conceptualizations, as is the case in attempts to "broaden the genealogy of intersectionality" by erasing race from the identity categorizations and power relations, quintessentially rewriting history and rebranding the concept (Bilge 2013). This type of reworking can be pinned on the circumstance that the concept of intersectionality has traveled fast and far. The rate of travel of intersectionality has also resulted in scholars misemploying intersectionality by not fully explicating how it can explain or was evident in the phenomenon under investigation. Intersectionality has an alluring inclusivity hook that seemingly validates that a scholar is "down with the cause" and has embraced racial diversity; however, simply adding the term intersectionality along with a base definition in a publication because the sample includes women (or men) of Color, but not fully applying intersectionality, is inadequate. These rootless, reframed, or underemployed renderings of intersectionality can also be attributed to trending. The indication by some observers that intersectionality is simply a buzzword – that is, a term or concept that is currently in vogue but is fated to have a short life – is a misrepresentation. Deeming intersectionality as a transitory fad does not recognize that women of Color feminists and others have been conducting academic analyses under corresponding frameworks for many years. As Kimberlé Crenshaw (2011:233) argued, characterizing intersectionality as a buzzword "does not do justice to the academics and activists who use intersectionality to illuminate and address discriminatory situations that would otherwise escape articulation."

As indicated, intersectionality's base is in Black and women of Color feminist work. The terms *feminism* and *feminist* are not often connected with women of Color, yet, as Black feminist sociologist Patricia Hill Collins (2006:195) asserted, "US feminism is not now, nor has it ever been, the exclusive property of White, middle-class, or affluent women." Black feminist social critic Bell Hooks (2000: 11) argued that White women feminists have sometimes taken a condescending and possessive position in feminism and feminist movements:

> Frequently, white feminists act as if black women did not know sexist oppression existed until they voiced feminist sentiment. They believe they are providing black women with 'the' analysis and 'the' program for liberation. They do not understand, cannot even imagine, that black women, as well as other groups of women who live daily in oppressive situations, often acquire an awareness of patriarchal politics from their lived experiences, just as they develop strategies of resistance (even though they may not resist on a sustained or organized basis).

Although White women feminists "desperately wanted women of color to join *them*" (Roth 2004:195, emphasis in original text), the work of White feminists toward equality for women was not strongly influenced by the need to also address racial equality. To be sure, there are distinctive strains of feminism – or, as Benita Roth (2004) referred to it, "separate roads to feminism" – even if the feminist label is not routinely applied by and to women of Color. The intersectional activism efforts of US Black and Chicana feminists are well documented in a variety of intellectual, news, and entertainment media. Indigenous feminists have also played significant activist roles in the United States. Unfortunately, Indigenous feminists, along with Arab, Asian, and Asian American feminists, are the most obscure feminists in feminist theory, research, and activism (Green 2007; LaRocque 2007). LaRocque (2007:67) generally attributed this invisibility to Black and White authors who "seem unaware of our existence, both as politically situated women and/or as intellectuals and scholars."

Women of Color feminist activism and organizing and women of Color feminist theorizing and scholarly production are not separate entities; both endeavors are based in the significance and impact of distinct lived experiences, identity politics, and hierarchization and minoritization regarding women of Color. Moreover, women of Color feminisms and feminists are relationally situated in a custom that involves an exchange of knowledge (Cho *et al.* 2013). Arguably, women of Color feminist scholars *are* activists. Beyond explicit participation in community organizing (outside of institutions of higher education), the critical academic work of women of Color feminist scholars is an act of resistance. The utilization of feminist of Color conceptualizations in scholarly work is still a risk for many women of Color scholars, who face greater pressure to justify and defend their theoretical frameworks and topics of inquiry and who are assumed to be incapable of objectively examining members of their own race×gender group (an indictment not typically lodged against Whites who study Whites). From gaining approval for masters and (especially) doctoral theses topics to successful defense of a doctoral dissertation to attaining a tenure-track position to being awarded tenure (see Gutierrez y Muhs *et al.* 2012), budding and established women of Color scholars, particularly in White-predominated colleges and universities, work to disrupt the White male racial frame. Granted, these challenges within an elite or elitist setting are different from other forms of individual everyday activism and collective organizing, but, unquestionably, feminists of Color all participate in some form of resistance and change activism.[1]

Naming and claiming feminisms and feminists

Broadly, feminism has been identified as a "political program working to empower women, to ensure them autonomy and control over their lives in a way that does not impede the autonomy or contribute to the exploitation of other women" (Laughlin *et al.* 2010:101). What is typically referred to as "mainstream feminism" – and, sometimes, "Western feminism" or simply "feminism" – is the work and ideology that are readily recognized by the general public. In "mainstream feminism," the primary identity attribute concern is gender (Hooks 2000; Laughlin *et al.* 2010). In considering the reach of "feminist thought," one assertion contended that "feminist thought suffers from a white middle-class bias. The privileging of white and middle-class sensibilities in feminist thought results from both who did the theorizing and how they did it" (West and Fenstermaker 1995:10). This pronouncement was written as a *mea culpa* by the White feminist authors for overlooking and not addressing the racial and classed differences in "doing gender" in an earlier publication (see West and Zimmerman 1987). Even the authors' declaration, however, is laden with the assumption that there is but *one* feminist thought and that women of Color did *no* feminist work. This demonstrates the marginalization of and inattention to feminist work that has been undertaken by women of Color. This exercise of disregard is one that has long been in existence, but, thankfully, is showing signs of dwindling, as evidenced by the growing deployment of intersectionality. Because "mainstream" indicates a default, regular, or normal method, I refer to the well-known efforts of feminism, typically forwarded by groups comprising a White women majority, as *colorblind feminism*. This designation is not to slight the efforts of these trailblazers; colorblind, in this context, references how the racial identity of women is or was not a major impetus for the recognized and recognizable movement, and how White women feminists believe or believed gender was *the* prominent factor connecting *all* women.

Women of Color have long expressed difficulty in identifying with colorblind feminist theory and activism because of its focus on gender as the sole aspect of womanhood and because the lives and concerns of White women (especially middle socioeconomic class White women) were placed at the forefront of the liberation efforts (Beal [1970]1995; Chow 1987; Collins 2000a; Crenshaw 1989; Huhndorf and Suzack 2010; Laughlin *et al.* 2010; Roth 2004; Sanchez-Hucles *et al.* 2012; Yamada 1981 [2001]). Women of Color regularly convey that they not only deal with issues of gender inequality, but with racial inequality, as well (Baca Zinn and Thornton Dill 1996; Crenshaw 1991; Segura and Facio 2008). It is this state, feminists of Color argue, that relegates women of Color to an invisible class, and can pull these women's loyalties in two directions: feeling the need to choose between being loyal to gender-equality ideas or being loyal to their racial or ethnic community. Often, the choice has been made by a woman of Color to place her efforts in, and side with, the latter, even if the lives of women and girls are set aside to address general race-group issues (like institutional racism) or the plights of male counterparts. Feminists of Color, therefore, can be seen as either standing alongside or parallel to both colorblind feminism and antiracism/progressive race perspectives or standing astride each of these perspectives.

With regard to naming the different strains of feminist action and theory, the work by women of Color feminists is typically identified by the group's identity. For instance, critical race feminism, Black feminism, Latina feminism, Indigenous feminism, third-world feminism, and multiracial feminism. Black women advocates of gender and race equality only began to describe themselves using the term *feminism* in the 1970s (Cole 1995). In support of attaching the descriptive term, Collins (1996:13) suggested, "Using the term 'black feminism' disrupts the racism inherent in presenting feminism as a for-whites-only ideology and political movement. Inserting the adjective 'black' challenges the assumed whiteness of feminism and disrupts the false universal of this term for both white and black women." Women in general are often reluctant to adopt the term *feminist* because of the negative connotation of the word (Freedman 2002) and for fear of being denied attention and love from men because feminism is often viewed as a man-hating cause (Hooks 2000). Women of Color have difficulty attaching themselves to the term because feminism has generally been associated with Whites and Whiteness (Anderson 2010; Brown 1992; Collins 1996; Smith 2005b). Even though Black women espouse ideas of feminism, Black feminist anthropologist Johnetta B. Cole (1995) affirmed that Black women are reluctant to appropriate a feminist classification to describe themselves, in part because of distorted images (by media and others) of feminists. Writ large, although many women of Color have rejected identifying themselves using the feminist term or have not publicly identified themselves with the term, they are certainly cognizant about situating their political, activism, research, or theoretical work within a feminist context.

Among women of Color practicing woman-centered activism and producing woman-centered theory, the self-naming varies. While I choose to use *Black feminist* to identify myself and my work, and in this book I identity women of Color doing work considered to be feminist using the same term or an analogous term (Chicana feminist, Indigenous feminist), many women of Color have opted to identify their feminism by adopting other labels. Some women of Color have opted for *womanist*, a term coined by Black feminist novelist Alice Walker (1983:xi) to specifically designate "a black feminist or feminist of color." For Walker, "Womanist is to feminist as purple to lavender" (xii). Some Latina feminists have used *feminista* and *mujerista*, *muxerista*, and *xicanisma*. Feminista is often simply the Spanish translation of feminist, but also specifies the work of those involved in Chicana, Latina, and Latin American feminist movements (Delgado Bernal *et al.* 2006).[2] Feminist scholar Anita Tijerina-Revilla (2009:48) described a *muxerista* as someone who identifies as a Chicana or Latina feminist, fighting against all modes of social oppression. *Muxerista* was created from *muxeres*, a self-descriptive term for grassroots activists in Chiapas, Mexico, who fought for the autonomy of the Indigenous populace in Chiapas (Zapatistas). The *muxerista* expression captures a Latina's identity as a *mujer* (woman) who is, at the same time, feminist and activist. "The 'x' replaces the 'j' to denote a connection to indigenous ancestry/language and anticolonial struggle. It also signifies the multiplicity, complexity, and intersectionality of a Chicana/Latina activist identity" (p. 49). Similarly, the "x" is used in *xicanisma*, according to literary scholar Ana Castillo (1994), to rename Chicana feminism and emphasize indigeneity. Tijerina-Revilla differentiated *muxerista* and *mujerista*, indicating that both classifications have a grassroots social justice orientation, but *mujerista* emphasizes a strong theological component, while the "articulation of a *muxerista* consciousness rarely invokes a connection to theology…[and] is rooted in the theoretical framings and actions of the women themselves" (p. 49). For some purveyors, *mujerista* has extended beyond a discrete theological understanding, and is often viewed generally as a Latina-oriented womanism (Delgado Bernal *et al.* 2006). Finally, some contemporary young feminists of Color are identifying as *hip-hop feminist* or *crunk feminist*, on which I elaborate later in this chapter. Whether using *womanist*, *mujerista*, *muxerista*, *feminist*, or any other term, or not using a term at all, the actual grassroots and wide-reaching work that is being done by women of Color advocates and scholars for women's rights is what reigns as important. For women of Color who have appropriated the *feminist* term, we have redefined it to reflect our lives, principles, and causes.

(Re)Tracing feminist journeys

Colorblind feminist activism and theory comprises three eras of development, typically referred to as *waves*, which began in the 1700s. The waves reference underscores the occasions when middle-class White women were especially active and these activities were well publicized (Laughlin *et al.* 2010). Although contemporary feminist scholars are beginning to question the utility of distinguishing the colorblind feminist movement in the United States, Canada, and Europe into cohorts, generations, or waves (Aikau *et al.* 2007; Laughlin *et al.* 2010), the wave descriptor has been referenced since the late 1960s, and is recognizable to a broad, nonfeminist audience. Further, a reading of literature on women of Color feminism in the United States demonstrates that women of Color feminist action has been an unremitting enterprise, and does not neatly align with the waves. In addition, other feminist women have not been included in the waves, such as women in the working classes, women with limited physical abilities, lesbians, and elder women (Laughlin *et al.*

2010). Nevertheless, I retain the three-wave timeline to trace colorblind feminism since its usage in academic and public discussions persists; but I juxtapose that history with the paths traveled by women of Color (particularly in the United States) on their feminist journeys.

The birth of feminism?

Certain Indigenous feminist thought claims that the feminist concept was actually originated by Indigenous women and adopted by White women or, at the least, "was simply a way of life to our ancestors," where women in many Indigenous cultures were valued, held equal status with men, and, in some cases, were authority figures (Anderson 2010:82; see also Green 2007; Smith 2005b). Cree-Métis feminist Kim Anderson (2010:89) concluded, "women's organizing is an Indigenous thing: our pre-colonial societies were sustained by women's work, women's councils, women's ceremonies, and women's languages" (see also Henning 2007). Conversely, it must also be noted that Métis feminist Emma LaRocque (2007) questioned the claim that all or most Indigenous societies on the North American continent were *non*sexist.

Hooks (2000) maintained that, unlike many White women who enjoyed the "feminist lifestyle" because it provided them the opportunity to meet and bond with other women, Black women have always had a sense of sisterhood. It is often assumed that Black women were not contributors in the development of feminist ideology and the efforts toward gender equality (King 1988; Roth 2004; Springer 2005). Though typically not included in common depictions of the colorblind feminist movement, by reading the works of Black women who considered themselves to be feminists, or were identified as such by others, we find that Black women have undeniably been involved in liberation efforts since the early 1800s (King 1988), and perhaps even dating to the 1600s, when African women who were captured and then enslaved in the so-called "New World" made attempts (also exhibited by Black slave women throughout the entire period of slavery) to resist the multiple forms of oppression and brutality by their slave masters (Beal 1975; Davis 1971; Guy-Sheftall 1995; Marable 1983).

The *first wave* of colorblind feminism in the United States began in the eighteenth century, borrowing from the efforts introduced in England, where organized groups of (mostly) White women and a few men began to demand equal gender rights in employment, education, and voting (Freedman 2002). Their campaign goal focused much attention on the abolishment of slavery. Even though White women were involved in fighting for equality between the sexes and against slavery, many still held racist attitudes (for example, support of racial segregation) or completely ignored the concerns of women of Color (Cotera [1980]1997; Davis 1983). White women leaders of this first wave also downplayed the immediate concerns of working-class White women, such as salaries and working conditions, arguing that the primary focus should be on voting, which would, in turn, bring gender equality.

At the start of the colorblind feminist movement, Black women were cognizant of White feminists' inattention to Black women's plight and began to speak in public forums on issues related to them. The advent of *organized* Black feminist efforts are traced to the nineteenth century (at least beginning in the 1830s), when Black women such as Ida B. Wells, Maria Stewart, Anna Julia Cooper, and Sojourner Truth spoke openly on Black women's affairs and breaking free from oppressive gender roles (Beal 1975; Giddings 1984; Guy-Sheftall 1995). Although their efforts were supported by notable Black male activists Frederick Douglass and W.E.B. Du Bois (Marable 1983), these women's public declarations of racism, as well as sexism – in particular, sexism by Black men – did not go without criticism from men and other women in the Black community (Guy-Sheftall 1995; Marable 1983). Detractors in the Black community did not want the general public to be privy to their in-group unrest and they felt more energy should be placed on securing freedom from slavery and on racial justice in general, and that attempts to gain equality for Black *women* within and outside of the Black community needed to be set aside. Fear of the Black community's reaction to Black women advocating for themselves was often not a concern among these women. One of the most significant illustrations of this valiance is seen with the work of slavery abolitionist and women's suffragist Sojourner Truth. It was Truth's 1851 speech at the Ohio Women's Rights Convention that began to bring White women and all men in the abolitionist and women's rights movements to acknowledge Black women in their struggles (Davis 1983). Although historian Nell Painter (1996) has critically questioned that Truth actually spoke the now legendary and widely used phrase "Ain't I a Woman?"[3] repeatedly in her speech to the congregation,[4] Painter recognized that the *symbol* Truth has come to personify is important not only for Black feminists but for all feminists. This symbol came to mean that *all* women's (varied) experiences and struggles were important to consider in the universal fight for gender justice. Truth's invitation to speak at this meeting was also important because very few women of Color were extended invitations to join White women feminists at their conventions in these early years of the first wave of colorblind feminism (Cotera [1980]1997).

In the 1890s, the first Black women's clubs were established in response to lynching of Blacks, sexual abuse of Black women, the need to improve family life, and other issues specific to the lives of Black women (Davis 1983; Giddings 1984; Guy-Sheftall 1995). The founding of these clubs is considered to be the first formal and organized Black women's feminist movement (Guy-Sheftall 1995). The leading members of these clubs tended to be women who did not work outside their homes, and thus were not of lower income status, but the Black women's clubs were distinguished from White women's clubs by the Black club members' attention to the matter of racism (Davis 1983). "Indeed, their own familiarity with the routine racism of US society linked them far more intimately to their working-class sisters than did the experience of sexism for white women of the middle classes" (Davis 1983:129–130).

From the start of the first wave of the colorblind women's movement until the early twentieth century, although other women of Color in the United States were not involved in organized feminist efforts to the same extent as Black women, there was, nonetheless, involvement among them to fight for racial equality and gendered racial equality. Mexican and Puerto Rican women worked alongside male co-ethnics in their families and communities to seek racial equality after the United States acquired territories that belonged to Spain (Puerto Rico) and Mexico (the current southwestern region of the

United States) (Segura and Facio 2008). In 1911, political activist and journalist Jovita Idar Juárez established La Liga Femenil Mexicanista (the League of Mexican Women) in Laredo, Texas. Most members of *la liga* were working class, but formally educated, Mexican American women who operated schools for their community's children, educated women workers, and provided food and clothing to recent immigrants from Mexico (Cotera [1980]1997; Del Castillo 2005). Undoubtedly, Idar was a feminist, as is evident in her criticism of the oppression of women under Catholicism and her attempts to persuade women that they were not men's servants and should work toward economic independence. Concurrently, in the eastern United States (New York City and Florida) and the Caribbean, Puerto Rican-born Luisa Capetillo, accompanied by several like-minded women (see Hewitt 2005), worked for labor workers' rights, equal voting rights for women, and education and social services for working mothers. A volume of essays written by Capetillo was published in 1911 entitled *Mi opinion, sobre las libertades, derechos y deberes de la mujer, como compañera, madre y ser independiente* (*My Opinion on the Liberties, Rights, and Duties of the Woman, as Companion, Mother, and Independent Being*). Considering the era, writing and distributing this book was a daring move for a woman to take, because Capetillo's essays addressed many taboo issues, "from prostitution and sexual oppression in marriage to domestic labor, religious tyranny, education, women's work, politics, and motherhood" (Hewitt 2005:125).

Many other women of Color participated in feminist activities, but they represented smaller numbers and did not begin to mobilize collectively in greater numbers until the 1960s. Even so, they were engaged in meaningful resistance to being stripped of their land and shipped to boarding schools (Indigenous populations), being imprisoned in "war relocation camps" (Japanese Americans), and being targeted by police and legislators as sexually immoral carriers of disease (Chinese Americans).

The first wave of colorblind feminism in the United States is reported by some to have ended in 1920 with the ratification of the Nineteenth Amendment to the US Constitution, which granted women the right to vote (see Guy-Sheftall 1995; Laughlin *et al.* 2010). But there are clear indications that Black and Chicana feminists did not waver in their activism because of the amendment, particularly since few women of Color were actually able to vote during this time because of disenfranchisement practices carried out by Whites, including intimidation that dissuaded women and men of Color from voting or registering to vote and requiring poll taxes and proof of citizenship (Cotera [1980]1997; Hooper 2012). Women of Color who advocated feminist ideas from the 1920s through the 1950s (the start of the second wave of the colorblind feminist movement) included in their agenda "passing a federal anti-lynching bill, unionizing themselves as workers, achieving economic independence, securing birth control, enhancing their educational status, and improving the working condition of domestics" (Guy-Sheftall 1995:78). Although Mexican Americans and Puerto Ricans in the United States were racially reclassified as *White* with the 1940 census, they still faced marginalization, discrimination, and exclusion from the country's ruling class (Oboler 1995). Mexican American women also regularly feared deportation (Cotera [1980]1997; Ruiz and Sánchez Korrol 2006). In sum, simply because voting rights had been afforded to (some) women, and the world wars allowed opportunity for increased employment opportunities for women in general, this did not signify the conclusion of women of Color feminist work.

The climax of feminism?

The *second wave* in the colorblind feminist movement began in the 1960s after the relatively uneventful, quiet four decades for White women feminists (Guy-Sheftall 1995). This wave is characterized by continued dissatisfaction with women's second-class status (that is, second to men) (Hooks 2000). Unfortunately, there still remained an aura of racism and classism among some of the leaders of this movement. *The Feminine Mystique*, the 1963 book written by White feminist Betty Friedan, founder of the National Organization of Women (NOW), is proclaimed to be the source that initiated contemporary feminism (Parry 2010). Without doubt, Friedan's book and activism had significant influence on gaining equal rights for women. Regrettably, like many of the White feminists during the first wave, Friedan failed to acknowledge the existence of women of Color and poor White women, as evident in her book, which was limited to the lives and experiences of middle-class White heterosexual women (Hooks 2000; Parry 2010). While other theoretical models of color-blind women's liberation included a cross-section of socioeconomic class, it was still the case that race and ethnicity were neglected as factors affecting the lives of women of Color (Lewis 1977). Despite this omission, some forms of collaboration occurred with the different groups. Smith (1983) contended that just as White women had used the Black equal rights movement to support and advance their cause in the nineteenth century, they did so again by attaching themselves to Black organizations in the 1960s.

Some White women feminists during the second wave also misinterpreted Black women's struggles because these White feminists based their perceptions of Black women on stereotypical beliefs and images (Hooks 2000; Smith 1983; Springer 2005). Some White feminists believed that the failure of Black women to participate in feminist bonding groups was due to their assumption of Black women as already having been liberated – at least liberated from *Black* men's attempts at asserting patriarchal practices. This was based on the belief that all Black women were *strong* Black women holding positions of power within the Black community and the Black family (Hooks 2000; Smith 1983). Criminologist Freda Adler (1975:140) captured this perspective about Black women's "liberation" after the abolishment of slavery in her book *Sisters in Crime: The Rise of the New Female Criminal*:

> In a grimly sardonic sense, the black female has been "liberated" for over a century. Expediency not aspiration, necessity not preference thrust this upon her many years ago when circumstances coerced her out of the traditional American female role of submissiveness and compelled her into the masculine role of dominance. It was not a position she sought, but one she accepted. She needed no liberation movement to gain the right to head a single-parent household, to be free within her home from masculine authority, to find a job outside the home, and to have parity with or superiority over black men. But therein lay the rub .... She attained pseudo liberation, not real

> liberation. Her emancipation extended to the ragged fringes of the black world, but hardly beyond. She was no more free than animals in a zoo who are transferred from a cage to a compound. True, she had extended her range of movement within a confined area, but the borders were narrow, strictly defined, and hemmed all about by the white world.

Although Adler recognized that Black women were not liberated outside "the black world," she still assumed there to be parity among Blacks, regardless of gender. Adler continued with this line of reason when specifically addressing criminal activity among Black women. She hypothesized that as White women became more liberated during the colorblind women's movement of the 1960s and 1970s, they would begin to reach similar offending rates as Black women, who had already been "liberated as criminals":

> Black women have been "liberated" as criminals for many years. In the century that has elapsed since the era of slavery, black women have freed themselves from the fetters of male domination, while, ironically, white women are still fighting to loosen the socioeconomic chains that have kept them in psychological bondage to their husbands. Today black women generally shy away from or even openly scorn the women's liberation movement. Liberation – in the sense of living on their own, being the breadwinner for large families, existing free from male control – has been theirs for years. They did not have to fight for it; it is liberation without options and, in consequence, it is often a cruel mockery of liberation.
>
> (p. 152)

These views of Black women are also apparent in the infamous Daniel Moynihan (1965) report, *The Negro Family: The Case for National Action*. The Democratic US senator and academician asserted that this *strong Black woman* was responsible for the problems within the Black community. Moynihan argued that because the Black woman spent a large amount of time working outside the home, she neglected her duties as wife and mother, therefore causing juvenile delinquency among Black children and the devalued status of Black males within the social structure. Therefore, these Black women contradicted the so-called traditional role to which women should adhere: the submissive heterosexual woman who caters to her husband and procreates, and whose main or, preferably, only form of work is to care for her children.

Scathing, paternalistic views of Black women's lived experiences and personal actions and agency within the Black community and in society-at-large continued to motivate Black women feminist activists to organize. Black women feminists during the 1960s and early 1970s were involved in the predominant Black Power, civil rights, and colorblind women's rights movements, working alongside Black men and White women. A few Black women held leadership roles within Black Power organizations, but a number of Black male leaders of organizations operating during the Black Power movement deemed Black women as secondary and espoused sexist views and practices, including Malcolm X (Nation of Islam), Stokely Carmichael (Student Nonviolent Coordinating Committee), and Eldridge Cleaver (Black Panther Party) (Marable 1983; Williams 2008). Some Black women within these groups also adopted or internalized a subordinate status to Black men (Marable 1983; Smith 1983), including Elaine Brown (1992:367), the "chairman" of the Black Panther Party from 1974 through 1977, who shared, "Sexism was a secondary problem. Capitalism and racism were primary. I had maintained that position even in the face of my exasperation with the chauvinism of Black Power men in general and Black Panther men in particular." Brown later came to realize that the "feminists were right. The value of my life had been obliterated as much by being female as by being black and poor. Racism and sexism in America were equal partners in my oppression. Even men who were themselves oppressed wanted power over women." Prejudiced attitudes toward non-normative sexualities were also problematic in Black Power organizations, and lesbian activists of Color faced additional challenges within the movements.

In response to the failure of the Black Power, civil rights, and colorblind women's rights movements to address race *and* gender matters particularly important to Black women during the 1960s and 1970s, and the inability for Black women to be viewed as equal partners in the movements, Black women feminists organized in larger and more sustainable groups (Collins 2006; Combahee River Collective 2000[1983]; Guy-Sheftall 1995; Lewis 1977; Roth 2004; Springer 2005; White 1999; Williams 2008). Although lesbians within some Black feminist organizations faced discrimination and prejudice (Springer 2005), these groups tended to include a cross-section of Black women by social class, which was different from what the colorblind feminist movement had accomplished at that stage in their liberation efforts (Lewis 1977). Many of these Black feminist groups, such as the National Black Feminist Organization, the National Alliance of Black Feminists, and the Combahee River Collective, were short-lived, but they had an undeniable impact on consciousness-raising by Black women and other women of Color (Harris 2009; Hooper 2012; Roth 2004; Springer 2005).[5] The Combahee River Collective (2000[1983]:264), a group of self-declared Black feminists that was formed in Boston in 1974, specified an intersectional perspective in the group's seminal 1977 statement: "The most general statement of our politics at the present time would be that we are actively committed to struggling against racial, sexual, heterosexual, and class oppression, and see as our particular task the development of integrated analysis and practice based upon the fact that the major systems of oppression are interlocking."[6]

Regrettably, as occurred during the Black feminist efforts of the nineteenth century, Black women were continually pressured – either self-inflicted or by others – to choose either the fight for Black liberation/nationalism or the fight for women's liberation (Cleaver 1997; Cole and Guy-Sheftall 2003), and the writings of some Black women feminists during the 1970s and 1980s were met with antagonism from several members of the Black intellectual community (Cole and Guy-Sheftall 2003; Guy-Sheftall 1995). These Black feminist authors were protesting and resisting via their written works not only the social injustices they and other Black women suffered in US society and globally, but also the strife within the Black community. Some Black male scholars and professionals felt betrayed and were angered by the depictions of Black men in both the fictional and nonfictional compositions. Consequently, these men deemed it necessary to retaliate in what they *believed* was in kind, and wrote seething articles replete with Black woman-hating prose (Guy-Sheftall 1995; Harris 2009). It appeared some Black men of this time felt threatened by what Black feminists were making known about their interpersonal relationships with Black men and did not want to be vulnerable to the societal responses to the images recounted by these women. Despite the condemnation of their work during this period, Black women feminists made significant and lasting contributions.

Chicana feminists' involvement in human rights movements during the 1960s and 1970s was similar to Black feminists' experiences. In El Movimiento, Chicanas and Chicanos pushed for *Chicanismo*, a Chicano cultural nationalism that was analogous with the Black Nationalism movement (García 1997). By way of a number of rural and urban grassroots organizations, El Movimiento fought against institutional racism and discrimination of Mexican Americans. In particular, César Chávez, after organizing for voter registration through his Community Service Organization in the 1950s, cofounded with Dolores Huerta in 1962 the National Farm Workers Association, later called the United Farm Workers of America (UFW). Chávez's wife, Helen Chávez, also figured heavily in development of the UFW. Even though Helen Chávez's efforts were "behind the scenes" since she was involved in administrative and supportive efforts, she played a fundamental role in building the organization (Rose 1990). In Denver, Colorado, Rodolfo ("Corky") Gonzales organized the Crusade for Justice to improve the educational, economic, and housing conditions of Chicanas/os and to fight for social justice for Chicanas/os in general (Vigil 1999), with Chicanas fighting alongside the men. Chicanas also became heavily involved in college student groups such as United Mexican American Students (UMAS) and Movimiento Estudiantil Chicano de Aztlán (MEChA) (Roth 2004).

Although Chicana feminists' earlier organizing efforts in the 1960s pushed for maintaining alliances with their male counterparts and Chicano organizations (Roth 2004), similar to the experiences of Black women feminists, Chicana feminists struggled within the Latino movements because of *machismo* (sexism/genderism) and domination by the men (Cotera [1980]1997; García 1997; Oboler 1995). In popular and scholarly depictions, Dolores Huerta and Helen Chávez are seldom recognized for their significant roles in the movement to organize farm workers and Mexican Americans because praise was given to those who appeared to dominate the movement: male organizers (Oboler 1995; Rose 1990). Chicana feminist lesbians often faced discrimination from El Movimiento devotees (men *and* women), who saw lesbian feminists as "a double threat to the family" (Roth 2004:154–155); that is, these women were seen as rejecting "traditional" womanhood – the "Ideal Chicana" (García 1997) – as they wanted both equal participation in the movement and were not going to set up a home with a man. Also like Black feminists, in attempts to join forces with White women feminists, Chicanas did not feel welcome, and, as indicated by Chicana feminist Marta Cotera ([1980]1997:229), women of Color "could fill volumes of examples of put-downs, put-ons, and out-and-out racism shown to them by the leadership of the [women's] movement."

Chicana feminists subsequently formed their own organized groups, both within and outside of the male-dominated movement, such as Las Hijas de Cuauhtémoc (The Daughters of Cuauhtémoc), the Comision Femenil Mexicana (Mexican Women's Commission), and the Concilio Mujeres (Women's Council). A number of influential newspapers, newsletters, and journals were also established and published by and for Chicana feminists (García 1997). But as Roth (2004:169) noted, Chicana feminists "coordinate[d] their organizations much more closely with the broader Chicano movement – that is, men – than was the case in either White or Black feminism." Ultimately, Chicana feminists maintained alliance with El Movimiento and distanced themselves from White feminist efforts (Roth 2004).

Corresponding to Black and Chicana feminists' efforts, Puerto Rican women in the United States had a role in Puerto Rican civil rights movements and organizations. Specifically, the Young Lords Organization (which later changed its name to the Young Lords Party), which was founded in 1969 in New York and was based in the Young Lords street gang of Chicago, saw women members making concerted efforts to gain equality within and outside of the group (Enck-Wanzer 2010; Oboler 1995). However, in 1970 in Young Lords Party's newspaper, *Palante*, the Central Committee of the party penned "The Young Lords Party Position Paper on Women," which provided a scornful overview of the state of Puerto Rican and Black women in US society and within their respective racial and revolutionary groups. Surrounded by pictures of revolutionary women of Color – some wielding rifles – the treatise spoke of some of the many forms of exploitation of Puerto Rican and Black women, including sterilization and sex work (prostitution). Regarding sex work, the author of the piece extended the definition beyond women of Color being forced into exchanging sex for money because of their poor economic statuses, to the ways in which many women of Color are treated in "unskilled" jobs in hospitals and offices. In these jobs, women had been "subjected to racial slurs, jokes, and other indignities ... [and] are expected to prostitute themselves and take abuse of any kind" (p. 13). The Central Committee asserted that the issuing of its position paper was necessary to educate members of the party, both men and women, about the role that women had and should play in their resistance efforts. The article placed blame across gender: "We criticize those brothers who are 'machos' and who continue to treat our sisters as less than equals. We criticize sisters ... who do not join in the struggle against our oppression." The push was for organization members to take responsibility and resolve internal strife in order to better organize as a group.

In Canada and the United States, indigenous women feminists formally mobilized during the 1960s and 1970s (Huhndorf and Suzak 2010). The Native Women's Association of Canada (NWAC) formed in 1974 to address equal human rights for Indigenous women in Canada (Green 2007; Huhndorf and Suzak 2010). In the same year in the United States, and as an extension of the American Indian Movement to address women's issues, the Women of All Red Nations (WARN) was founded. Issues of sovereignty, decolonization, and violence against women were – and continue to be – the major undertakings by Indigenous feminists. Regarding Arab American and Asian American feminists, although their numbers and representation have been small in comparison with other women of Color feminists (Chow 1987; Jarmakani 2011; Naber 2006; Sanchez-Hucles *et al.* 2012), they expressed similar concerns regarding women's equality and the impact of living multiply oppressed lives. Mitsuye Yamada (1981[2001]:35) asserted that Asian American women came to organized feminist efforts later "because we Asian American women have not admitted to ourselves that we were oppressed." Feminist sociologist and community activist Esther Ngan-Ling Chow (1987) recognized that the ethnic diversity among Asian American women served as another barrier to forming an Asian American feminist collective. Even so, a number of Asian American women – though relatively small – joined forces with Asian American civil rights groups. These women endured experiences similar to Black, Latina, and Indigenous women's experiences in mixed-gender/sex groups; that is, Asian American women were typically relegated to subordinated roles and faced sexism from male group members (Chow 1987).

As demonstrated in the work of the Young Lords Party, in which Black and Puerto Rican women joined forces, there were a few other efforts to have women of Color feminists collaborate. Black feminist activist Frances Beal established the Third World Women's Alliance (TWWA) in 1968 in New York City (and, later, a second branch in California) to bring all women of Color together to jointly organize. Beal found her way to the establishment of the TWWA starting with the Black Women's Liberation Committee, a caucus of the Student Nonviolent Coordinating Committee (SNCC) that evolved into the Black Women's Alliance (BWA), an organization independent from the SNCC due to the sexist practices and beliefs of (some) male SNCC members discussed earlier. After Puerto Rican women joined the BWA, the group changed its name to the Third World Women's Alliance to allow for the opportunity to create an ideology that represented the experiences of *all* women of Color. The TWWA's activities included publishing a monthly newspaper titled *Triple Jeopardy: Racism, Imperialism, Sexism* (September 1971 through the summer of 1975), holding health information fairs in communities of Color, and organizing interactive theater and discussion groups in their "Liberation Schools" to educate communities of Color on imperialism, racism, and sexism. The group also attracted the attention of federal law enforcement, having been under investigation by the Counterintelligence Program (COINTELPRO) of the US Federal Bureau of Investigation from December 1970 to March 1974 (Springer 2005). Although all TWWA chapters had disbanded by 1980, the ideological legacy of the group remains. To the present, women of Color activists continue to unite with their feminist activist causes and publishing, while simultaneously respecting each group's need to independently confer.

The continuing significance of feminism

From the 1980s through the early 1990s, women of Color feminists continued to work to keep or get interests of women of Color on the agenda of the colorblind feminist movement. With the introduction of a new round of "get-tough" crime and social policies that disproportionately affected people of Color in working-class and low-income neighborhoods across the United States during the 1980s, community work and activism by women of Color did not falter (Collins 2006). Although there have not been movements at the same scale as those in the 1960s and 1970s, women of Color feminist collectives and organizations have remained active and new collectives and groups have formed. Women of Color feminist movements also infiltrated the Ivory Tower; in the past four decades, the endeavors of feminists of Color in the previous generation afforded greater opportunities for women of Color, including *critical* and *progressive* women of Color. Academic research addressing social concerns from a woman of Color feminist standpoint flourished, including a greater presence in scholarly publishing venues. Women of Color feminist scholars authored theoretical critiques and empirical articles employing feminist theory based in the multiplicative marginalized identity standpoint. There was great need for the incorporation of intersectional and oppositional viewpoints into the academic world.

Feminist legal scholars who base their work in *anti*-essentialism (typically referred to as critical race feminists) were moved to focus on an intersectional approach, in part as rebuttal to feminist legal scholar Catherine MacKinnon's (1982) work on feminism and women's position in society. Anti-essentialism asserts that there is more than *one* essential voice of women. Collins (2000a:299) defined *essentialism* as the "belief that individuals or groups have inherent, unchanging characteristics rooted in biology or a self-contained culture that explain their status." Critical race feminist Angela P. Harris (1990) criticized MacKinnon's and others' use of essentialism regarding women's issues. Harris argued that MacKinnon and members of society in general assumed the existence of "an essential 'woman' beneath the realities of differences between women," thereby in recounting the experiences of these essential women, "issues of race, class, and sexual orientation can therefore be safely ignored or relegated to footnotes" (pp. 591–592). Further criticism of MacKinnon's essentialist standpoint by Harris concerned the matter of race identity versus gender identity for Black women. Harris argued that MacKinnon's use of essentialism indicates that the experiences of Black women will undergo a fragmentation, "as those who are 'only interested in race' and those who are 'only interested in gender' take their separate slices of our lives" (Harris 1990:589). In defense of essentialism as it relates to gender, MacKinnon (2002) disagreed that feminism does not consider all women's experiences and that anti-essentialism would be anti-feminist, because "[f]eminism does not see women as the same; it criticizes this view" (p. 73). Moreover, MacKinnon found that "[f]eminism does not claim that all women are affected the same by male power or are similarly situated under it – just that no woman is unaffected by it" (p. 73). The debate persisted (and *persists*), however, as women of Color feminists and other anti-essentialist feminists continued to encounter researchers and theorists who employ a feminist framework but do not take into account the varied experiences of women due to their social positions and identities. In referring to the issues raised regarding Anita Hill's reports of sexual harassment during the 1991 US Senate hearings for Clarence Thomas's confirmation to the US Supreme Court, Black feminist literary scholar Nellie Y. McKay (1993:276) wrote that White women feminists "forgot that for Black women, issues of gender are always connected to race .... Black women cannot choose between their commitment to feminism and the struggle with their men for racial justice." Kimberlé Crenshaw (1991:1244) echoed this stance, stating that within feminist and antiracist discourses, which are formed "to respond to one *or* the other, the interests and experiences of women of color are frequently marginalized within both" (emphases in original text). Thus, the struggles of women of Color in the United States continued to remain a concern for women of Color feminists even though many observers believed feminist and antiracial movements to have ended with the enactment of civil rights and women's rights laws and policies.

According to common feminist rhetoric, we are currently in the *third wave* of *the* feminist movement, which reportedly began in the 1990s, even though many of the feminists who came to feminist consciousness during the second wave are still active in their efforts. In this current delineation of the waves, it is difficult to differentiate between them as a stage in time or as an identity (of some feminists) whereby, for instance, a White feminist active in the 1960s and 1970s comes to understand the ideas promoted by third-wave feminists. The third wave is, ostensibly, a movement that was founded by White women and some women of Color born during the early years of the second wave (late 1960s through 1970s) (Baumgardner and Richards 2000; Clay 2008; Laughlin *et al.* 2010; Peoples 2008; Springer 2002). The third wave focuses on bringing the ideas of second-wave feminism up to date and relevant to the lives of younger women, typically in their twenties and early thirties (Baumgardner and Richards 2000). Third-wave feminists aver their ideology is more sensitive to the differences among women and claim to include variations by race, ethnicity, class, sexuality, and nationality, and that its membership mirrors this diversity. As such, there was a move away from *colorblind* feminism, and toward giving greater attention to anti-essentialism. This was an important shift, since arguments continued to be made that feminist theory was based in a White racial-cultural frame and failed to provide an appropriate base for understanding experiences of women without social privilege (Crenshaw 1989).

Although there is now increased acceptance of a variety of feminisms, whether belonging to the second wave or the third wave or no wave, feminist critics continue to question whether today's White women understand that their perspectives may not be indicative of all women's realities, and that White women's views may still be racist and classist (Collins 2006; Hernández and Rehman 2002; Hooks 2000; Sanchez-Hucles *et al.* 2012). Indeed, feminist historian Leandra Zarnow (in Laughlin *et al.* 2010) warned that third-wave White scholars who claim an inclusivity stance and employ intersectionality in their work must reflect on their privileged social positions. Many women of Color feminist organizations of today welcome White women, under the condition that they are especially attuned to their privileged status in comparison with women of Color (and many feminists of Color participate in White-dominated feminist organizations). Other feminist of Color organizations purposely maintain a stance in which only women of Color are allowed membership. One such organization is INCITE! Women of Color Against Violence, which does welcome genderqueer individuals and transwomen of Color into the group.[7] INCITE! essentially picks up where the Combahee River Collective ended in its efforts at advocating against violence experienced by women and transpeople of Color. Efforts like those carried out by INCITE! members epitomize the type of efforts put forth by many contemporary women of Color feminists. INCITE! was established in 2001 as the result of a conference on violence against women of Color held at the University of California, Santa Cruz, in April 2000, which was organized to address the frustrations of women of Color who were working within antiviolence and racial justice organizations (INCITE! 2006). Andrea Smith (2005a), a founding member of INCITE!, contended that the "mainstream antiviolence movement" in the United States places women of Color in a precarious position. Women of Color subjected to sexual and other forms of violence by intimate partners, strangers, and others "are often told they must pit themselves against their communities, often stereotypically portrayed as violent, to begin the healing process" while members of the women's communities "often pressure women to remain silent about sexual and domestic violence in order to maintain a 'united front' against racism" (p. 151). As is evident, today's women of Color continue to face similar problems to women of Color in previous generations, and, therefore, believe it necessary to organize apart from White women in order for the focus to always remain on women of Color. INCITE! assembles women of Color across age, but some contemporary feminist groups place especial focus on younger women of Color, as indicated previously regarding the third-wave initiative.

Many young women of Color doing feminism today do not utilize the third-wave moniker, instead opting for signifiers that reflect contemporary music genres created by people of Color, such as hip-hop feminists and crunk feminists. References to a hip-hop feminism began to appear in the late 1990s, and were based on the new feminism of women of Color who were of the hip-hop generation. The hip-hop generation was originally identified by some to refer to those individuals born between the years of 1965 and 1984 (Kitwana 2002), yet in present times the hip-hop generation tends to reference current adolescents and young adults. Thus, it is unclear whether the older members of those classified as the original hip-hop generation, who are now in their late thirties and forties (such as myself), are involved in, have a place in, or are welcomed into hip-hop and crunk feminist collectives because of the younger ages of the feminists heading these collectives. (To be sure, I support younger feminists of Color claiming a "space" solely for them.) Literature that has provided an explanation of and contributions to hip-hop feminism include Joan Morgan's (1999) *When Chickenheads Come Home to Roost: My Life as a Hip-Hop Feminist* and Ruth Nicole Brown's (2008) *Black Girlhood Celebration: Toward a Hip-Hop Feminism Pedagogy*, and the anthologies *Home Girls Make Some Noise! Hip Hop Feminism Anthology* (Pough et al. 2007) and *Wish to Live: The Hip-Hop Feminism Pedagogy Reader* (Brown and Kwakye 2012). In *From Black Power to Hip Hop: Racism, Nationalism, and Feminism*, Collins (2006) maintained that women of Color feminists of the hip-hop generation are living in a different political reality and have different personal paths to feminism than those of women of Color feminists in the 1960s and 1970s. Hip-hop generation women are less likely to begin (or, for original hip-hoppers, *have* begun) their path to feminism in college or state bureaucracies like the previous generation, but more likely to be mobilized by popular culture and mass media. Hip-hop and crunk feminists are defining and diffusing their feminism within the present era and state of society, using the best tools and methods of communication and mobilization at their disposal or, as Kimberly Springer (2002:1077) put it, "fresh modes for developing collective consciousness." Groups like the Crunk Feminist Collective provide a space – most of which is occupied virtually in Internet social media – for younger sets of feminists of Color.[8] This group, founded by young scholar-activists (junior untenured professors) Brittany C. Cooper and Susana M. Morris, aspires to "articulate a crunk feminist consciousness for women and men of color, who came of age in the Hip Hop Generation, by creating a community of scholars-activists from varied professions, who share our intellectual work in online blog communities, at conferences, through activist organizations, and in print publications" (http://www.crunkfeministcollective.com). Hip-hop feminists and crunk feminists have built upon the work and theorizing of women of Color feminists who came before. Whitney A. Peoples (2008:42), scholar-activist member of the Crunk Feminist Collective, surmised, "Where hip-hop feminists claim second-wave black feminists are suffering from outmoded social and political strategies, second-wave black feminists argue that hip-hop feminists lack social and political strategies altogether. While hip-hop feminists might possess a theoretical approach to hip-hop, they have yet to produce a clear example of their theory in practice."

While Collins's (2006) focus in *From Black Power to Hip Hop* is on the hip-hop *generation(s)* of feminists and not on actual hip-hop music, in the afterword to *Home Girls Make Some Noise!* (Pough *et al.* 2007), Joan Morgan asserted, "By embracing hip-hop, we had the potential to complicate black feminist thought in critical ways. We could begin to bridge the generational gap .... [A]s hip-hop feminists we had shit to say and a lot to offer, but nobody was asking us to join the conversation" (p. 478). While there have been some critiques of women of Color embracing the term hip-hop to describe their feminism because of the misogynist lyrics and images in some hip-hop music and videos, many hip-hop feminists of Color retain the identifier, believing that hip-hop music and culture possess the ability to mobilize young women of Color to radicalize and liberate themselves in today's culture (Peoples 2008). In an ethnographic study of two nonprofit organizations geared toward urban youth of Color in Oakland, California, sociologist Andreana Clay (2012) investigated the development of activism by the youth in the programs. Clay discovered that popular culture, especially hip-hop, was a major source for mobilizing contemporary youth to organize around social injustice issues.

Defining intersectionality

As seen in the tracing of the pronouncements of women of Color over the past (at *least*) 200 years, awareness of simultaneous oppressions by race *and* by gender *and* by sexuality *and* by socioeconomic class (*and* by an unlimited number of other identities) is not a novel concept. *Intersectionality* is frequently deployed as a collective, broad term to label this idea of woven identities of women of Color (and others), but a review of the literature related to and preceding the coining and specification of intersectionality yields a variety of terms and phrases used to describe the experiences of women of Color, based in multiple interlocked and subjugated identities.

Scholar-activist Frances M. Beal ([1970]1995) wrote of the burden of the Black woman's disadvantaged status based on gender and race as a *double jeopardy*. Beal also discussed the added burden of economic exploitation experienced by Black women (in the United States and within many locations throughout the world), although it is not included in her labeling, nor in her TWWA newspaper, *Triple Jeopardy: Racism, Imperialism, Sexism*, which, as mentioned previously, broadened the concept to all women of Color. Beal's intent with the jeopardy terms was to stress the multiple sources of oppression of women of Color. Black feminist sociologist Vivian V. Gordon (1987) used the term *trilogy of oppression* to reference gender, race, and economic exploitation. Gordon claimed that Black women are often confronted with determining which form of oppression is most important. Deborah K. King (1988), another Black feminist sociologist, went even further and advocated using the term *multiple jeopardy* to describe Black women's oppression, because Black women often undergo even more forms of subjugation, and to signify that these categories of oppression impact Black women simultaneously. Likewise, critical race feminist Adrien K. Wing argued that "women of color are not merely White women *plus* color or men of color *plus* gender. Instead, their identities must be multiplied together to create a holistic One when analyzing the nature of the discrimination against them" (2003:7; emphases in original text). Wing (1997:31) used the term *multiplicative identity* to capture the identity of women of Color: "The actuality of our layered experience is *multiplicative*. Multiply each of my parts together, 1 × 1 × 1 × 1 × 1, and you have *one* indivisible being. If you divide one of these parts from one you still have *one*" (emphases in original text). Further, regarding Black women, Wing wrote, "I am asserting that the experience of black women must be seen as a multiplicative, multilayered, indivisible whole, symbolized by the equation one times one, *not* one plus one" (p. 32, emphasis in original text). Collins (2006) used the phrase *matrix of domination* to reference the organization of interlocked oppressions, specifying that individuals' experiences vary, dependent on the location of their social identities within the various identity hierarchies (gender, race, sexuality, and so on). For example, a Vietnamese American woman will experience life in the United States differently from a Vietnamese American man because the man's gender will elevate him along the gender hierarchy, perhaps providing him with some social benefits; however, the Vietnamese man will not fare as well as a White man, whose race places him higher on the race scale. Whereas most of the examples of interlocked multiple identities listed here specifically addressed Black women's experiences, all women of Color can be considered within these analyses. All told, feminist scholars Maxine Baca Zinn and Bonnie Thornton Dill stressed that "the lives of women of color cannot be seen as a *variation* on a more general model of white American womanhood" (1996:329; emphasis in original text).

Crenshaw employed the same interpretation of identity interconnectivity and oppression in conceptualizing intersectionality. In her 1989 legal article, "Demarginalizing the Intersection of Race and Sex: A Black Feminist Critique of Antidiscrimination Doctrine, Feminist Theory and Antiracist Politics," Crenshaw provided examples of US legal cases where judges denied the multiplicative identity of Black women, refusing to acknowledge that claims could be made based on race discrimination *and* sex discrimination. To all intents and purposes, the courts argued that Black women could not demonstrate that they had been discriminated against as *Black women*. In opposition, Crenshaw illustrated how discrimination by race *and* by gender can occur simultaneously by analogizing the experiences of Black women with automobile traffic that moves through adjacent and intersecting street lanes: "If an accident happens in an intersection, it can be caused by cars traveling in any number of directions and, sometimes, from all of them. Similarly, if a Black woman is harmed because she is in the intersection, her injury could result from sex discrimination or race discrimination" (p. 149).

In "Mapping the Margins: Intersectionality, Identity, Politics, and Violence Against Women of Color" (1991) – more frequently cited regarding the concept of intersectionality, especially in criminology, than her 1989 article – Crenshaw expanded on the social underpinnings of intersectionality. Crenshaw described three forms of intersectionality: structural, political, and representational. *Structural intersectionality* refers to sociostructural elements and institutions that place women of Color at a disadvantage. *Political intersectionality* refers to women of Color feminists straddling the (colorblind) feminist agenda and the antiracist agenda, and struggling to get the voices of women of Color heard and their experiences integrated into these agendas. *Representational intersectionality* considers the images of women of Color and how the intersections of women of Color are not critically interrogated based on image production of women of Color by others. Crenshaw (1991) focused on the intersecting mechanisms of race and gender and did not explicitly address how sexuality, nationality, and class, among other identities and statuses, further compound one's experiences; yet she did stress that the concept of intersectionality can and should take these other identities and statuses into account. For Crenshaw, the most pressing issue is not that the classifications exist; rather, in her conceptualization of the identity and power categorizations in intersectionality, the importance lies in the social principles affixed to the categories and the resultant hierarchies that are created.

There has been immense application of intersectionality as a concept by many scholars, throughout many academic disciplines, and across many identities, but intellectual dissonance has ensued. Discourse has focused on (1) the use or exploitation of intersectionality to understand experiences beyond certain groups (that is, its use with those who are not Black women), (2) the co-opting or misappropriation of intersectionality by certain scholars, (3) the precise definition of intersectionality, and (4) the capacity or strength of intersectionality as a theoretical or methodological tool (I address this final point in the next section of this chapter). Feminist theorist Sirma Bilge (2013:410) observed that divergences regarding intersectionality – similar to the fate of other traveling perspectives that transcend disciplines and societies – have resulted in intersectionality's "widespread misrepresentation, tokenization, displacement, and disarticulation" and reflect "power struggles, opportunity structures, and turf wars" within academic disciplines.

Legal scholar Jennifer C. Nash (2008:4) argued that there are some "unresolved questions" regarding intersectionality, including Black women serving as "prototypical intersectional subjects." Nash argued that scholars need to determine whether intersectionality is about Black women and other "multiply marginalized subjects" or whether it is applicable to all identities and all placements within the social power structure. In her view, Nash questioned intersectionality's "reliance on black women as the basis for its claims to complex subjectivity" (p. 8), asserting that because it remains situated in Black feminist thought, intersectionality is limited to being applied only to Black women. Nikol G. Alexander-Floyd (2012), a Black feminist legal theorist, argued for a refocusing of intersectionality solely on the experiences of Black women, or women of Color generally, and is especially critical of scholars who dissociate intersectionality from women of Color. Alexander-Floyd declared that some definitions of intersectionality are broader than the original conceptualization, as indicated in her understanding of intersectionality: "centering research and analysis on the lived experiences of women of color for the purpose of making visible and addressing their marginalization as well as an ethos of challenging business as usual in mainstream disciplines' habits of knowledge production" (p. 9). Alexander-Floyd charged that intersectionality's application to other groups is an affront to women of Color and a departure from what she believed was the original purpose of intersectionality. She referred to this as a "bait-and-switch," where a scholar employing intersectionality does not earnestly consider the perceptions of women of Color, and concluded that the use of intersectionality among social scientists is an approach that is "post–black feminist" and "disappears or re-marginalizes black women" (p. 9). Bilge (2013:407) also expressed concern about the reformulation of intersectionality, which she indicated has been "commodified and colonized for neoliberal regimes," particularly in Europe. Yet Bilge's emphasis is not on confining intersectionality to women of Color, nor on delineating the identity of the scholars who have used or who could use intersectionality. In what she deemed the *Whitening of intersectionality*, Bilge indicated that this Whitening excises race from the array of identities and dismisses the experiences of women of Color – a practice especially prevalent among European feminist scholars about whom Black feminist scholar Gail Lewis (2013:870) also alerted, "there is a disavowal of the relevance and toxicity of the social relations of race."

Unlike Alexander-Floyd's conviction that intersectionality be utilized only when considering women of Color, many protagonists and practitioners of intersectionality – *including* Kimberlé Crenshaw – believe that intersectionality can reach beyond application solely to women of Color. Addressing the misreading of and rampant debate surrounding her original articles on intersectionality, Crenshaw (2011:230) recently explicated that because we *all* exist within "the matrix of power," intersectionality is applicable to all individuals, concluding, "Intersectionality represents a structural and dynamic arrangement; power marks these relationships among and between categories of experience that vary in their complexity." In addition, two special journal issues published in 2013 provided a timely assessment and improved understanding about intersectionality: "Intersectionality: Theorizing Power, Empowering Theory" in *Signs: Journal of Women in Culture and Society* (2013, volume 38, issue 4) edited by Sumi Cho, Crenshaw, and Leslie McCall, and "Intersectionality: Mapping the Movements of a Theory" in *Du Bois Review: Social Science Research on Race* (2013, volume 10, issue 2) edited by Devon W. Carbodo, Crenshaw, Vickie M. Mays, and Barbara Tomlinson. One conclusion put forward is that intersectionality was introduced as a "heuristic *term*" used to attend to the "vexed dynamics of difference and the solidarities of sameness in the context of antidiscrimination and social movement politics. It exposed how single-axis thinking undermines legal thinking, disciplinary knowledge production, and struggles for social justice" (Cho *et al.* 2013:787; emphasis added). Thus, there is an element that is a constant and must always remain fixed in designating what intersectionality *is*: *social-power differentials based on the social ordering of social attributes that are multiple, multiplicative, and inseparable for each individual.* Although there is the ability and endorsement to extend the application of intersectionality beyond women of Color, the original tenets of intersectionality must remain intact; to do otherwise is to unravel or nullify intersectionality, thereby morphing the concept into something altogether different.

If I take liberties with the English language and remove the connective notion of the intersectionality term, we are left with what could be termed *sectionality*, with *sectionalize* used as a verb and defined as to attempt or to desire to segment identities and to attend to only one identity categorization. As should be discernible to this point and to be demonstrated throughout the remainder of the book, the sectionalization of identities may not provide a scrupulous analysis of individuals' lived experiences. The attributes of an intertwined identity cannot be untangled, but, dependent upon the setting, individuals are able to "hide" certain facets of their identity (a gay Cuban American man passing as heterosexual), and certain identity attributes are responded to (and internalized) differently in the different settings. In the latter condition, one can envision how the interactions of a middle-class, college-educated Black woman change when (a) spending private time with her partner and their children, (b) convening in a closed space only with other Black woman, (c) interacting with co-workers at her White male-dominated place of employment, or (d) browsing and trying on clothing in a high-end store staffed and mainly frequented by White women. In these different settings, the other parties will configure her identities differently, but they are not likely to separate them and to think of her unidimensionally. Even if she does not engage in *social shapeshifting*[9] in any of these settings, thereby presenting and performing (by way of attitude, speech, posture, style of dress, hairstyle, and so on) in the same way in all settings, the responses to her will still likely vary based on how the group has configured and interprets her multiplicative identity as a Black woman. Sectionalization in the real world of our social actions and interactions can rarely occur. Carried forward, then, sectionalization in social-scientific research and theoretical conceptualization can be viewed as an incomplete or faulty interpretation of the social world.

Using intersectionality

The multiple academic applications of and explorations and dialogues about intersectionality have resulted in some inconsistency in how intersectionality is to be used. So the question remains: Is intersectionality a theory, a perspective, a paradigm, an epistemology, a methodology, or a research method, or some combination of any of these? Based on the current state of intersectionality and my appraisal of the ways in which intersectionality has been and can be used in academia, I respond to this question regarding the use of intersectionality generally and within the context of the criminology discipline.

US English dictionaries simply define a *paradigm* as an example, a pattern, or a model. Within the disciplinal realm of academia, science, and research, there is not a sole definition or understanding of a paradigm. One oft-mentioned explanation of a paradigm is that tendered by philosopher of science and historian Thomas Kuhn. As demonstrated by Kuhn (1962/1970), particularly in his book *The Structure of Scientific Revolutions*, scientific research in each discipline is dominated by one paradigm ("normal science") until a major scientifically progressive force is able to unseat the existing school of thought and invoke a paradigm shift. Kuhn questioned the existence of scientific truths and demonstrated that social and historical contexts affect the types of scientific knowledge that are classified as laudable (Dillon 2010). Kuhn specified that the "great works" of science became paradigms because they were "sufficiently unprecedented to attract an enduring group of adherents away from competing modes of scientific activity" and they were "sufficiently open-ended to leave all sorts of problems for the redefined group of practitioners to resolve" (p. 10). Although his paradigm concept is often applied in the social sciences, Kuhn's seminal and widely disseminated ideology actually served to show that there is no theoretical consensus among theories in the social science disciplines, therefore a paradigm cannot exist within these disciplines (Dogan 1996; Eckberg and Hill 1979). Regarding the use of Kuhn's definition of a paradigm within sociology, "the term comes most often to mean no more than a general theoretical perspective" (Eckberg and Hill 1979:929). Within criminology, scholars have also utilized a distinct understanding of a paradigm (even, again, when citing Kuhn) and have identified a criminology paradigm.

In the United States, social-scientific perspectives – in particular, the influence of social environment factors – have dominated the discipline of criminology since the early 1930s[10] (Cooper *et al.* 2010; Ellis *et al.* 2008; LaFree 2007; Schmalleger 2014). Thus the social science school of thought, led by theories based in sociology and social psychology, would be classified as the dominant paradigm within criminology. However, because there are many types of social science applications, or "theoretical fragmentation" (Cooper *et al.* 2010:332), to explain crime, criminality, and legal responses, it might be argued that the socio-theoretical perspectives within criminology could be viewed as paradigms. In this way, feminist criminologists Meda Chesney-Lind and Merry Morash's (2013) and Claire Renzetti's (2013) use of the term paradigm to categorize feminist criminology is plausible. Renzetti affirmed, "there is no single, unitary feminist *perspective* in criminology" and explained:

> Feminist criminology is a *paradigm* that studies and explains criminal offending and victimization, as well as institutional responses to these problems, as fundamentally gendered, and that emphasizes the importance of using the scientific knowledge we acquire from our study of these issues to influence the creation and implementation of public policy that will alleviate oppression and contribute to more equitable social relations and social and social structures.
>
> (p. 13; emphases added)

Based on the general understanding of Kuhn's conceptual definition of paradigm, however, an area of intellectual thought cannot be considered a paradigm until it becomes a *worldview* implicated in theory and research of a particular scientific subject or discipline. By this definition, neither feminist criminology nor intersectionality can be described as a paradigm or, more appropriately, *the* paradigm within criminology. Feminist-based perspectives and theories within contemporary criminology are still on the fringe and are viewed as a *boutique perspective* or *theory*. Within feminist studies and women's studies an argument can be made that intersectionality *is* the paradigm. McCall (2005:1771) declared that "intersectionality is the most important theoretical contribution that women's studies, in conjunction with related fields, has made so far." And, undoubtedly, the use of intersectionality is tremendously popular. There appears to be, at a minimum, anecdotal evidence that intersectionality has reached Kuhn's first specification ("sufficiently unprecedented to attract an enduring group of adherents away from competing modes of scientific activity"). This is seen in the move away from using essentialist or unidimensional feminist theories and incorporating an intersectional approach. Based on the inconsistency surrounding the intersectionality concept, it has undeniably met Kuhn's second specification ("sufficiently open-ended to leave all sorts of problems for the redefined group of practitioners to resolve"). Certainly, others may deny this assertion that intersectionality is a paradigm, recognizing that it has only reached the status of perspective or theory within feminist, women, and gender studies.

As indicated previously, paradigm is often used (or misused) interchangeably with *perspective*. A perspective is a general viewpoint in appraising an issue (Farley 2012), and "perspectives contain assumptions: things that we suppose to be true without testing them.... Perspectives and assumptions form the background of theorizing" (Allan 2010:8–9). In addition, perspectives can be viewed as comprising three elements: "[1] An approach to a topic that helps to determine the kinds of questions that are asked about the topic. [2] A theory or set of theories describing what are believed to be the realities of the topic. [3] Stated or unstated values concerning potentially controversial issues related to the topic" (Farley 2012:81). Some observers locate women of Color feminist theories into broader perspectives, such as colorblind feminism and postmodernism. The postmodernist (or poststructuralist) perspective or theories assert that "no truth is possible and that all knowledge, whether produced by academics or by ordinary people in their everyday lives, is infused and distorted by power" (Dillon 2010). Postmodernist research thus has a strong focus in exploring the social construction of reality, particularly with textual analysis in deconstructing (or dismantling) language and linguistic code binaries (such as man/non-man, White/non-White, White male/Black female, good/bad, rational/emotional) in order to "challenge the function of knowledge in legitimating power relations" (Collins 2000b:53; Dillon 2010). Feminist of Color theories may appear to fit squarely within the postmodernist perspective, but, in actuality, feminist of Color theories (and some colorblind feminist theories) lie outside the postmodernist tradition. By extension, intersectionality is also *not* a postmodernist concept. Because there is no absolute truth within the postmodern perspective, Collins recognized that antiracist, classism, and feminist theories were not desirable and could not be realized because, within postmodernism, no group can affirm the best explanation or understanding of any "truth." Collins (2000b:59) pondered, "who benefits from a methodology that appears unable to construct alternative explanations for social phenomena suitable for guiding political action; legitimates its own authority via exclusionary language; and dismantles notions of subjectivity, tradition, and authority"? Basically, postmodernist conceptualization is *postracial* and *postfeminist*, in that the scope is to dilute or disallow the continued significance of race and gender (as well as other identity categorizations) in present-day society.

Intersectionality is also typically placed within the coterie of *the* feminist perspective, and is even claimed by some as the "brainchild of [colorblind] feminism" (Bilge 2013:413). Certainly, placing feminist of Color theories and intersectionality within the broad (colorblind) feminist perspective is warranted because of the shared focus on gender equality, but I contend that, because of the colorblind feminist perspective's history (and, for some feminists, the continuing practice) of ignoring or not considering the prominence of race in the lives of women of Color, and in order to acknowledge multiple generations of women of Color who have evaluated their lives from an intersectional perspective, intersectionality (and similar conceptualizations) must be considered within the feminist of Color perspective, a perspective that has flanked or, at most, straddled colorblind feminism and antiracism/progressive race perspectives. This is aligned with Bilge's (2013:420) observation, "Reframing intersectionality as a creation of '[colorblind] feminism' … effectively erases a landmark oppositionality from which intersectionality emerged: feminists of color confronting racism within feminism."

As specified, theories fall within perspectives. A *theory* is a proposition or logical and formal explanation for why or how a phenomenon exists or functions. Theories are developed from and tested in systematic observations. Indeed, a theory should be able to be tested for "its accuracy in describing reality" (Farley 2012:510). I assert that intersectionality can be both a perspective and a theory and that one definition can be used to describe both: *intersectionality perspective* and *intersectionality theory* denote the supposition (perspective) or proposition (theory) that individuals have multiple intertwined identities that are developed, organized, experienced, and responded to within the context of the social structure and its dis/advantaged ordering. As a theory, it is the job of individual scholars to determine the precise process of how intersectionality theory is able to explain the matter under investigation. In Chapter 4, I present some of the phenomena or topics in criminology that embody the tenets of the intersectionality perspective, including street-level violence in underprivileged urban communities of Color and the government's treatment of Latino and Black boys; Black women's experiences and responses to intimate partner abuse; and Black, Latina, and White women's actual lived experiences within an illicit street drug and sex market in the wake of the increased drug enforcement and imprisonment during the 1980s and 1990s. I place the studies in Chapter 4 within the intersectionality perspective, as opposed to intersectionality theory, because the majority of the researchers did not explicitly use the intersectionality label in their theoretical conceptualization and a few of the researchers built specific theories from their investigations, including Beth E. Richie's (1996) gender entrapment theory and my Black feminist criminology and dynamic resistance concepts (2006, 2008).

Intersectionality has also been associated with the research process, from who can do research to applied research practices. *Epistemology* is the theory of knowledge and knowledge production. It is an interrogation of what is or should be "regarded as acceptable knowledge in a discipline" (Bryman 2012:27) and "who can be a 'knower' … [and] what kinds of things can be known" (Harding 1987:3). Collins's (2000a) view on individual and group standpoints is easily translated to an *intersectionality epistemology*. Because intersectionality is inclusive of many identities and standpoints and is born from Black feminist thought, it would be natural (and necessary) that the selected group speak from its own standpoint about the subject under academic investigation; therefore, "those ideas that are validated as true by African-American women, African-American men, Latina lesbians,

Asian-American women, Puerto Rican men, and other groups with distinctive standpoints, with each group using the epistemological approaches growing from its unique standpoint, become the most 'objective' truths" (Collins 2000a:270). An intersectionality epistemology is represented in the studies detailed in Chapter 4. A review of the methodology and the methods used in the qualitative studies in particular (not included in the study summaries provided) demonstrates the importance the researchers placed in the informants, seeing *them* as the experts in relating their experiences.

As mentioned earlier, Nash (2008) identified unresolved questions regarding intersectionality. Another of these questions is "the lack of a clearly defined intersectional methodology" (p. 4), referring to the lack of clarity in how to study intersectionality (see also McCall 2005). First, it is important to distinguish methodology from method, the former of which is commonly used as a heading in a journal article to describe the methods used to conduct the research. *Methodology* is "a theory and analysis of how research should proceed," while *method* is "a technique for (or way of proceeding in) gathering evidence" (Harding 1987:2). The various strains of intersectionality's definition have caused uncertainty among some scholars about how to conduct research under an intersectional approach. Feminist sociologists Hae Yeon Choo and Myra Marx Ferree (2010) provided an answer to those who question or are skeptical of intersectionality's role in conducting research, indicating that a researcher must first understand intersectionality as perspective or theory to incorporate it into any research method. Choo and Ferree offered that studies can improve upon "normal science" by incorporating a "more dynamic, process-oriented, nonhegemonic intersectional analysis" (p. 147). And an analysis is intersectional when it adopts an understanding of "the problem of sameness and difference and its relation to power" (Cho *et al.* 2013:795), thus underscoring what intersectionality *does* rather than what it *is* (see also Carbado *et al.* 2013). Thus, it is not about developing a new research method to incorporate an intersectional analysis; there are plenty acceptable existing methods that can be used to answer research questions. Instead, it is possible to develop an *intersectionality methodology* that determines how a research project can be guided by issues raised by intersectionality and then establishes the most appropriate methods to be used to answer the research question while being mindful of an intersectional framework. An overwhelming amount of research based in intersectionality has utilized qualitative methods, but quantitative researchers studying racial discrimination must also make intersectionality a fundamental aspect in their research (Harnois and Ifatunji 2011). In their longitudinal lifecourse study of residents living in poverty in Baltimore, Maryland, sociologists Karl Alexander, Doris Entwisle, and Linda Olson (2014) directly incorporated a method into their statistical analyses that attends to multiplicative identity. They made a compelling argument for stratification of the sample by identity attributes:

> Had we taken a different approach, contrasting the experience of African Americans against whites, on the one hand, and of women against men, on the other, [the intersectional] disparities would not have emerged.... They would not because the earnings differences at issue are not simply a matter of race or of gender, but rather of race and gender jointly as bases of stratification. The disadvantage of women is not the same for whites and blacks, and that of African American men is more different still.
>
> (p. 158)

In sum, in scholarly undertakings, intersectionality can be seen or used as an intellectual perspective, a theory, an epistemology, and a methodology, and can aid in research methods. Further, intersectionality has a place in criminology, and has a *right* and a *need* to have that place in criminology.

Illuminating intersectionality

Kimberlé Crenshaw's seminal articles – "Demarginalizing the Intersection of Race and Sex" (1989) and "Mapping the Margins" (1991) – provided a broader presence of women of Color feminist thought into colorblind beliefs about feminism by creating the term *intersectionality* to describe what women of Color had been expressing about their experiences for several generations. Black feminist activism, thought, and theory and critical race theory are the major strains that built the intersectionality approach (Alexander-Floyd 2010; Carbado *et al.* 2013; Nash 2008). Since Crenshaw's articulation of intersectionality, much debate has surrounded its definition and to whom it is applicable. Although critical race theorist Devon W. Carbado (2013:815) articulated that "the genesis of intersectionality in Black feminist theory limits the ability of some scholars both to imagine the potential domains to which intersectionality might travel and to see the theory in places in which it is already doing work," intersectionality as based in Crenshaw's (1989, 1991) conceptualization has since been adopted in many disciplines (Carbado *et al.* 2013; Cho *et al.* 2013). The concept of intersectionality has also reached beyond US scholarship, with a prominent showing in Europe. British feminists adopted the ideology alongside US feminists since the concept was originally disseminated in the English language and there had already been intersectional analyses on the lives of women of Color in the United Kingdom (see Anthias and Yuval-Davis 1983; Brah and Phoenix 2004). Other European countries, such as France (*intersectionnalité*), Italy (*intersezionalità*), Spain (*interseccionalidad*), and Scandinavia (*intersektionalitet*), are in the early stages of welcoming intersectionality into mainstream feminist thought (Lykke 2003; Lutz *et al.* 2011); but intersectionality practitioners are (rightly) concerned about the forsaking of *race* within European adoptions of intersectionality.

As a Black woman who studies the lived experiences of Black women, I identify with Alexander-Floyd's (2012) and Bilge's (2013) criticisms of the White-washing or Whitening of intersectionality theory's original usage. However, because the application of intersectionality theory (or intersectionality perspective) has proliferated and been expanded to analyze the experiences of individuals who are not women of Color, as Black feminists, we should work toward reminding those using this "new" concept in ways that recognize Crenshaw's intentions and roles in developing the concept and the Black feminist activism and theory that preceded it. I strongly believe the principal goals of intersectionality's origination are needed in considering *all* lived experiences, regardless of the identities individuals hold. Other feminists of Color also support this view (see Baca Zinn and Thornton

Dill 1996; Cho 2013; Cho *et al.* 2013; Crenshaw 2011). I believe the field of criminology, in particular, has too often and for too long ignored or disregarded the importance of socially constructed identities and how they affect or are affected by crime, criminal offending, and formal sanctioning of polity-defined acts. Instead of keeping such revered theorizing to ourselves (that is, only Black women theorizing only about Black women), and since there has already been some necessary, though still small, movement toward employing intersectionality theory for analysis of experiences of other groups, we should *encourage* its expanded use while simultaneously never forgetting the tremendous challenges faced by Black women and other women of Color and the many transgressions against women of Color that are resisted every day.

Notes

1 For instance, as Collins (2000a:203) illustrated, "a Black mother who may be unable to articulate her political ideology but who on a daily basis contests school policies harmful to her children may be more an 'activist' than the most highly educated Black feminist who, while she can manipulate feminist, nationalist, postmodern, and other ideologies, produces no tangible political changes in anyone's life but her own."
2 *Feminista* is also the Polish word for feminist.
3 Sometimes worded as "Ar'n't I a woman?" (See Oliver Gilbert 1998[1850], *Narrative of Sojourner Truth*, http://digilib.nypl.org/dynaweb/digs/wwm97268/@Generic__BookView, last accessed January 15, 2015).
4 Painter (1996) has argued that convention secretary Marius Robinson's account of Truth's speech, which does not record any statements of "Ar'n't/Ain't I a woman?," is closer to Truth's actual wording than Harriet Beecher Stowe and Frances Dana Gage's account written 12 years after the convention.
5 See Kimberly Springer's (2005) *Living for the Revolution: Black Feminist Organizations, 1968–1980* for an in-depth examination of the Third World Women's Alliance (1968–1979), the National Black Feminist Organization (1973–1975), the Combahee River Collective (1975–1980), the National Alliance of Black Feminists (1976–1980), and Black Women for Organized Action (1973–1980). The groups had vibrant, but short, histories. Springer provides a detailing of the life span of these organizations, including their disbandment due to insufficient funding, conflicts within the organization and between organizations, and burnout "as they attempted to capture the momentum of the civil rights and women's movement protest cycles by mobilizing large numbers of black women around feminist issues" (p. 18).

6 Springer's (2005) research and in-depth interviews indicate that the Combahee statement's reference to "heterosexual oppression" referred to the group's denouncement of heterosexism or homophobia. Also, see Springer for similar mission statements of other Black feminist organizations that reflect an intersectional perspective (pp. 116–117).

7 The INCITE! Women of Color Against Violence gender statement on membership reads: "When we say women of color and trans people of color, we mean people of color who experience violence and who identify as women, transgender, queer, gender non conforming, Two Spirit, lesbian, bisexual, bull daggers, aggressives, dykes, gay butch, studs, genderqueer, and those whose experiences are generally marginalized by movements resisting violence. We lift up the important work already being done by trans people within the INCITE! network. Some INCITE! chapters and affiliates already support transpeople of color leadership and are working to integrate a gender justice analysis into every aspect of our work and organizational culture" (http://www.incite-national.org/page/vision#sthash.eqWdwe41.dpuf).

8 As of August 2014, the Crunk Feminist Collective's Facebook site has more than 32,000 "likes" and followers, and there are more than 19,000 followers of the Collective's Twitter account.

9 Others would refer to what I call *social shapeshifting* as *code-switching*. Code-switching has been applied beyond its original and dictionary definition of "the practice of alternating between two or more languages or varieties of language in conversation" (http://www.oxforddictionaries.com/us) to refer to the way we change our social behaviors and presentation in different social settings (see Anderson 1999). I believe social shapeshifting is a more fitting term, for a combination of reasons. First, the term *shape* can be amended more than the term *code* to refer to social behaviors like attitude, speech, posture, style of dress, hairstyle. Second, *to shift* can encompass a complete switch, but can also designate only a slight modification in the way an individual presents self. Finally, shapeshifting in folklore, mythology, and fiction refers to the ability of a being to physically transform into another being or form. An analogous "down-to-earth" example considering the case of the middle-class Black woman in different settings, is for this woman to wear her hair in a straightened style that more closely resembles how Whites style their hair. But at home or with other Black women, she may opt to wear her hair in a "natural" wash-and-go style that reveals a thicker and curlier texture. Nevertheless, all individuals can and do engage in social shapeshifting, but for those with subjugated identities, there often exists the social pressure to follow the social standards often set by a society's majority.

10 See Nicole Rafter (2009), for an overview of criminology's history, and the discipline's paradigms and paradigmatic shifts; "Biological theories dominated nineteenth-century criminology, and eugenics, a particularly virulent biological theory, dominated late nineteenth century… [but], this preference for biological answers and solutions was supplemented by a strong undercurrent of sociological criminology" (p. 303).

3

REDUXING CRIMINOLOGY

An intersectional assessment of identity- and power-blind research and theory

Critiques abound of orthodox criminology's failure to consider the impact of interconnected social identities or statuses on participation in illicit activities, dealing with victimization, working in the criminal legal system, and establishing criminal laws and policy. For some time, feminist criminologists have pushed for intersectional analyses in criminology, yet we still face similar experiences to the one recounted by criminologist Kathleen Daly (1993) over two decades ago during a session at the 1991 conference of the American Society of Criminology (ASC). This special session comprised fledgling criminologists who posed questions to former ASC presidents. Daly directed her questions to Ronald Akers, Travis Hirschi, and C. Ray Jeffery. Daly asked the highly regarded criminologists if the persons they considered while conducting their research on crime had a specific race, gender, or socioeconomic status. Hirschi responded that his image of a lawbreaker was someone *without* those identities, indicating that "The offender is everyone – they have no qualities of class, race, or gender." Daly attempted to have a discussion about Hirschi's statement: "I said, 'Yes, that's what I find extraordinary.' At that point, John Laub, the moderator, checking his watch, suggested it was time to close 'on that extraordinary note'" (p. 66). During the same time period, Kimberlé Crenshaw (1989, 1991) also raised questions within the field of law and legal studies and for scholars doing social science research about inclusive and holistic responses regarding women of Color. In "Mapping the Margins," Crenshaw (1991) critiqued social-scientific research for not adequately considering the experiences of women of Color. Crenshaw commented at length on criminologist Gary LaFree's (1989) analyses in his book *Rape and Criminal Justice: The Social Construction of Sexual Assault*. Crenshaw appreciated LaFree's attention to the discrimination of Black men who rape White women. Likewise, Crenshaw appreciated that LaFree raised the issue of White men who rape Black women but are not punished to the same extent as Black men who rape White women. Crenshaw acknowledged that LaFree clearly demonstrated that Black women are subordinated on both gender and race hierarchies when it comes to the processing of rape cases in the criminal legal system. Crenshaw asserted, however, that for LaFree, "the differential protection that Black and white women receive against intraracial rape is not seen as racist because intraracial rape does not involve a contest between Black and white men" (p. 1277). Crenshaw was critical of this polarized analysis of gender and race, thereby leaving Black women's experiences indiscernible and insufficiently assessed. Crenshaw underscored that by the time LaFree reached his overarching inferences at the closing of his monograph, Black women have disappeared. In supporting arguments like Crenshaw's, which refute viewing interconnected identities as irrelevant, criminologist James W. Messerschmidt (2013:124) declared that "to better understand crime generally, we need to bring criminology 'out of the closet' by supporting extensive historical and contemporary research on the relationship among sexualities, gender, race, class, and crime."

Criminology includes the study of a large array of people, institutions, practices, and acts and behaviors, which includes assessments of criminality, victims, laws, and the criminal legal system. As this is a broad scope, this chapter focuses on research and theory that explain individuals' involvement in acts deemed deviant and criminal. I focus specifically on self-control theory developed by Michael R. Gottfredson and Travis Hirschi and lifecourse perspectives on crime,[1] particularly the age-graded theory of informal social control developed by John H. Laub and Robert J. Sampson and the intergenerational transmission theory of Peggy C. Giordano. Self-control theory and theories within the lifecourse criminology perspective are among the most popular contemporary theories in criminology and are repeatedly tested by other criminologists.

The critique of the studies I include in this chapter is not intended to belittle the contributions made by the scholars who conducted the research; indeed, I commend any who use their scholarly aptitude to work toward making sense of our world. Nor do I make the critiques to create enemies or to encourage continued discord among criminological perspectives. I offer this assessment because, in keeping with the strong propositions made over the past few decades by women of Color feminists and their allies, we must *center* the experiences of the "subjects" of inquiry based on the pronounced impact of socially constructed identities on those experiences. It is quite likely that criminologists whose work I analyze in this chapter *did* consider intersectional qualities of their study samples, so my critique is based on the tendered work products available for review (that is, the *published* analyses). In order to progress as a science, just as has been done over the nearly 140 years since Cesare Lombroso's (1876) *L'uomo delinquente* (*Criminal Man*), criminology must regularly question how research is conducted and conceptualized. In doing so, we must be sure to not privilege White experiences that erase the rich experiences of people of Color. Additionally, as intersectionality is a concept built on the centering of Black women's experiences (and, as indicated by Crenshaw (1991), the experiences of all women of Color), criminologists must always be mindful that many individuals exist on the differentially situated planes. Under this framework, to consider the experiences of White men engaged in criminal behavior is to acknowledge that many others are not equally situated and that the privileges afforded to White men, even those behaving badly, place them in advantageous situations. Legal scholar Paul D. Butler (2013) recognized this in his consideration of the intersectionality perspective for comparing the lived experiences of Black women with those of Black men. This comparison often yields the idea of *Black male exceptionalism*, an assertion that Black men as a group in the United States is the race×gender group doing the worst. Butler advised, "The challenge is to highlight the particular ways in which Black men are marginalized without marginalizing the experiences of Black women in the process" (p. 486).

Gottfredson and Hirschi's self-control theory

For more than 25 years, Gottfredson and Hirschi's general theory of crime and criminal behavior, interchangeably referred to as the self-control theory, has held the attention of criminologists. Gottfredson and Hirschi's seminal piece of work delineating their theory is *A General Theory of Crime* (1990), which is one of the most cited publications within criminology.[2] They considered both the *propensity* to commit acts deemed criminal, delinquent, and deviant (*criminality*) and the *act* (*crime*), and contended that the theory can apply to any individual across all characteristics (gender, race, class, and so on) and all locations (for example, across neighborhoods and across countries). A major tenet of the theory is the influence of child-rearing practices and the proclivity of some children to later engage in criminal or deviant behavior because of low self-control developed during childhood. Gottfredson and Hirschi asserted that "low self-control is not produced by training, tutelage, or socialization" (pp. 94–95). The main source of low self-control is "ineffective child-rearing" (p. 97). They identify the following elements in child-rearing that will foster low self-control in a child: a parent's poor emotional attachment to the child, poor parental supervision, a parent's lack of recognition and punishment of deviant acts by the child, criminal behavior by the parent, a large number of children in the family, a "single-parent" home, and a mother who works outside the home. Regarding the impact of parental criminality on low self-control, Gottfredson and Hirschi indicated that "people lacking self-control do not socialize their children well," assuming that – because it is a *general* theory of crime – the parents committed criminal acts because they have low self-control. Gottfredson and Hirschi also identified that the school setting is another major social institution that can instill low self-control. They argued that, in the United States, "the school has a difficult time teaching self-control," primarily because of "the lack of cooperation and support it receives from families that have already failed in the socialization task" (p. 106). Essentially, in their explication of the way in which self-control is developed in children, Gottfredson and Hirschi argued that parents cannot socialize their children to have low self-control ("low self-control is *not* produced by training, tutelage, or *socialization*"), but they *can* socialize their children to have high self-control ("people lacking self-control do not socialize their children *well*").

Gottfredson and Hirschi identified several behavioral commonalities and desires among individuals who engage in adverse behaviors that signify a low degree of self-control. Criminal acts satisfy one's needs immediately and simply. Individuals with low self-control are less cautious than those with high self-control; therefore, the criminal acts generate the excitement and risk sought out by those with low self-control. Individuals with low self-control are typically unable to make lengthy commitments, resulting in difficulty in maintaining long-term employment and relationships with others; thus, criminal acts that provide few long-term benefits are an allure to those with low self-control. Many crimes do not require higher levels of cognitive ability, so those with low self-control do not need to have academic or reasoning proficiencies in order to engage in most criminal activities. Since crimes typically cause the victims to suffer, this demonstrates the self-centeredness and insensitivity among individuals with low self-control. In sum, Gottfredson and Hirschi stressed, "people who lack self-control will tend to be impulsive, insensitive, physical (as opposed to mental), risk-taking, short-sighted, and non-verbal, and they will tend therefore to engage in criminal and analogous acts" (p. 90). They also indicated that "victims and offenders tend to share all or nearly all social and personal characteristics" (p. 17), but they only addressed offending, not how low self-control increases the probability of becoming a victim of crime.

Gottfredson and Hirschi maintained that low self-control persists throughout one's life and that the causes for an individual engaging in crime are likely to be the same at any age. Therefore, criminal offending will persist and only be interrupted by factors such as natural biological and physical maturation that limit activity in aging adults. Unlike desistance or lifecourse theories that attribute attachment to social institutions as the basis for "aging out" of crime, Gottfredson and Hirschi contended that maintaining steady employment and having a home, girlfriend or wife, or children *do not* affect criminality. When relaying this lack of support for the effects of employment and intimate relationship status on aging out of crime, Gottfredson and Hirschi are specifically referring to research and theorizing about individuals identified as heterosexual males. Citing others' and their own research, Gottfredson and Hirschi imparted that individuals (*heterosexual boys and men*) with jobs and girlfriends have been found to be just as or more delinquent than the unemployed and the unattached.

Although Gottfredson and Hirschi held that self-control theory is applicable to all crimes and deviance (that is, behaviors *they* identify as criminal and deviant), they noted the typical acts to which they were referring: (a) "common crimes" (p. 25), which include burglary, robbery, auto theft, "white-collar crime," embezzlement, drug and alcohol use, rape, and murder, and (b) "events theoretically equivalent to crime" (p. 42), such as "having children out of wedlock" (p. 90), pregnancy during adolescence, sexual promiscuity, adultery, unexcused absences from school or work, accidents (for example, motor vehicle accidents and house fires), overuse or abuse of alcohol, and cigarette smoking. Gottfredson and Hirschi emphasized that the undesirable activities of each person are eclectic, so there is no specialization in any particular crime or analogous behavior. Yet they did indicate that certain offenses committed by certain individuals are not appropriate for consideration under self-control theory, postulating that "complex, difficult crimes are so rare that they are an inadequate basis for theory and policy" (p. 119). One of these "exotic crimes" is the act of terrorism (p. 119). In response to ensuing critiques by criminologists that there is a contradiction in the theory if it is developed to apply to all crimes committed by all individuals, but it is not to be used to account for individuals committing terrorist acts, Hirschi and Gottfredson (2001) provided a caveat and clarification. Fundamentally, they do not consider terrorist acts to be "criminal" or "deviant." They argued that a high level of self-control is typically prevalent among those engaging in acts deemed as terrorism because these acts "are assumed to reflect commitment to a political cause or organization" and terrorists "do not act without regard for the broad or long-term consequences of their acts" (p. 94). Therefore, as they originally argued – and, generally, still do (Hirschi and Gottfredson 2008) – the theory can apply to "all crimes."

Hirschi and Gottfredson (2008: 231) maintained that even if an individual possesses a predisposition to commit a crime or imprudent act, their theory is situated in the classical criminological theory of *free will* and in "a tradition that sees actors making choices based on the objective elements of the situation." They also insisted that a criminal act cannot happen if there is not an *opportunity* to commit the crime. Essentially, in comparison to high self-control individuals, individuals with low self-control are more vulnerable to temptations and then act impulsively on their desires if there is the opportunity to do so. Hirschi and Gottfredson warned that not all individuals with low self-control will engage in adverse behaviors, as it takes more than just having low self-control; alternatively, they asserted that those who do engage in adverse behaviors (typically) have low self-control (except, again, for "terrorists" (Hirschi and Gottfredson 2001)). In response to critiques about the role of opportunity in their theory, Gottfredson and Hirschi (2003:9) stated, "To say the opportunities for crime are ubiquitous is not to say that opportunities for any particular crime are ubiquitous." Thus, they appeared to have softened their original proposition that all individuals have opportunity to commit all forms of crime by recognizing that it is impossible for each individual to commit any type of criminal, delinquent, or deviant act if, for instance, that person does not even have access to engaging in that act. In response to the critiques (see especially Goode 2008), Hirschi and Gottfredson (2008:221) contested that opportunity is not a requisite component of their theory and the main sources of crime are due to an individual's need to satisfy immediate and effortless gratification, to provide excitement or thrills, and to provide "relief from momentary irritation."

In keeping with the comprehensive nature of self-control theory, Gottfredson and Hirschi proclaimed that there is no need for specialized theories or for the use of more than one criminological theory (although they subsequently backed away on this latter point). They are critical of criminological theories that are developed to explain a specific population or a specific criminal activity and of criminological theories that incorporate a binary perspective:

> In criminology it is often argued that special theories are required to explain female and male crime, crime in one culture rather than another, crime committed in the course of an occupation as distinct from street crime, or crime committed by children as distinct from crime committed by adults.
>
> (Gottfredson and Hirschi 1990:117)

Hirschi and Gottfredson (2008) reasoned that there is no need for *gendered* theories of crime because the reasons or explanations for criminal activity are the same across gender/sex. They claimed that the gender differences found in criminal activity (that girls and women commit less crime than boys and men) are due to the gender differences in parenting, including greater monitoring, recognition, and punishment of girls' activities. The different parenting methods (by gender of the child) then affect self-control and, as a result, different choices are made between the genders about committing crime, with girls and women less likely to choose to get involved in criminal activities. Regarding race, Gottfredson and Hirschi (1990) argued that self-control, more than opportunity, accounts more for the different offense rates among racial and ethnic groups.

> There are differences among racial and ethnic groups (as there are between the sexes) in levels of direct supervision by family, and thus there is a 'crime' component to racial differences in crime rates, but, as with gender, differences in self-control probably far outweigh differences in supervision in accounting for racial or ethnic variations. Given the potentially large differences among racial groups in the United States in the elements of child-rearing … it seems to us that research on racial differences should focus on differential child-rearing practices and abandon the *fruitless* effort to ascribe such differences to culture or strain.
>
> (p. 153; emphasis added)

The main scope and principles of self-control theory have remained the same since Gottfredson and Hirschi's initial presentations of the theory. Hirschi (2004) took umbrage, however, at what he believed was improper measurement and conceptualization of the theory (see Grasmick *et al.* 1993). Hirschi hoped to bring attention back to the "elements of cognizance and rational choice" in the theory (p. 542). He also attempted to bridge self-control theory with his mid-twentieth-century social bond/social control theory. This theory specified that crime and delinquency are less likely to occur if certain bonds are intact: to others, especially parents (attachment); to placing energy and effort into activities, such as education and occupation (commitment); to the time involved in prosocial activities that leaves little time to engage in criminal behaviors (involvement); and to acceptance of a common value system (belief) (Hirschi 1969). Gottfredson and Hirschi's (1990) conceptualization of self-control theory suggested that social bonds are unstable over the lifecourse, but Hirschi (2004:543) rejected this and most recently has stated that social bonds are stable and internalized and that the social bond and self-control "are the same thing." Hirschi redefined self-control – which he says is in keeping with the original concept – to mean "the tendency to consider the full range of potential costs of a particular act" (p. 543), explaining that if individuals do not wish to lose their attachment, commitment, involvement, and belief bonds then they will not engage in crime. Those who have weak social bonds are low in self-control and, therefore, are more likely to engage in crime and analogous behaviors.

Evaluating self-control theory

A few years after the publication of *A General Theory of Crime*, Hirschi and Gottfredson (1995:140) provided a modified interpretation of their proposition by proclaiming, "although we argue that self-control is a general cause of crime, we do not argue that it is the sole cause of crime." But it appears that even though they acknowledge other theories are available to explain the commission of criminal acts, they maintained that the self-control theory can explain all criminal behavior (with only a few exceptions) committed by all individuals, even when faced with the frequently lodged misgiving that "it is not entirely clear that self-control is the principal cause of all crime types, at all ages, for all persons" (Piquero 2009:164). In order to determine the robustness of self-control theory, a large amount of research has been undertaken to test the theory (Buker 2011; Goode 2008; Pratt and Cullen 2000), and a growing amount of research is incorporating Hirschi's (2004) reiterations of the theory (see Bouffard *et al.* 2014; Brown and Jennings 2014; Higgins *et al.* 2008; Morris *et al.* 2011; Piquero and Bouffard 2007; Ward *et al.* 2012). The ensuing investigations have had mixed outcomes, resulting in the theory being fully supported, partially supported, rejected, or expanded upon (Buker 2011; Goode 2008; Gottfredson 2006; Pratt and Cullen 2000). The variations in how self-control is defined and measured in quantitative analyses further serve to augment the variety of findings (Benda 2005; Geis 2008; Gibson *et al.* 2010; Tittle *et al.* 2003). Additionally, the theory has been assessed based on its soundness and sensibility (but not on direct tests of the theory), including questioning the meanings of the theory's main elements. Some critics have suggested that the self-control theory does not do well in explaining crime in locations outside the United States (Alvarez-Rivera and Fox 2010; Marenin and Reisig 1995; Tittle and Botchkovar 2005; Wang *et al.* 2002). Because of the varied results in the numerous tests conducted on the theory, many scholars question if the theory is truly generalizable to all crimes, individuals, or groups.

Designations of crime and deviance in self-control theory

Gottfredson and Hirschi's declaration that all, but not *all*, crimes and theoretically equivalent events can be evaluated under self-control theory is inconsistent and baffling. As described previously, they did not designate terrorism as a crime, and "civil disobedience" (Gottfredson 2011:42) was also not included for the same reasons.[3] To be sure, there is continual debate among academicians, politicians, and criminal legal system agents about the definition of terrorism; yet, historian Charles Townshend (2011:3) disputed, "there is no specifically 'terrorist' *action* that is not already a crime under the ordinary law" (emphasis added). Thus, we are left unclear as to which crimes, and which people, are *not* to be included when employing self-control theory. In highlighting Hirschi and Gottfredson's (2001) characterization of terrorist acts as noncrimes, criminologist Gilbert

Geis (2008:207) concluded that, for Hirschi and Gottfredson, "a crime that does not meet their definition of a crime is to be consigned to limbo. The theory thereby can be said to explain only what it can explain, not all that it claims to explain." Questions have also arisen for researchers about the applicability of the theory to "white-collar" or corporate offenses, indicating that these types of offenses are complex and multidimensional and cannot be evaluated with the simplistic and one-dimensional attribute of low self-control (Friedrichs and Schwartz 2008; Simpson and Piquero 2002).

Another element of Gottfredson and Hirschi's theory that is scrutinized by criminologists is the concept that individuals do not specialize in certain criminal activities. The research findings are quite mixed in this area, but several studies have found that specialization is common among those participating in crime (Deane *et al.* 2005; Iovanni and Miller 2008; Moffitt *et al.* 2000; Osgood and Schreck 2007; Wright *et al.*1995) or that specialization is common among those participating in crime, but during shorter periods over the lifespan (DeLisi *et al.* 2011; McGloin *et al.* 2007; Sullivan *et al.* 2006).

Also of concern with self-control theory is the inclusion of certain behaviors "similar to crime." Gottfredson and Hirschi swept a large number of acts into the behaviors they considered analogous to crime. While it is commendable that they included behaviors outside of what the polity determines to be criminal, their selection of what those acts are and their supposition that these behaviors are a result of low self-control and opportunity and choice can be problematic. Gottfredson and Hirschi did not consider differential socioeconomic effects and cultural, racial, or religious dynamics that can have greater influence when considering truancy, children born to unmarried couples, and accidents. Gottfredson and Hirschi's inclusion of these so-called acts analogous to crime appears to be based on the definition of objectionable behaviors according to a colonialist, White, middle-class framework. This dominant/majority group belief system is addressed by criminologists Otwin Marenin and Michael D. Reisig (1995:512) in their (sardonic) valuation of self-control theory within a Nigerian context:

> Imprudent individuals have failed to incorporate the dominant values of society into their psyche and motivations and,

> hence, act as deviants.... [P]eople socialized to self-control and prudence do not act in criminal and deviant ways ... because they do not reject the controlling standards and values of their reference group.

Generalizability of self-control theory across race/ethnicity and sex/gender

Over the two decades since the publication of *A General Theory of Crime*, during which it has propagated as a standard in theoretical criminology textbooks and curricula, scholars have questioned the applicability of self-control theory across race/ethnicity and sex/gender (Blackwell and Piquero 2005; Flavin 2001; Gabbidon 2010; Unnever and Gabbidon 2011), and raised concern about the absence of socioeconomic class in the theory (LaGrange and Silverman 1999). As was established in Chapters 1 and 2, each of these elements is important when considering social behaviors. There have been relatively few studies conducted to test invariance by sex or gender and/or race or ethnicity in considering the differing effects of low self-control on crime and analogous behaviors to support or reject Gottfredson and Hirschi's claim that their theory is gender and race neutral (Gabbidon 2010; Gibson *et al.* 2010; Higgins and Ricketts 2005; Piquero 2009). Although gender and race are typically included as control variables in quantitative criminological studies, gender and/or race – and, especially, the *intersection* of gender and race – have only occasionally been empirically or theoretically scrutinized in research testing self-control theory. In comparing racial groups or gender groups and their respective levels of self-control and involvement in bad acts, some research has supported the principles of self-control theory across gender groups (see Burton *et al.* 1998; Cochran *et al.* 1998; Higgins 2004; LaGrange and Silverman 1999) and across race groups (see Morris *et al.* 2006; Vazsonyi and Crosswhite 2004). In those studies that did include racial comparisons, most of the research compared Blacks with Whites. But recent research demonstrated the generalizability of self-control theory to Indigenous groups (Morris *et al.* 2006) and Latinas and Latinos (H.V. Miller *et al.* 2009; Shekarkhar and Gibson 2011). In spite of research that has supported the soundness of self-control theory, other examinations are less supportive and some scholars question the theoretical applicability of a genderblind and race-blind standpoint.

Gottfredson and Hirschi's lack of acknowledgment that gender and race *do* matter may be reflected in some of the research undertaken to test self-control theory that has resulted in mixed findings. In testing the connection between low self-control and delinquency for Black and White youth, George E. Higgins and Melissa L. Ricketts (2005) found that low self-control had an effect on delinquency for Whites but not for Blacks. Alexander T. Vazsonyi and Jennifer M. Crosswhite's (2004) research on southern US rural Black youth found that low self-control predicted alcohol and other drug use, school misconduct, vandalism, and "general deviance" for boys and girls alike. For assault and theft, even though low self-control predicted involvement in these offenses for Black boys, it did not do so for Black girls. Similarly, using data from the Project on Human Development in Chicago Neighborhoods, Zahra Shekarkhar and Chris L. Gibson (2011) discovered that low self-control predicted Latino male youths' participation in property crimes (such as shoplifting and destruction of property), but not that of Latina youth, and that low self-control predicted both Latina and Latino youths' participation in violent crimes.

In contrast to Gottfredson and Hirschi's proposition that gendered parenting affects self-control and leads to differential offending rates by gender, Shekarkhar and Gibson found that "parental warmth, hostility, and level of supervision did not have statistically significant influences on violent offending" (p. 72) – thus not supporting the proposition that differential parenting of boys and girls attributes to gender differences in self-control. Brenda Sims Blackwell and Alex Piquero (2005) tested self-control theory (in conjunction with power-control theory) to investigate how low self-control is developed among and between female and male children. Although Blackwell and Piquero found that low self-control is a factor in the commission of crime among girls and boys, they demonstrated that the types of household and socialization by parents vary and, therefore, will have differential effects on children's development of self-control. For instance, patriarchal, egalitarian, and any other styles of family and child management must be considered when evaluating the effects of parenting on *all* children's self-control, and as it relates to ultimate participation or nonparticipation in crime and deviance. In another focus on the existence or effect of differential parenting by gender, Constance L. Chapple and colleagues (2010:1128–1129) found in their test of the theory using Children of the National Longitudinal Survey of Youth (NLSY79-Child) data that "boys' self-control was significantly predicted by greater school and neighborhood socialization … maternal monitoring and attachment, and, negatively, by mother's use of physical discipline." In their statistical modeling, however, they were unable to predict the origin of girls' self-control, as compared with boys, and why girls have higher levels of self-control than boys.

Many scholars have established that gender differences in criminal offending are much more complex than Gottfredson and Hirschi allowed for in their theory development (Blackwell and Piquero 2005; Iovanni and Miller 2008; Miller and Burack 1993; Nofziger 2010). Early on, feminist scholars panned self-control theory for its inadequate attention to gender construction and the strong effects of a patriarchal social structure (Miller and Burack 1993; Pettiway 1997). Moreover, self-control theory was developed from the analysis of quantitative data with predominantly male samples (Iovanni and Miller 2008); consequently, the theory was primarily geared toward attempting to understand criminal and deviant behavior engaged in by males. Variations in the effect of gender in tests of the theory may be attributed, at least partially, to the different ways self-control is measured in quantitative analyses (Tittle, Ward, and Grasmick 2003). Sociologist Stacey Nofziger (2010) conducted a quantitative analysis in which she was able to provide a more nuanced explication of the role of gender in self-control theory than did Gottfredson and Hirschi. Nofziger considers, more specifically, the impact of gender identity, as opposed to sex assignment or biological sex, on self-control and subsequent criminal behaviors. Nofziger analyzed survey results of a convenience sample of 252 students in an introductory sociology course at a university in the southwestern region of the United States. Using a gender identity scale meant that some women in the study identified with conventional masculine characteristics and some men identified with conventional feminine characteristics. Nofziger observed, "When gender identity is accounted for, sex no longer directly influences self-control. This indicates that self-control is not linked to sex, but instead gender identity, and implies that the gender socialization practices that develop feminine traits in particular also produce greater self-control" (p. 45). Nofziger did not find a connection between masculinity and crime or deviance, concluding that "it is not men being masculine" that factors into the commission of crime, but levels of self-control and femininity that *prevent* the occurrence of criminal activity (p. 45). In effect, Nofziger's study supported self-control theory, but demonstrated that self-control is connected with gender identity, not a biologically based sex assignment. In spite of this finding and of other supportive research, skepticism of self-control theory's ability to be broadly applied across genders remains. In what Gottfredson and Hirschi have conjectured to account for gender differences in the commission of crime – that is, variations in low self-control and opportunity to do crime – these underpinnings do not provide an exhaustive account of the many sources of behavior that aid in explaining different offending rates by gender (Bottcher 2001; LaGrange and Silverman 1999). Criminologists LeeAnn Iovanni and Susan L. Miller (2008:130) offered, "self-control as a general construct may be so at odds with female life experience that it may not even vary enough among girls or women for it to be a useful predictor of female involvement in crime."

Perhaps Iovanni and Miller's reflection explains the findings of a study conducted by criminologists Jeff Bouffard, Jessica M. Craig, and Alex R. Piquero (2014). They tested Hirschi's (2004) reconceptualized self-control theory by having convicted felony offenders (194 women and 819 men) answer questions about a drunk-driving vignette during their first week of entering a correctional facility. Based on the self-control theory, low self-control leads to criminal behaviors for all genders; thus, the men, *and* the women, in the research sample are in prison due to low self-control that led them to engaging in crime and ultimately being convicted. The investigation demonstrated that the study's self-control measures were independently associated with the men's self-reports of their likelihood to drive drunk. None of the self-control measures were independently associated with the likelihood of drunk driving among women. The study authors did not reflect on these different outcomes. Perhaps the women were not as honest as the men in the self-reporting of the likelihood to drive drunk, or maybe each of the 194 women were in prison for convictions based on false accusations. While these propositions are implausible, what would Gottfredson and Hirschi attribute to the gender-variant findings in the study if they insist that women commit crimes for the same reason as men? Bouffard, Craig, and Piquero contemplated that although the findings for the women in their study "may be related to the smaller sample size, ours is not the first study to find that self-control may operate differently between the sexes" (p. 12).

Gottfredson and Hirschi's admonition that it is unnecessary to construct theories for specific types of crimes or specific types of people contrasts with many criminologists' beliefs that certain crimes and the people committing those crimes warrant independent investigation. In considering the ability for self-control theory to explain men's violence against women, Iovanni and Miller (2008) stressed that the theory represses or ignores the impact that gender and power have on relationships and the social structure. Intimate partner abuse committed by a man against a woman involves the long-term benefit of one individual maintaining control over the other (Iovanni and Miller 2008), which is in direct contrast to Gottfredson and Hirschi's proposition that the commission of a crime only results in a short-term benefit. Terrie E. Moffitt and her colleagues (2000) considered the issue of intimate partner abuse in comparison with "general crime." Although they established in their longitudinal study of 849 women and men in New Zealand that there were no differences by gender in the motivations for intimate partner abuse, they did conclude that "the same individual who attacks someone [who is not an intimate partner] *impulsively* in a bar, at a sports event, or during a robbery may use violence *strategically* to control his or her partner in the privacy of home" (p. 223; emphases added).

Iovanni and Miller (2008) considered the application of self-control theory to the commission of sexual violence (in particular, outside the context of an intimate relationship, where sexual violence often occurs as a form of intimate partner abuse).[4] Gottfredson and Hirschi's (1990:89) downgrading of this form of *gendered* violence to a form of violence where a person (man) simply participates in immediate gratification by engaging in "sex without courtship" demonstrates their lack of understanding of the prominent role that control and power play in sexual assault. Rebutting Gottfredson and Hirschi's claim, Iovanni and Miller cogently declared, "rape occurs in the absence of *consent*, not in the absence of dating" (p. 137; emphasis in original text).

Challengers of the self-control theory conclude that culture, social structure, and institutional and polity practices must be factored into an analysis and conceptualization when attempting to determine the variations in the commission of crime by race/ethnicity, sex/gender, socioeconomic class, and other social statuses (Greenberg 2008; Iovanni and Miller 2008). Gottfredson and Hirschi's unworldly conceptualization was panned by criminologist Gilbert Geis (2008:212) in one of his fervent assessments of the self-control theory: "It is not poverty, not discrimination, not absence of equal opportunity to live a decent life, but poor parenting that must assume the blame for criminal behavior by different segments of the population." In a literature review of 44 studies based on self-control theory, criminologist Hasan Buker (2011) summarized that although parenting and parental socialization is important in the development of self-control, other factors also contribute to it. Buker reported that, based on the findings of previous studies, future research must seek to determine the sociostructural, cultural, and familial factors that intervene in parental effects on children's self-control, including neighborhood settings, religiosity, and family structure (see also Iovanni and Miller 2008; Pratt *et al.* 2004; Unnever *et al.* 2003).

In one of their recent replies to critiques of their theory, Hirschi and Gottfredson (2008) stood by their proposition that self-control theory is applicable across different groups. They argued, "the critics are wrong" and "demographic factors, real and imagined, pose no threat to the theory" (p. 218). In support of the challengers of Gottfredson and Hirschi's self-control theory, and based on what I have presented in this monograph thus far for the incorporation of an intersectional criminology, the impact of social identities and power dynamics must be incorporated into any social-scientific conceptualization of crime. Gottfredson and Hirschi's measured refusal to consider identity politics and broader sociostructural forces, even in the face of numerous compelling critiques, is narrow and flippant.

Lifecourse perspectives on crime

Another predominant theoretical perspective in criminology is the lifecourse perspective. There are several theories based in this perspective, and many lifecourse studies utilize longitudinal data to develop lifecourse theory. The most popular of the criminological lifecourse theories is probably John H. Laub and Robert J. Sampson's age-graded theory of informal social control. Laub and Sampson (2003:33) explained, "The major objective of the life-course perspective is to link social history and social structure to the unfolding of human lives. A life-course perspective thus looks to within-individual variations over time, regardless of whether one is interested in understanding persistence or desistance in crime." They "believe that a life-course perspective offers the most compelling and unifying framework for understanding the processes underlying continuity (persistence) and change (desistance) in criminal behavior over the life span" (p. 13). In comparison with Gottfredson and Hirschi's self-control theory, lifecourse criminology theories provide more promising explanations when considering the issues generated with intersectionality. However, intersectional criminologists still have concerns about lifecourse theories.

Laub and Sampson's age-graded theory of informal social control

Having progressively built upon their theoretical premise for three decades, Laub and Sampson have been deservedly lauded for their work on the lifecourse perspective in criminology. In what they term the age-graded theory of informal social control, they underscore the strong effect of social ties and informal social control in the persistence and desistance in crime and deviant behaviors. In their books *Crime in the Making: Pathways and Turning Points Through Life* (1993) and *Shared Beginnings, Divergent Lives: Delinquent Boys to Age 70* (2003), Laub and Sampson used data secured from a longitudinal study originated by Sheldon Glueck and Eleanor Glueck (1950, 1968). The Gluecks' project is considered to be the longest longitudinal study in existence. The study sample includes 500 boys classified as delinquent and 500 boys classified as non-delinquent, born between 1924 and 1932. The Gluecks' study consisted of three waves between 1939 and 1963. The first wave of data collection (interviews) occurred between 1939 and 1948 (at or near age 14), the second wave between 1949 and 1957 (at or near age 25), and the third wave between 1957 and 1963 (at or near age 32). There was a sample retention rate of 92.6 percent for the second interview and 87.6 percent for the third interview. Participants did not take part in the follow-up waves for a number of reasons, including refusal, death, or because they could not be found. The Gluecks collected data by means of psychiatric interviews with participants, physical assessments, parent and teacher reports, and police, court, and correctional institution records. To analyze the assessments and reports, each delinquent boy was matched with a non-delinquent boy (a matched-pair research design) by age, ethnicity, intelligence (based on an IQ assessment), and neighborhood socioeconomic status. All the boys grew up in low socioeconomic class neighborhoods in central Boston when they were first enrolled in the study. All the participants were identified as White, so ethnicity referred to English (25 percent), Italian (25 percent), and Irish (20 percent) backgrounds, with the remainder identified as American, French, German, Scandinavian, Slavic, Spanish, and Jewish (Laub and Sampson 2003). Conducting longitudinal research like this is rare. Criminologists can learn much about the social effects of crime by tracking individuals throughout their lives, which is what Laub and Sampson have provided by picking up where the Gluecks left off with the research participants. Laub and Sampson coded, recoded, and reanalyzed the data originally collected under the Gluecks' direction.

In *Crime in the Making*, which was the first full delineation of lifecourse criminology, Sampson and Laub highlighted the significance that social ties have during the entire lifecourse, and the ways in which behaviors are affected by informal social controls. The central idea of the age-graded theory of informal social control is "the dynamic process whereby the interlocking nature of trajectories and transitions generate *turning points* or a change in life course" (Laub and Sampson 1993:304; emphasis in original text). Trajectories are long-term, lifetime pathways made up of many transitions. A person's life has multiple interlocking trajectories, such as a work trajectory, an education trajectory, a health trajectory, and a criminal behavior trajectory. Transitions are changes in roles or statuses, such as leaving home to start college, getting a first job, or getting married. Turning points are major events that can cause a life path to be redirected; they are lasting changes, not temporary diversions. For the Glueck men, events such as getting married, securing and maintaining stable and legal employment, and serving in the military were identified as significant turning points, particularly in relation to the men's criminal activity.

Sampson and Laub concluded that individuals are more likely to engage in crime when their societal bonds are weakened in force or effect. Although basing their theory in Hirschi's (1969) social bond/social control theory, which focused on the formation of youth criminality when important social bonds (family, peers, school, community) are weakened or broken, Sampson and Laub departed from Hirschi's bond theory by incorporating the influence of life events that occur in adulthood. For instance, Sampson and Laub evaluated the effects of marriage, adult employment, and marital status on the continuation of or desistance from crime. In describing a process of "cumulative disadvantage," Sampson and Laub (1997:145) declared that "childhood antisocial behavior and adolescent delinquency foster adult crime through the severance of adult social bonds." That is, the accumulation and continuation of disadvantageous life events served to prevent the discontinuance of censured behaviors into adulthood.

Laub and Sampson conscientiously acknowledged in their 2003 monograph, *Shared Beginnings, Divergent Lives*, that the theoretical propositions offered ten years before in *Crime in the Making* left a number of areas in need of significant modification of some elements. This included heeding the observation of behavioral scientist John Modell (1994) that the interpretive analysis of the original interviews was lacking due to treating the respondents as variables instead of as persons. In response, in their follow-up study, Laub and Sampson

(2003) focused on the 500 participants from the Glueck study who were classified as delinquent. They conducted their own set of "detailed life-history interviews" with 52 of the men in 1993 when they were aged 61 through 69. Laub and Sampson also gathered the participants' local, state, and national criminal legal system records and searched for and collected any death records. Since 25 of the men had died by the time of the Gluecks' follow-up study at age 32 (years 1957–1963), Laub and Sampson only included the remaining 475 participants in their re-examination. Their study is exceptional in that it follows a group of boys-to-men over a 60-year period. While this new investigation highlighted in *Shared Beginnings, Divergent Lives* did not yield different results in the major turning points for the men, Laub and Sampson advanced their previously established age-graded theory by incorporating the interactive process of "human agency and choice, situational influence, routine activities, local culture, and historical context" (p. 9).

Sampson and Laub (2005:37) defined human agency as "the purposeful execution of choice and individual will."[5] They contended that the men were cognizant and deliberate in their choice to continue participating in criminal activity or to make efforts to desist from crime. "It appears that offenders desist as a result of a combination of individual actions (choice) in conjunction with situational contexts and structural influences linked to important institutions that help sustain desistance" (Laub and Sampson 2003:145). Laub and Sampson referred to this mechanism as "situated choice" to demonstrate that individuals "are active participants in the construction of their lives" (p. 38).

Laub and Sampson conceived that "routine activities" could either entice individuals into criminal activity or away from it. They concluded that marriage assists with desistance from crime among men because the routine activities of offenders are changed. The theorists asserted that marriage limits the amount of time the men spend with their male peers, including peers who participate in criminal activities. The men can also become involved with their wives' family members, who may assist in modifying the men's routine activities. Ultimately, Laub and Sampson argued that marriage serves as a form of informal social control, in that a spouse has "direct supervision" of her or his partner. They also maintained that marriage is the stage at which the men transitioned into true adulthood:

> Although it now may seem retrograde, the men we are studying came of age when getting married meant becoming a man and taking responsibility. Marriage also meant having someone to care for and having someone to take care of you. This view became even more evident once children entered the family.
>
> (Laub and Sampson 2003:43)

An additional analysis (after the publication of *Shared Beginnings, Divergent Lives*) of the 52 in-depth interviews with the Glueck men in their 60s resulted in the finding that there is a significant association between marriage and crime, with an approximate 35 percent probability (the average of the outcomes of all models employed in the study) that being married would reduce criminal activity (Sampson *et al.* 2006).

The age-graded theory of informal social control demonstrates that the discontinuation of criminal behavior as a person ages is not simply about getting older. The concepts of routine activities, personal agency and situated choice, and cultural and structural factors are also important for understanding a person's movement in and out of criminal activity during their lifecourse. In a reassessment of the theory, Sampson and Laub (2005) modified their stance on turning points, now indicating that turning points include not only singular (and sometimes rare) events, but also frequently recurring events and the long-term and dynamic processes of life events.

Evaluating the age-graded theory of informal social control across race/ethnicity and sex/gender

Laub and Sampson's age-graded theory has garnered much attention in the way of assessing its theoretical soundness. Yet, a relatively small amount of research has been conducted on the applicability of the age-graded theory across racial and gender groups (Caudy 2011; Gabbidon 2010; Piquero, Farrington, and Blumstein 2007; Piquero, MacDonald, and Parker 2002). The theory tests have resulted in mixed findings. In relation to the objective of this book, and like the assessment of Gottfredson and Hirschi's self-control theory, I focus on the theory's ability to adequately address the social impact of race, gender, and race×gender.

Laub and Sampson (2003:40) specified that "turning points take place in a larger structural and cultural context. Group processes and structural determinants (for example, race and ethnicity, social class, and neighborhood) need to be considered in the process of continuity and change in criminal behavior." And elsewhere they write, "Among the disadvantaged, things seem to work differently. Deficits and disadvantages pile up faster, and this has continuing negative consequences for later" (Sampson and Laub 1997:153). Support for this can be found in research conducted by sociologist Anastasia S. Vogt Yuan (2010) to explicitly test the age-graded theory. In comparing the aging out of substance use among Blacks and Whites, Vogt Yuan discovered that even though Blacks have lower alcohol and other drug use at earlier ages, by middle-age years the cumulative disadvantages that many Blacks face are correlated with less of a decline in use or abuse as compared with Whites. Vogt Yuan determined that the lack of "high-quality conventional social roles" (p. 4) – work, economic conditions, relationship quality, and family structure – among Blacks affected their "deviance" in later life. This research indicated that greater structural disadvantages for Blacks led to higher numbers of Blacks who were single parents, nonresidential parents, or married or single without children, which led to less of a chance of their declining substance use in comparison with Whites.

Clearly, Laub and Sampson acknowledged the important role of structural and cultural context and differential disadvantages. And some research has supported their theory. Curiously, however, the theorists too easily generalize that their theory can explain the experiences of all men (and women, as indicated in a quote below), even those who live in different regions of the United States and those who do not identify as White or with a White ethnic identity. While they do mention in the concluding chapter of *Shared Beginnings, Divergent Lives*, "why should we be concerned about white boys?" (p. 282) and cite Paul E. Tracy and Kimberly Kempf-Leonard's (1996) critique of *Crime in the Making* for disregarding race, Laub and Sampson then resumed their disregard of this notion and declared that the theory that was built on the experiences of the Glueck men can be applied to all individuals. They concluded, "we believe that the patterns of persistence in and desistance from crime that we have uncovered are more general than specific with respect to place, historical time, gender, and race" (Laub and Sampson 2003:283). As I have already proposed, *all* individuals can be considered from an intersectional framework. Simply because a research sample comprises only White men does not mean that issues of race and gender and sexuality do not need to be considered. Laub and Sampson missed the opportunity to say something about the White male experience. Regarding the Glueck men, they concluded, "It seems that some, but by no means all, men who desisted changed their identity as well, and this in turn affected their outlook and sense of maturity and responsibility" (Laub and Sampson 2003:147). Incorporating an intersectional analysis might result in a different or expanded assessment, where if men of Color (particularly, Black, Latino, and Indigenous men) "changed their identity" after building a prosocial and crime-free life, racial discrimination may redirect or reverse the trajectory of desisted men of Color. Criminologists Alex Piquero, John M. MacDonald, and Karen F. Parker (2002:667) argued that these "differential levels of disadvantage faced by racial groups" can more appropriately serve as "*breaking* points" (emphasis added).

Some tests of the age-graded theory have shown mixed results. If only considering the White research participants – the sample for Laub and Sampson's theoretical development – then the age-graded theory is supported in a multiple race sample. Criminologist Amie L. Nielsen (1999) discovered that the age-graded theory was unable to explain the trajectory of alcohol drinking among Blacks (all genders). For Whites, getting married lessened drunkenness, but marriage had no effect on alcohol use among Blacks, and only a small effect on Latinas/os. Nielsen created and included interaction terms, which speak to the goals of an intersectional analysis. Some of the interactions reached statistical significance. For instance, Nielsen concluded, "although men got drunk more often than women, the effect of being male was greater for Hispanics than for the other two groups" (p. 144). Criminologist Jessica M. Craig (2014) tested Laub and Sampson's theory by analyzing two waves of the National

Longitudinal Study of Adolescent Health (Add Health) dataset of nationally representative US respondents. The study included the initial Add Health survey data collected during 1994 and 1995, when respondents were 13 through 18 years old, and the fourth-wave data collected from 2007 to 2008, when the participants were ages 24 through 32. Craig considered marriage and parenthood, major elements of age-graded theory, to determine their effects on offending patterns. The analysis was unable to support the propositions of the age-graded theory across race once the control variables of bond with mother, bond with teachers, age, gender, family structure, socio-economic status, religiosity, education level, and current employment were introduced. For White respondents, as predicted by the theory, getting married and becoming a parent led to a desistance from criminal behaviors. Among Black respondents, however, neither marriage nor parenthood was correlated with any changes in offending. For Latinas and Latinos, the results were split, with a decrease in criminal activity aided by marriage but not parenthood.

Other tests of Laub and Sampson's theory also demonstrated mixed results, but regarding gender. If considering only the male research participants – the sample for Laub and Sampson's theoretical development – then the age-graded theory is supported in a multiple-gender sample. Lifecourse researchers Elaine Eggleston Doherty and Margaret E. Ensminger (2013) considered the age-graded theory proposition of the effect of marriage on offending for a sample of nearly one thousand Blacks living in a Chicago community. Analyzing data from the Woodlawn Project, a longitudinal Chicago study that began in 1966 with first-grade children who were interviewed again at ages 16, 32, and 42, Doherty and Ensminger found variations by gender in the marriage effect. Although few men in the study were married by the age of 32 (approximately one-third), marriage was determined to decrease offending of all crime types measured (violent, property, and drug offenses for which community members were regularly arrested). The status of marriage resulted in different outcomes for Black women. While the married women's involvement in property crimes decreased, there was no decrease in violent crimes or in overall crime rates, and for drug crimes there was an increase among married women. Doherty and Ensminger concluded that the findings for women do not necessarily disprove the age-graded theory, since Laub and Sampson (2003) cautioned that the pacifying or protective effect of marriage on criminal behavior was more likely relevant for men than for women. Doherty and Ensminger offered a caveat regarding the role of diverse cultural aspects that may be at work: "[T]his study did not address the mechanisms by which marriage impacts a reduction in offending. Thus, while a marriage effect seems to exist for these urban African American males, questions remain as to whether the mechanisms that are proposed for Whites similarly apply to this population" (p. 121).

It may also be necessary to question the causal or correlational direction in the marriage–offending relationship. Sociologists Ryan D. King and Scott J. South (2011:118) shared that "criminological theory has generated more interest in the question of whether marriage deters criminal offending than whether criminal offending impedes marriage." Consequently, in their examination of data from the longitudinal, United States-based National Youth Survey, the researchers found that engagement in criminal behaviors was associated with male respondents' delay in getting married. Regarding *race*, marriage, and crime, King and South found no evidence that the striking differences in self-reported offending rates between Black and White respondents – with Blacks reporting more offenses than Whites – explain the prominent differences in marriage rates – with Blacks marrying less than Whites. Therefore, a connection at the aggregate level between crime and marriage, if there is one, remains unknown or unclear. From the few recent quantitative studies presented here that sought to determine if Laub and Sampson's theory is supported across race or gender classifications, it is evident that we cannot say definitively that this is the case.

Giordano's intergenerational transmission theory

The criminological studies conducted by criminologist Peggy C. Giordano and her colleagues incorporate a lifecourse perspective and provide incredibly nuanced analyses regarding gender, well beyond those done by Laub and Sampson and other lifecourse criminological studies (see Blumstein *et al.* 1986; Tonry *et al.* 1991). Within her lifecourse analyses, Giordano (2010) has highlighted a revised social learning perspective by incorporating concepts of self and identity, agency, and emotion. Giordano investigated the lives of children whose parents, during adolescence, participated in the first wave of the Ohio Life-Course Study in 1982. Like Laub and Sampson's (2003) research based on the research initiated by the Gluecks, Giordano's study comprised participants who were first interviewed while institutionalized in a juvenile corrections facility. This original sample included 127 girls, with 38 percent identified as African American, and 127 boys. The respondents averaged 16 years of age during the first wave. The second wave of the project occurred in 1995, when the participants were on average 29 years old. This first follow-up study comprised 210 participants. The second follow-up investigation occurred in 2003 at an average age of 38, and included 153 participants from the first wave, 123 of whom were parents. The focus of this third wave of the project was on parenting and the children of the original respondents. At the time of the third wave of the study, of the original respondents who could be located and who had children, at least one biological child (aged 10 to 19) was interviewed.

Giordano's lengthy and rigorous study also involved control groups of youth. In 1981, 941 youths, half of whom were identified as African American, were interviewed for the Toledo Youth Survey. Seventy-seven percent of these were interviewed in 1991 and 1992 for the Toledo Young Adult Survey, at an average age of 29 years. The comparison group used for the third wave of the Ohio Life-Course Study was the Toledo Adolescent Relationships Study, in which 1,300 teenagers were asked similar questions to those posed to the children of the original respondents in the lifecourse study. Not only were the samples of Giordano's studies racially diverse, she found that persistence and desistance in crime varied by race and gender. Classifying desisters as those who had no known arrests for polity-defined criminal activity according to official records and self-reports, after the third wave of the study it was determined that of the original Ohio Life-Course Study participants, 53 percent of females and 36 percent of males (at approximate age 30) were "stable desisters." By race and gender, 60 percent of White women were desisters, while only 41 percent of Black women had desisted, which is even lower than the desistance rate of 43 percent for White males. Meanwhile, only one-quarter of Black men were deemed stable desisters at the time of the second adult follow-up. Regarding drug use, even though the study found more drug use among White youth during the first wave, an analysis of the third wave yielded results in which Blacks reported higher drug-use rates than Whites (52 percent versus 35 percent). Within race, Black men's drug-use rates were significantly higher than those reported by Black women (59 percent versus 48 percent), but there was no significant difference in use between White women and White men. Another racial group outcome found in the third wave was that Black respondents were more likely than Whites to appear in the lowest income category (US$0 to US$14,000 annually).

Clearly, *something* is going on with these dissimilar race×gender outcomes in Giordano's research projects. Giordano was especially careful to include a racially diverse sample in her research design and clearly recognized that race and gender are important to factor into the analysis. Alas, as is the pattern in many criminological studies, only descriptive information is provided and no conceptualization is proffered for these race×gender differences.

In addition to quantitative findings, some of the narratives presented in Giordano's (2010) monograph, *Legacies of Crime: A Follow-Up of the Children of Highly Delinquent Girls and Boys*, include cases that provide an abundance of substance for an intersectional analysis. For instance, Giordano reports that study participant Daniella "spoke at length about her negative feelings about having the darkest skin of any person in the family and her belief that her mother treated her lighter-skinned sibling with more love and care" (p. 109). One of Daniella's children, 17-year-old Maurice, had numerous challenges (as did several of Daniella's eight children), including multiple school suspensions due to behavior deemed problematic within the school setting. Maurice discussed his experience at one of the several schools he attended: "It ain't my type of school. I think it's because there aren't a lot of blacks there. I just feel like I don't fit in.... [T]he people there are nice but I just feel like I don't fit in" (p. 114). Without being privy to the researchers' field notes and the complete texts of the interviews (which would show, among other information, whether questions were asked specifically about the informants' racialized experiences at home, school, and elsewhere), I am certainly not equipped to suitably interpret Daniella's and Maurice's experiences. Based merely on the excerpts, an intersectional analysis would take into account how Daniella's identity was developed in a complex racialized society where sediment of structural discrimination and institutional racism seeped into and sullied interactions among the Black community and within a Black family. These societal functions demonstrate how stratification based on skin color within Daniella's own home and in greater society may have affected her lived experience, including her involvement in crime during her youth and adulthood. Of course, racial bias and colorism are only part of Daniella's life history. She is a survivor of abuse by her stepfather and a Girl Scout troop leader. These traumatic events must also be bundled with the context of Daniella's entire life, experienced as a *Black* girl/woman. An intersectional analysis of the experiences of Daniella's son Maurice, especially with the advantage of him being part of a longitudinal study, would demonstrate how his feelings of racialized marginalization may have impact on his education trajectory and other trajectories. If Maurice experiences "breaking points" (Piquero *et al.* 2002) during his lifecourse, an intersectional analysis would identify how the breaking points are related to his braided identity as a *Black* male and subsequently prompted a redirection of a trajectory.

Like Laub and Sampson (2003), but to a much greater extent, Giordano included the concept of identity formation in her research. "Consistent with our social-psychological approach, we argue that it is critical to consider identity-formation processes, since the child's emerging identity gives added coherence to developing attitudes and emotions, eventually fostering either similarities with one's parents or a break with family traditions" (Giordano 2010:3). Although Giordano paid significant attention to identity formation of the children in the third wave of the study, she did not explicitly address the impact of one's *race×gender* on the formation of identity. For instance, Maurice had some trouble in school ("talking back to my teachers" and "clowning in class, being disrespectful"). "In spite of these problems at school and his short stay in the juvenile-detention facility,

Maurice does not consider himself a delinquent" (p. 114). Maurice cited his father as a positive source who led Maurice "in the right direction" and "to do the right stuff" (p. 115). Again, an intersectional analysis would incorporate the import of Maurice's interconnected identities on his lived experiences. It might include how the perception of Black boys and men as the *criminalblackman* (Russell-Brown 2009) – the synonymy of "Black man" and "criminal" – affects how they navigate in various communities and the factors that might interrupt the internalization of this branding.

Unlike the Glueck men, Giordano found that for her study participants, neither "marital status nor job stability was systematically related to the odds that these women and men had desisted from crime" (p. 213). Giordano cited the work of feminist criminologist Beth E. Richie (1996) regarding women in abusive relationships being "compelled to crime," but she failed to incorporate Richie's findings and conceptualization that emphasized the importance of interconnected identities and different experiences for women by race (which I describe in Chapter 4 as an exemplar of intersectional research). A female study participant, Amanda, exemplified what Giordano referred to as the "direct transmission" of "definitions favorable to the violation of law and 'techniques' for engaging in these behaviors" from Amanda's father: "He taught me to fight like a guy, fight like he does. I don't smack, pinch, or pull hair. I fist fight" (p. 144). While the study allows us to learn more about the experiences of girls transitioning into adulthood, and their involvement in deviant behaviors during this transition, Giordano failed to provide a complex and multifaceted investigation into the implications of gendered scripts or narratives like the one imparted by Amanda (whose race was not identified). In discussing their protective stances regarding their children, original Ohio Life-Course Study respondents "directly communicate[d] that violent retaliations are sometimes an appropriate response" when they vowed to avenge harms their children suffered ("I'll kill him and go to jail") and taught their children to defend themselves ("hit her back hard enough to let her know," "beat the shit out of him"). Giordano concluded that these lessons increased "the ratio of definitions favorable rather than unfavorable to the violation of law" (p. 162). The expectation in many societies is that individuals avoid engaging in violent behaviors and that it is antithetical to teach one's offspring and other children to be ready to fight. Alternatively, as we see in many accounts that weave racial stigma, social isolation and marginalization, economic deprivation, and malleable gender roles (particularly for girls and women), engaging in violence goes beyond simply considering intergeneration transmission.

Reduxing criminology

An excessive amount of criminological research offers only demographics of the individuals being studied, and does not tease out and interrogate intersectional identities, but then sweepingly applies the findings to all persons. Criminologists must at least ponder the impact of individuals' interconnected, multiplicative identities in any research conducted involving the actions of people, whether as offenders, victims, criminal legal system agents, or lawmakers and policymakers. Of course, in certain instances, there may be no differences between the factors that impel individuals to behave in certain ways and make certain decisions. For example, there may be no variations in the proclivity for car theft between a young Arab American solidly middle-class heterosexual man and a middle-aged White working-class transgender man. But it is imperative to investigate any possible intersectional effects before assuming the experiences of these men are neutral by race, gender, sexuality, *and* class, and can be generalized to any men, or others, committing motor vehicle theft. Arguably, with intersectional criminology's focus on the influence of interconnected identities and the power structure, as a theoretical perspective it travels better than lifecourse theories and the self-control theory across individuals, groups, and places.

As a general theory of crime, Gottfredson and Hirschi (1990) argued that their self-control theory is applicable across race, gender, age, and culture, and across (most) types, targets, and sites of crimes. Hirschi (2004) clarified and amended elements of self-control theory, but the general precepts of the theory remain and misgivings persist about the applicability of the theory across diverse groups. This is also the situation with Laub and Sampson's (1993, 2003) age-graded theory of informal social control based on follow-up studies of the men in the Gluecks' longitudinal research project on delinquency. Some research that has tested age-graded theory to determine its applicability across race and gender has discovered that the theory may not be substantiated for all populations. What is unfortunate about Laub and Sampson's analysis is that the researchers did not address how the social condition of being White men may render different life outcomes from those of men of Color. And even though Giordano (2010) was mindful of gendered effects within her longitudinal studies and included a diverse set of research participants, her analysis did not fully appreciate the *intersectional* realities of the research participants.

It may be the case that a criminological theory can only be applicable to a certain group within a society. This is not a problem. It is not a problem for there to be a theory that may *only* explain the *majority* of individuals in a particular society who participate in crime, violence, or substance abuse (for instance, US White men), just as it is not a problem to have a theory that may only explain the behaviors of a subordinated group or a group that comprises only a minority of a population. Criminologists who focus on social factors that influence crime need not feel pressure to find a theory that can explain the entire population in one society, especially if it is a heterogeneous society where individuals and groups are situated within different castes and classes. This is even the case for intersectionality. If criminologists believe that the tenets of intersectionality only apply to women of Color, then that, too, is not a problem. The takeaway, then, is that socially constructed weaved identities are real and must be taken into consideration – and not insolently abandoned at the periphery – when studying crime, deviance, and justice, which operate in and are affected by a *social* world.

Notes

1 Gottfredson and Hirschi's (1990) self-control theory has been identified as a lifecourse criminology theory by some criminologists (e.g. Wright et al. 2015), but it is often discussed outside of the lifecourse perspective.

2 According to Google Scholar (scholar.google.com), *A General Theory of Crime* (1990) has been cited in other publications 6,800 times (as of August 10, 2014).

3 Gottfredson (2011:37) included civil disobedience alongside terrorism as events to exclude from analysis under self-control theory, because these "violations of the criminal law are not easily characterized as harming others in pursuit of short-term personal gain at the risk of longer-term personal cost."
4 Some would argue that in an intimate relationship that involves one partner engaging in control/power and abuse/violence of the other partner that sex is never consensual because control/power remain constant, even if specific acts of physical violence are intermittent.
5 Scholarly debate prevails about definitions of *human agency* (Ahearn 2001; Emirbayer and Mische 1998). Comaroff and Comaroff (1997:37) opined that agency is an "abstraction greatly underspecified, often misused, [and] much fetishized these days by social scientists."

4

INTERSECTING CRIMINOLOGY

Exemplars of intersectional perspectives in criminological research and theorizing

Criminologist Christy A. Visher (1983) provided one of the earliest applications of an intersectional approach in criminology with her article "Gender, Police Arrest Decisions, and Notions of Chivalry." In analyzing data from 1977, Visher not only sought to learn the differential impact of arrests of Black women and girls, but also was acutely aware of the unique experiences and stereotypes of Black females that affected their propensity for arrest. Although Visher did not explicitly reference Black feminist theory in explaining the Black woman's plight, she was mindful that the experiences of Black females in the criminal legal system are likely to be different from the experiences of Black males and White females. Since research conducted in the late 1800s by sociologist W.E.B. Du Bois (1899), it has been well documented that Blacks suspected of criminal activity are more likely to be arrested than White suspects. In the antebellum and postbellum United States, Black women were not free of over-punishment or false accusation simply because they were women. Black women did not fit the ideal of true womanhood (an ideal reserved for White women, and arguably still applicable today), therefore, not only were they deemed undeserving of protection, they were often over-criminalized for minor offenses and were often criminalized for their own victimizations (Battle 2014). Visher's (1983) study was one that began to bring new attention to Black women's experiences with crime and the criminal legal system. Visher determined that women and girls who "violate typical middle-class standards of traditional female characteristics and behaviors (i.e. white, older, and submissive) are not afforded any chivalrous treatment during arrest decisions" (pp. 22–23). Specifically, "young, black, hostile women" were not provided the same protections as older women and White women.

Although Visher's article appeared three decades ago in *Criminology*, the journal that is considered by some standards to be *the* top journal in the field of criminology, it is bewildering that many criminologists still do not hypothesize and theorize that arrests and other criminal legal system procedures may differ across race and gender due to the social construction of racial and gender identities. Although an abundance of feminist criminologists and other scholars now stress the need to provide an intersectional context on girls' and women's experiences, ethnographer Cindy D. Ness (2010:157) argued that in a number of analyses, girls and women are still "primarily viewed through the lens of gender with the variables of race and class effectively fading into the background." Nevertheless, a strong and growing collective of criminologists *has* made attempts to bring the significance of interlocked identities in criminology to the fore. Feminist researchers, in particular, took the lead in incorporating an intersectional approach in criminological investigations. It has been natural for many feminist criminologists to reject essentialism and embrace the importance of interlocked identities, diverse experiences, and social inequities. Since most feminist criminological research has focused on the experiences of women and girls, this is where we see much of the intersectional analysis. Some of the most recognized intersectional research on crime, criminality, or justice, is that conducted about the lives of Black girls and women in the United States; in comparison, few intersectional studies have placed attention on girls and women (or any gender) of other races and ethnicities, although there is a fast-growing interest in broadening *whom* we include in our studies. In example, feminist criminologist Natalie J. Sokoloff (2005) compiled a large selection of intersectional analyses of excerpts of mostly previously published articles and books on violence against women in *Domestic Violence at the Margins: Readings on Race, Class, Gender, and Culture*. This comprehensive collection not only brings attention to the experiences of violence in the lives of women of Color, it also includes the experiences of poor women, White women, and non-Christian women. In addition to some of the monographs and journal articles I review in this chapter, Sokoloff's anthology signified the growing importance of de-essentializing women who are subjected to abuse and violence. Intersectional criminological research conducted with other sexes or genders is also multiplying. There is an increasing body of research on men and boys that provides an intersectional analysis, most of which incorporates the role of masculinity into the theoretical examination. And although severely lagging in criminological research generally, intersectional studies on the crime-related experiences of transgender or genderqueer individuals is also showing growth (Woods 2014).

Criminological research that has employed an intersectional approach has not always explicitly referenced intersectionality, particularly in earlier works. Accordingly, the research featured in this chapter is research that was conducted in the spirit of intersectionality or from an intersectional perspective. As I detailed in Chapter 2 regarding research methods, because a large proportion of research conducted within women's studies, gender studies, and ethnic studies – the fields at the forefront of using intersectionality – employs qualitative methods, an abundance of the research with an intersectionality focus has been conducted using a qualitative method. Qualitative studies composed of small numbers of participants (relative to quantitative survey studies) often have qualitative researchers disseminating their research interpretations with a caveat about generalizing the observations to other populations – frequently due to pressure by, and misunderstanding among, those not well-versed in qualitative methods about the generalizability of this work. If qualitative researchers do indicate that their outcomes are generalizable to a larger population, which is seldom, "the reference is not to the statistical relation of the sample to the greater population, but to common patterns in social interaction and social life" (Warren and Karner 2010:7). I take the time to interject these methodological explanations here because most of the research projects (including my own) detailed in this chapter used qualitative methods and the reader will detect some common themes across the findings. At different times, in (mostly) different places, and typically working solo (sans research associates) in the field, many of us have discovered similar patterns in our respective settings. Included in this chapter is only a selection of exemplar criminological studies that have utilized an intersectional approach. These projects explored victimization experiences with and responses to violence and abuse, involvement in polity-defined criminal activity, and legal criminalization and punishment.

Navigating transgressions in public and private settings

Intersectional analyses of violence against women incorporate the impact of a multitude of structural, institutional, and cultural elements to understand (1) the proliferation of violence against women; (2) the social welfare, medical, and legal responses to violence against women; and (3) the women's decisions in dealing with the abuse. The theoretical contribution of Cherokee activist and feminist scholar Andrea Smith (2005a) provides a foundation for understanding the connection between legacy, supremacy, identity, and individual experiences with violence. In *Conquest: Sexual Violence and American Indian Genocide*, Smith recognized sexual violence as one of the weapons in patriarchy, colonialism, and racism disproportionately used against Indigenous women and other women of Color in the history of the United States. She deftly conjoined the initial detrimental effects of colonization to the present violations of Indigenous women, and connected all that occurred between these two periods. Smith stressed that European colonizers imported this system of degradation from the misogynistic, violent, and oppressive European society to the "more peaceful and egalitarian nature of Native societies" (p. 18). European colonizers regularly sexually victimized Indigenous women. Beginning in earnest in the late 1800s, Indigenous children were systematically removed from their homes and placed into boarding schools (on and off the reservations) where they underwent assimilation to European customs and Christianity – what Smith deemed a form of "cultural genocide." The boarding school practice was an act of violence and violation by itself, but children also faced physical, sexual, and mental abuse by their custodians. Smith also included in her definition of sexual violence (1) the US government's attempts to control Indigenous women's reproductive rights by targeting the women with sterilization (by coercion or deception) and long-acting hormonal contraceptives; (2) environmental racism ("raping of the land"); and (3) appropriation of Native spiritualities and cultural practices. Smith asserted that the result of the lengthy history of degradation of Native women, communities, and land is an internalized self-hatred among Indigenous peoples. Further, the violent behaviors of the colonists were eventually internalized among Indigenous men and perpetrated against members in their communities (women and children in particular), although the majority of perpetrators of sexual violence against Indigenous women in North America continue to be White men. In thinking about individual behaviors, Smith's exposition reminds us that the mechanisms and "culture" orchestrated by the sociostructural system and the policies enacted by groups in power, both past and present, contribute to violence and other transgressions and the varied individual responses to conflict. This theme is seen in much of the research contained in this chapter.

Studies on the experiences of Black girls and young women living in distressed inner cities demonstrate how violence differentially impacts multiply oppressed groups. The works of Nikki Jones (2010) and Jody Miller (2008) offer two examples. In her book *Between Good and Ghetto: African American Girls and Inner-City Violence*, Black feminist criminologist Nikki Jones provided an exploration, rich description, and explanation of inner-city Black girls' management of the transgressions they encountered in their homes, schools, and neighborhoods. Jones's study involved conducting a three-year ethnographic study in Philadelphia that included participant observation in a healthcare-initiated violence reduction program and the in-depth interviews with youth she met in the program. The violence and resultant "street justice" (Anderson 1999; Jones 2010) that is often inescapable in many distressed inner cities across the United States is not solely directed at and experienced by boys and men; girls and women also live within these spaces and are confronted with multiple oppressive, abusive, and violent circumstances. Further, girls and women navigating in these multifarious violent environments are faced with complex and conflicting expectations for expressing their intersecting identities. Jones's treatise adds to the small body of criminological research that has explicitly considered Black women's identity, particularly the salience of the *strong-Black-woman* maxim. Jones strongly situated her examination of Black girls' responses to violence and use of violence within Black feminist and intersectional contexts, sure to include obligatory gender performance of girls and women in the United States. Jones declared:

> The intersection of gender, race, and class further complicates the degree to which girls measure up to gender expectations. African American, inner-city girls in the United States are evaluated not only in light of mainstream gender expectations but also by the standards of Black respectability: the set of expectations governing how Black women and girls ought to behave. (p. 8)

In criminologist Jody Miller's (2008) ethnographic study presented in her book *Getting Played: African American Girls, Urban Inequality, and Gendered Violence*, she and her research team conducted semistructured interviews and surveys with 75 young Black women and men, ages 12 through 19, living in economically disadvantaged neighborhoods in St. Louis, Missouri. The youth had been labeled as "at risk" or involved in delinquency. The surveys collected information about "sexual harassment, sexual coercion and assault, and dating violence" (p. 14) that the young men or their friends engaged in or that the young women experienced. The semistructured in-depth interviews, which were conducted after the completion of the survey with each youth, then built upon the information gathered in the survey. Both Miller and Jones discovered numerous strategies that the girls and young women in their respective studies engaged in to stay safe. The young women in Miller's study often isolated themselves in their homes and used male relatives and neighbors as escorts to get home and gained comfort in their beliefs that their family and friends would shield them from dangerous situations. The young women were also somewhat comforted when there was visible neighborhood police presence. But based on direct and indirect experiences, distrust and lack of faith in beneficial police intervention caused the young women not to view the police as a reliable source of protection. The self-imposed isolation due to the need to protect themselves resulted in the young women being unable to take full part in the public community that was essentially "*male* space" (p. 65; emphasis in original).

The girls in Jones's study adapted to their environments using what Jones referred to as "situated survival strategies." The girls delicately balanced "unrealistic physical and behavioral expectations of the good African American girl … and the behavioral expectations of the code [of the street], which encourages the adoption of aggressive postures or behaviors that are typically expected of boys and men" (p. 53). In poor inner-city settings such as the one where Jones conducted her research, it is important even for the "good" or "pretty girls" who attempt normative feminine displays to be identified as being willing and able to fight. Indeed, Jones reminds us, "Violence is generally considered femininity's polar opposite" (p. 76); however, as demonstrated by the girls' narratives, "[s]ometimes you got to fight" (p. 7). The girls' lives were compounded by racialized, gendered, and classed canons, leaving Jones to conclude that "this negotiation of overlapping and, at times, contradictory survival and gender projects emerges new forms of femininity that encourage and even allow girls to use physical aggression when appropriate without sacrificing any and all claims to a respectable feminine identity" (p. 155).

Jones's findings on girls' propensity to fight differed from the experiences of the girls and young women represented in Miller's study, who tended to use violence only in dating relationships, which were all heterosexual. In these contexts, "girls' violence was conceptualized as ineffectual and framed as stemming from their 'out-of-control' emotions, young men's violence was recognized as a serious threat" (Miller 2008: 196). The girls who initiated violence did so in response to being frustrated with boyfriends' emotional detachment and accusations of boyfriends' infidelity. Interestingly, none of the girls who had been physically abused by a male intimate partner reported that they responded with violence, which is notably different than findings from other studies (such as Jones's study and my study described below) that examine violence against Black girls and women.

The Black women I have interacted with in the context of learning about their experiences with abuse and violence also accentuated the power of identity and the lack of power in the social structure similar to that found in Jones's and others' research. One of these projects, detailed in my book *Battle Cries: Black Women and Intimate Partner Abuse* (2008), included in-depth interviews with 40 heterosexual Black women who had been in abusive intimate relationships. The women were diverse by class and education level, and lived in or near Denver, Colorado, at the time of the study. My study emphasized how Black women's identity influences their responses to intimate partner abuse and how others respond to Black women subjected to intimate partner abuse.

The women who shared their life histories with me spoke of distressing encounters with abuse exacted by family members during their youth (for a portion of the women) and by intimate partners during adolescence and adulthood. Regarding common terms used in criminology and the criminal legal system, such as offender and victim, the women did not readily embrace these terms even though they were certainly victimized and some of them were arrested for physically retaliating against their abusers. The term they did embrace was *strong Black woman*; which, more accurately, was an *identity* that began to be formed during childhood. Never viewing themselves as passive, because of their propensity to fight back most of the time and because of their self-identification as a strong Black woman, the women were unable to see themselves as victims, and being a "battered woman" was not part of their identity. In addition, in using violence to respond to the violence committed on them by their boyfriends and husbands, the women did not view themselves as engaging in masculine behaviors. They simply believed themselves to be responsible for protecting themselves, their children, and their property, as they felt they were left to fight their battles without assistance from others. To be sure, embracing a strong-Black-woman identity and being seen that way by others because of the women's presentation of self or because of typecasting of Black women in this role, the women were often deprived of familial, spiritual, emotional, social, legal, or medical support.

Although the term "survivors" is an accurate way to describe women who endure, and live through, intimate partner violence, I concluded in *Battle Cries* that "because battered Black women continue to confront racial, class-based, and other struggles, such as the need to avoid entering subsequent abusive relationships, the use of the term 'survivor' assumes that their struggles have concluded" (p. 191). Here is where I employed the term *resisters* to focus on the women's fervent responses to abuse and utilized what I call *dynamic resistance* to capture the women's "distinctive life-chances, influenced by race, gender, sexuality, class, violence, abuse, and other characteristics, and their dynamic responses to these life-chances" (p. 191). Many Black women, regardless of whether they have been subjected to intimate partner abuse, "are resisters of racism, colorism, sexism, heterosexism, and sexualization in the Black community and in general US society," which solidifies their identity as *strong* Black women (p. 191). This is not to downgrade the grievous offense of abuse against Black women and girls but to demonstrate that identities, either self-imposed or ascribed by others, differentially situate women (and men) in society, thus resulting in varied and unique experiences with abuse. This project resulted in my development of *Black feminist criminology* as a theoretical concept (Potter 2006). The tenets of Black feminist criminology are cultivated from Black feminist theory and critical race feminist theory. Black feminist criminology incorporates interconnected identities, interconnected social forces, and distinct circumstances to better theorize, conduct research, and inform policy regarding victimization of and criminal offending by marginalized individuals. The theory views Black women and other women of Color from their multiple marginalized and dominated positions at three levels – structural/societal, community, and familial and interpersonal relationships – and how these affect each woman as an individual within the context of victimization and criminal offending.

Several recent studies have highlighted how immigration is yet another layer to be multiplied into the identities of women of Color subjected to abuse by their intimate partners while navigating the unfamiliar cultural and legal terrain within the United States. These studies employed an intersectional analysis. Margaret Abraham (2000) evaluated the narratives of 25 immigrant South Asian women who endured intimate partner abuse and the women's resistance efforts and assistance received by South Asian organizations that emerged to address violence against women in those communities. Hoan N. Bui (2004) examined the experiences of 34 Vietnamese immigrant women with abuse by their intimate partners and their dilemmas of interfacing with the criminal legal system under the constraints of their immigration status and loyalties to their culture and the abusers. Roberta Villalón (2010) conducted an ethnographic study in a nonprofit legal organization in Texas aimed at assisting refugees and undocumented immigrants. In the context of her work, Villalón also interviewed 17 Mexican and Central American women who were in abusive relationships and were undocumented residents in the United States (most of the abusers were also undocumented immigrants). Edna Erez, Madelaine Adelman, and Carol Gregory (2009) interviewed 137 women who immigrated to the United States from 35 countries. All the respondents had been subjected to intimate partner abuse, and all had sought assistance regarding immigration and/or intimate partner violence. This study "demonstrated that men who batter immigrant women, the majority of whom are immigrants themselves, have access to unique forms of domination and control, some of which are facilitated or even sanctioned by federal immigration law" (p. 51). In fact, the common finding among *all* these studies is that the experiences of the women of Color who are subjected to intimate partner abuse are further exacerbated by maintaining their culture while adapting to new cultures and being new immigrants in a country that is host to many laws and people who are hostile toward immigrants of Color, regardless of their citizenship status. In the case of the United States, protections for immigrants written into the Violence Against Women Act (VAWA) and the Victims of Trafficking and Violence Protection Act (VTVPA) demonstrate significant achievements made in the protection of all women in the United States who are subjected to gendered violence. Sadly, as demonstrated by Villalón, the VAWA and VTVPA preserve the social structure that is at work in US society because US immigration laws have historically prioritized those at the top of race, sex, national origin, and class hierarchies. Consequently, in practice, if a battered immigrant woman is even aware of the policies in place to protect her (Erez *et al.* 2009), the non-Christian poor immigrant woman of Color is left as the least likely person to be regarded a viable recipient of asylum via the VAWA or VTVPA provisions for abused immigrant women (Villalón 2010).

Considering the experiences of White women affected by crime and violence with intersectionality, critical social scientists Lois Weis and Michelle Fine and their co-authors explored the experiences of a subset of informants from a larger project (Fine and Weis 1998). The article "'I've Slept in My Clothes Long Enough': Excavating the Sounds of Domestic Violence Among Women in the White Working Class" (Weis *et al.* 1998) included interviews with 154 Black, Latina/o, and White low-income men and women ages 23 through 35 in Buffalo, New York, and Jersey City, New Jersey. In questioning the participants about family, religion, employment and education prospects, community/neighborhood, and contemporary social policies, the researchers learned of the many forms of violence prevalent in the participants' lives. I highlight here Weis and Fine's sample subset of 30 poor and working-class White women who shared their reactions to and navigation in abusive intimate relationships.

To understand working-class White women's experiences with economic hardship, prescribed gender roles, and intimate partner abuse, Weis and colleagues incorporated Joseph T. Howell's (1972) concepts of "hard living" and "settled living" that he formulated based on his ethnography of two White working-class families living in Washington, D.C. Hard-living women "float between different types of households, move in and out of welfare, and have less education and more (low-paying) employment," while settled-lives women "survive within what seem to be stable, intact family structures" (Weis *et al.* 1998:2). Both groups of women told of lives filled with years of abuse while in the care of their families of origin and later in their intimate relationships with men. The two groups diverged when it came to the option to disclose the abuse to others; the settled-lives women were less forthcoming in telling others about their abuse. "Living in violence may be better than living on the streets or losing custody of one's children. If she speaks, the 'settled' woman could pay the price of becoming 'hard living'" (p. 19). Relatedly, another difference between the groups was that the settled-lives women stayed entrapped in their abusive relationships in what, to outsiders, appeared to be "intact, stable marriages" (p. 16). To maintain this "stability" of partnership and some level of financial security, the settled-lives women stayed silent about the abuse. The settled-lives women often juxtaposed themselves with single Black mothers, who the respondents believed to be unproductive, over-reliant on government subsidies, and prone to crime and violence. The vilification of Black women aided the settled-lives White women in justifying remaining with their abusive partners. Weis and colleagues concluded that for the settled-lives White women to compare themselves with hard-living White women was too close to a situation in which they could find themselves and promoted anxiety, so they invoked an othering, stereotypical stance for Black women. Even in the face of economic hardship and of being subjected to unremitting violence, settled-lives White women attempted to uphold the middle-class family ideal. This is contrasted with hard-living women, who more frequently had escaped from the abusive partner and tended to be unmarried or living on their own, but faced impending poverty and homelessness – which, in turn, found the hard-living women feeling compelled to bring violent male intimate partners back into their homes in order to not slip deeper into financial distress. Although privileged by their racial identification and classification, the hard-living White women were observed by Weis and her colleagues to have "lived and spoke more like" the Black women interviewed in the larger sample. Even though sometimes faced with having to return to receiving assistance from an abusive partner, the hard-living White women rebuffed the patriarchal belief system of feminized domesticity and the violence that often accompanied it.

White women were also considered in Lisa Maher's (1997) ethnographic study of women drug users. Her study was solidly based in the interlocking identities of her study informants, which also included Latina and Black women. Maher conducted field research in Brooklyn, New York, where she observed women in street drug markets. Maher's aim with this project – acutely detailed in her book *Sexed Work: Gender, Race, and Resistance in a Brooklyn Drug Market* – was to contest both popular and academic (mis)representations of women crack users soon after the introduction of *crack* cocaine. In the late 1980s through the mid 1990s, widespread depictions of women involved in crime (1) presented these women as over-sexualized, (2) romanticized women's involvement in illicit drug markets, and (3) erroneously and irresponsibly reported a rise of violence perpetrated by women and girls. During the study, conducted over a four-year period, Maher observed more than 200 women drug users and regularly dialogued with 45 of them in the Bushwick neighborhood, an impoverished Latina/o community in central Brooklyn. In this social laboratory, the positioning and interactions of race and gender, in particular, were multifaceted and fluid. For instance, White women typically did not get into fights, instead opting for relationships with "powerful" men of Color in the neighborhood who would offer them some level of protection. Although the racial groups would interact within the context of their daily lives in the public setting of the neighborhood, tighter and more loyal connections tended to occur by race – Black women relied on Black women, Latinas relied on Latinas, and so on.

Maher's application of intersectionality in this project demonstrated that women drug users involved in the street drug and sex markets were responded to by street colleagues and customers based on their subordinated identities, with all women being subordinate to men in the underground markets, but where some women were afforded higher status than other women. Women in the study, mostly Latinas, were typically involved in the consumption of drugs, in dealing drugs when men were unavailable due to arrests, and in sex work in exchange for money or drugs to maintain their addictions. Although the identities or personas of age, immigrant status, and familial and neighborhood ties affected the way labor was divided in the drug and sex markets, Maher asserted that race and gender were the principal identities. Race and gender, together, determined the extent of the earnings for those working in the illicit drug and sex trades. White women sex workers were able to demand, and receive, higher rates for sex work than women of Color.[1] This cost differential is based partially on White women sex workers being more willing to engage in sex acts like anal sex and sadomasochistic sex

(S&M). According to Maher, however, greater desirability for White women sex workers was mostly attributable to racialized stereotypes about women, where consumers believed Black and Latina women to be violent like their male counterparts and that women of Color and the sex services they offer were devalued by male consumers. Regarding drug dealing, because street drug distributors considered White women as too conspicuous (to law enforcement officers) to work in drug sales, women of Color, especially the Latina "neighborhood girls," had an advantage over White women in this street market. Maher's study demonstrates the benefit of considering how the varied interconnected identities of the various parties differentially situated them in the street economy of illicit drugs and sex work. Maher stressed that these interactive dynamics are merely a reflection of the broader stratified social structure that orders individuals in dominant and subordinate statuses.

Bridging girls' and women's victimization and criminalization

In *Arrested Justice: Black Women, Violence, and America's Prison Nation*, Black feminist criminologist Beth E. Richie (2012) wrote of how Black women (especially, *poor* Black women) who have been subjected to abuse or violence are often confronted with suspicion that they are truly *victims* of a crime. They are often treated instead as criminals, violent aggressors, gender nonconformists, deserving of the abuse, or undeserving of assistance – or all of the above. The potency of *gendered×racialized×sexualized* stereotypes relegates Black women victims to the bottom of the social hierarchy. Moreover, factoring in socioeconomic class exacerbates the experiences of *poor* Black women victims.

In the same way that identities cannot be unraveled from each other, feminist criminologists have demonstrated that for girls and women, criminal activity cannot be easily disentangled, if at all, from a history of being subjected to abuse and violence (Belknap 2015; Daly 1992). Many studies have demonstrated that a large proportion of girls and women involved in illegal activities have abuse histories, with emphasis placed on the *path* from victimization to criminal activity – thereby named the *feminist pathways perspective* (Belknap and Holsinger 2006; for a review of feminist pathways studies, see Belknap 2015; DeHart and Lynch 2013; Pollock 2014; Zahn *et al.* 2010). The pathways approach is conceived of differently than (a) the research and theory that attempts to identify why people become victims and (b) the research and theory that maintains an overlap between victims and offenders, demonstrating that victims of crime are similar to criminal offenders. Gottfredson and Hirschi's (1990:17) self-control theory is within this tradition of "victim-offender overlap" research and theory, where it is determined that "victims and offenders tend to share all or nearly all social and personal characteristics," thus arguing that an individual's victimization can be explained by the individual's low self-control (for review of victim-offender overlap research, see Jennings *et al.* 2012). Feminist criminologists Meda Chesney-Lind and Noelie Rodriguez (1983) and Mary E. Gilfus (1992) conducted two of the earliest feminist investigations on the prominent connection between victimization and subsequent criminal activity among girls and women, revealing that the first arrest for the majority of the research participants was for unauthorized absences from home or school while they were children. During childhood, the respondents fled to escape the abuse they suffered from family members. Accordingly, much of the feminist research on women in criminology is all-inclusive in considering both victimization and criminalization and the contribution of the former to the latter, thus "blurring the boundaries between victim and offender" (Gilfus 1992:85).

Criminologists Emily J. Salisbury and Patricia Van Voorhis (2009:543) summarized the consensus of the pathways theory or perspective, which "recognizes various biological, psychological, and social realities that are unique to the female experience." The consensus of the research under this theory or perspective indicates that criminality of women is "(a) not typically seen with men, (b) typically seen with men but in even greater frequency with women, or (c) seen in relatively equal frequency but with distinct personal and social effects for women." Although the principles of intersectional criminology might be assumed to be captured within the "social realities" in this definition, the "social realities of *the* female experience" effectively disappears certain unique experiences between women. While many pathways theory enthusiasts incorporate an intersectional framework into their pathways analyses, many do not. I argue that an intersectional criminology perspective is *sure* to center racial identity and identity politics in research and conceptualization on girls and women. An intersectional perspective must be utilized if a thorough understanding of the "path" is to be gained. The blurring of victimization and criminalization is implicated differently based on one's social location, which is dictated by identity politics and a social structure (and its formal institutions and agents) based in supremacy.

Critical scholars argue that in the United States there is an overreliance on conservative policies to solve social problems and crime problems, which maintain the existing power structure where political and socioeconomic elites control marginalized individuals. Richie (2012) uses the term *prison nation* to describe this phenomenon (others have used the phrases *mass incarceration* or *the prison industrial complex*). Employing a figurative application, Richie broadened the notion of the prison nation to male violence against poor Black women by demonstrating how the strategic outcomes of the grassroots feminist antiviolence movement that began with 1960s activism were influenced by draconian policies developed during the rise of the prison nation. Richie traced the history of the political implications of the movement from the grassroots efforts to the broad adoption and acceptance of government-based efforts. She outlined this development in eight stages, starting with the 1960s activism and self-help by women personally affected by male violence, and ending with widespread public awareness and the institutionalization of practices to combat male violence toward women. The public discourse that ensued was that *every* woman has the potential to become a victim of male violence. Making this argument aided in neoliberal and conservative action for implementing policies to broadly address violence against women, including the initial enactment of the US Violence Against Women Act in 1994. Early in the antiviolence movement, utilizing criminal law and the criminal legal system to address violence against women was seen as an appropriate response. Indeed, Richie supports the use of systemic responses in certain situations; however, many unintended consequences stemmed from the dependence on using only official and legal mechanisms to solve the problem of violence against women. One of the unintended consequences has been an increase in arrests for women victims of intimate partner abuse who fought their attackers. Richie argued that, contrary to the intentions of making women safer with the institutionalization of intervention services for women victims of male violence, the conservative and governmental co-opting of the antiviolence movement's advocacy failed to benefit all women. She concluded, "We won the mainstream but lost the movement" (p. 97). Even though violence came to be thought of (in general public discourse) as a problem that could affect *any* woman – the "everywoman analysis" – Richie asserts that women of Color and poor women remained obscure. The representation of this "everywoman" became that of "a white, middle-class woman who can turn to a counselor, a doctor, a police officer, or a lawyer to protect her from abuse" (p. 92), and that it was *this* everywoman who was the emphasis in research investigations, social and legal support procedures, and public advertising campaigns. In effect, Black women and other women of Color were outside the purview of the *innocent* or *true* victim.

Richie detailed three preconditions for the proliferation of a prison nation that affects Black women victims of male violence: (1) divestment of social and material resources from low-income communities; (2) the co-opting of selected elements of the movements of White feminists (the everywoman emphasis) and Black liberation activists (the racial justice emphasis that excluded gender) that ignored the experiences of Black women (an *intersectional* emphasis); and (3) the criminalization of poverty and non-normative sexuality and gender roles among low-income Black women. Richie concluded, "[T]he buildup of America's prison nation – in terms of both ideology and public policy – leaves Black women who experience male violence at heightened risk that their victimization will be criminalized as opposed to their rights being protected" (p. 123). In the prison nation context, Black women – especially *poor* and *undereducated* Black women – are seen *first* as a problem. Seeing Black women as problematic precludes political and economic elites, legal system officials, and social services agents from seeing Black women as victims.

Criminalizing and punishing girls and women

Based in an intersectional perspective, an early exploration of the differential lived experiences, paths to crime, and treatment by criminal legal system agents is a study conducted by sociologist Regina Arnold (1990). Arnold considered the compounded social forces of patriarchy, racism, and economic marginality that led some Black girls and women to engage in activities regarded as criminal or delinquent. Essentially, Arnold concluded that being low- or no-income young Black girls and women means being at greater risk of being victimized and stigmatized by a variety of individuals and institutions. In her study of 50 Black women in a city jail and 10 Black women in a state prison in the United States, Arnold discovered that gender- and class-based oppression, along with criminal legal system officials blaming the women for their own victimization, was a pattern among the women she interviewed. This criminalization, at the time when the women were young girls, was exacerbated by their "structural dislocation" from their families and their schools during their formative years. The women's young lives were beleaguered by sexual abuse and other physical abuse, poverty, and inadequate educational experiences. This dislocation and lack of a stable familial alternative propelled the women early in their lives into proscribed deviant and delinquent behaviors, such as thievery, truancy, and running away from home, in what Arnold designated as their "active resistance to victimization" (p. 153). In return for their resistance, deviant and criminal labels were applied to these women from their youth and throughout adulthood. As the women continued engaging in criminal activity when they became adults, addiction to drugs became another obstacle to overcome.

When Arnold asked the women in her study to complete the statement "Crime is…" the women employed racialized comments and shared that they had not been prepared to participate in anything besides crime. For instance, Arnold's informants indicated that crime is "black people's support, if they're not working for a living" and crime is "the ultimate source of survival in the world of those who are black" (pp. 161–162). These enlightening statements illustrate the potency of race, socioeconomic standing, and other identifying factors in the women's lives, and demonstrate that there is an interactive aspect where these identifying factors only worsen the experiences of Black women.

Beth Richie also examined the circumstances that led women to engage in criminal activity, which is detailed in her monograph *Compelled to Crime: The Gender Entrapment of Battered Black Women* (1996).[2] Like the women-as-offenders studies existing at the time Richie conducted the research for *Compelled to Crime* (during 1991 and 1992), studies on abused women had predominantly been focused on the experiences of White women. To address this gap in the research, Richie, who had long worked as a feminist activist in the antiviolence movement, interviewed women detained at the Rikers Island jail in New York City. Richie conducted in-depth life-history interviews with 26 Black women and 6 White women who had been subjected to abuse by their intimate partners, and with 5 Black women who had not been subjects of partner abuse. *Compelled to Crime* is considered a seminal work in studies on women-and-crime and within feminist criminology because of the stirring findings on the varied responses of women subjected to intimate partner abuse, which were strongly connected to raced and classed experiences.

In not solely viewing the gender of the informants of her study, Richie found that racism (for Black women participants), poverty, inaccessibility of human-services programs, and aggressive crime policies compounded the women's lives and situations, ultimately steering them to participate in criminal or criminalized activities. Richie's interpretive analysis revealed, however, striking differences between the groups of women in the paths traveled to get to jail. The Black women who had been abused by their partners found their way to crime via *gender entrapment*. Richie explained that gender entrapment is "the socially constructed process whereby African American women who are vulnerable to men's violence in their intimate relationship are penalized for behaviors they engage in even when the behaviors are logical extensions of their racialized gender identities, their culturally expected gender roles, and the violence in their intimate relationships" (p. 4). Richie identified six stigmatized identities among the women who experienced gender entrapment. These identities comprised being women, being *Black* women, being low-income women, being abused women, being criminals, and being incarcerated women. Linking these stigmas, Richie concluded, "The African American battered women who are in jails for crimes that resulted from gender entrapment are among the most stigmatized group in contemporary society" (p. 161). Richie observed that the paths to crime among the White women she interviewed could not be explained by the gender entrapment theory. Even though they had been abused as children and by an intimate partner as adults, had low self-esteem, and were poor (the antecedents to their criminal activity), the White women had more social privilege than the Black women and the White women did not view that their future success would be stunted by a society hostile to their racial identity. The theory of gender entrapment also could not explain the paths of Black women who were not in abusive intimate relationships, whose paths to crime were commonly associated with drug-use addiction, poverty, friendships, and hopelessness for a positive future life.

Richie identified six paths that the women in her study had traveled. These were grouped into arrests for (1) some level of involvement (or assumed involvement) when the abuser killed the participant's child (abused Black women); (2) violent assaults, including homicide, against a man who threatened or attempted to harm the participant, but who was not the abusive partner (abused Black women); (3) forced sex work (abused Black women and abused White women); (4) property damage, including arson, and assaults against the abusive partner in the context of fighting back (abused Black women and abused White women); (5) property crimes (all Black women); and (6) drug-related offenses (all women). Richie observed that the women whose paths to illegal activities could be explained by the concept of gender entrapment – that is, Black women subjected to intimate partner abuse – participated in criminal offenses as (a) a means of delaying further violence by their intimate partners; (b) an extension of their loyalty to the Black men who abused them because of a sense of racial identity and unity, and the need to maintain some semblance of closeness with their abuser; (c) a perception of the duty to protect Black men from the racism they experience in the public sphere; and (d) a way to get arrested and incarcerated in order to escape the violence from their intimate partners, for at least a short period of time.

In considering the experiences women have once they are incarcerated in jail, sociologist Jill A. McCorkel (2013) conducted an ethnographic prison study to investigate the impact of US drug laws on the reworking of women's imprisonment *away* from rehabilitation and *toward* "tougher" practices, including increased reliance on privatized prison services. In the southeastern US prison where McCorkel did her research, as detailed in *Breaking Women: Gender, Race, and the New Politics of Imprisonment*, almost all of the prisoners interviewed had been living in or near poverty immediately before their incarceration, and the majority (77 percent) of the inmates were Black, while 17 percent were White and 6 percent were Latina. McCorkel conducted the study for four years from 1994 through 1998 and during a six-week follow-up in 2000. During the initial phase of the project, McCorkel spent many hours observing the prison happenings and completed personal interviews with 74 inmates and 29 state officials, private prison services company executives, and prison workers (including administrators, correctional officers, and counselors). In 2000, McCorkel conducted interviews with 12 prison staff members and 26 current and former inmates, many of whom had been interviewed in the first phase of the study.

McCorkel considered the prison and its occupants as a whole, but also specifically examined a privately operated drug treatment program housed within the prison. Beginning in the mid 1980s, in prisons and corrections departments across the United States, there was a move from a restorative and rehabilitative programming ideal to a punishment ideal of incapacitation, inmate control, and risk management. This was occurring in both men's and women's prisons, but with women's prisons changing at a slower pace than men's prisons. McCorkel labels the ideal that was practiced in the older system as *rehabilitative paternalism*, which is a quasi-familial and gendered method of control for women that is different from what was being done in men's prisons. That is, women were in need of parent-like guidance. This was a standard model in women's prisons until the sweeping national move to "get tough" on crime and criminals.

In the current era of a "new penology," the focus is on holding prisoners accountable, and encompasses a theme in which punishment and treatment are the same thing. McCorkel determined that this simultaneous method of punishment and so-called treatment among the prison officials and staff is done by way of "breaking down" each prisoner's self. In evaluating the prison drug treatment program, she discovered a "treatment" program replete with contradictions that simultaneously promoted the understanding and adoption of a "diseased self" and the abandonment of a woman's true self through a confrontational prison-based "therapeutic community" focused on combating drug addiction. McCorkel asserts that it is suspect that "the rehabilitative ideal disappeared at the moment when the number of African Americans surpassed the number of whites in the prison system" (p. 217).

McCorkel found that intertwined with the philosophical shift in imprisonment philosophy was the shift in the beliefs and perspectives of the prison workers she observed and interviewed. The workers designated the women prisoners as "good girls" or "real criminals." The good girls initially referred to the women in the pre-1980s era who found themselves in prisons that sought to reform or rehabilitate those who, but for bad and influential men in their lives, would not be in prison. By the 1990s, prison staff only referred to a minority of women as good girls – described as "vulnerable, innocent, and suffering from psychological problems attributed to childhood traumas, physical violence, and sexual victimization" (p. 77). The identification of women as real criminals began to dominate. Prison staffers characterized these women by using terms such as "manipulative, predatory, aggressive, addicted, and tough" (p. 77). These distinctions were solidly situated in a racial context. Generally, it was the Black women inmates who fit the criteria of and were referred to as real criminals, not the White or Latina inmates. The prison staff's racialized classification between "girls" and "criminals" was found not only among White staff; some Black staffers, including Black *women* staffers, also espoused racist and sexist presumptions about the prisoners. McCorkel observed, "In the prison, these images made the increase in African American women's incarceration rate appear to be an inevitable consequence of their own behavior and choices rather than as a function of poverty or broader changes in criminal justice policy" (p. 79). White women who entered the prison because of a drug-offense conviction were also typically deemed by the staff to be real criminals, but these inmates were seen as racial outliers. Between the mid 1980s and the present, as the shift occurred in the racial makeup of the inmates from a majority of White inmates to a majority of Black inmates, and from "good girls" to "real criminals," the prison workers thought it pointless to devote time to efforts to rehabilitate the women. In effect, Black women convicts – and the White women who committed crimes like Black women – were deemed irredeemable.

Consistent with McCorkel's research outcomes, Jody Miller (1996) found differential placement by race for girls who were adjudicated for committing delinquent acts. In her study based in Los Angeles, Miller discovered that White girls, as compared with Black and Latina girls, received significantly more recommendations for a treatment facility placement. While only 30 percent of Black girls and 34 percent of Latina girls received a treatment recommendation, approximately 75 percent of White girls were recommended for housing in a treatment facility. Miller concluded, "Paternalistic discursive frameworks were frequently called upon to explain the behavior of white and Latina girls, while punitive constructs were more likely to be used to describe African American girls" (p. 239).

The majority of people who are sentenced to correctional facilities will be released. Some releasees will continue to be supervised "in the community" by a legal system agent (such as a parole officer) or agency (halfway house, residential community corrections center). There exists an abundance of evidence that the general problems of the management of and programming for individuals in prison, as raised by McCorkel, do not prepare incarcerated persons with tools and resources that would be especially useful for post-incarceration success. Comparatively, there is a larger proportion of persons who are convicted (or adjudicated) and sentenced to do "street time" without first having to be incarcerated. This population also struggles with securing or maintaining adequate resources to sustain suitable living conditions *in addition* to challenges of remaining free of crime activity and alcohol or drug use. Criminologist Jennifer Cobbina and her colleagues (2014) investigated how women probationers and parolees dealt with occurrences of crime in their neighborhoods and whether their neighborhood environment affected the strategies they used to not recidivate. The researchers also considered if there were any variations by race regarding the dis/organization of the communities in which they lived. The mixed-methods study involved survey and semistructured interviews with 402 women aged 18 through 60 on probation (76 percent of sample) and parole in Michigan for a felony offense (256 informants provided usable narratives for the qualitative proportion of the study). Whites comprised about half (46 percent) of the participants and a third of the women identified as Black. A mix of Latinas, multiracial women, and women of "other" races made up the remainder of the sample. About half (53.5 percent) of the women were mothers of children 17 years old and younger and approximately 13 percent of the women were married at the time of the study. Only 17.4 percent of the women had full-time employment. Little more than half of the women who could work were employed and 85.2 percent of them had a yearly income of less than US$10,000. In reviewing only the descriptive statistics, it is clear the women endured some noteworthy circumstances. The qualitative and quantitative analyses provided a story of additional challenges that many of the women faced and managed.

As Cobbina and co-researchers expected, in comparison with the White women respondents, Black women perceived there to be more types of crime (visible or street crime) in their neighborhoods and they resided in neighborhoods with greater social disorganization. The most common personal crime-prevention strategy utilized by the women living in highly disorganized neighborhoods was to avoid persons engaged in criminal activity, including family members. The other strategies, in descending order by commonness, included staying home, avoiding all (or most) people, associating with prosocial (alcohol-, drug-, and crime-free) individuals, fully occupying their days with legal activities (work, childcare), remaining free of alcohol and other drug use, reflecting on the consequences of their previous criminal activity, and obeying the law. The women living in economically distressed neighborhoods were more likely than women living in more affluent neighborhoods to employ personal crime-prevention strategies that isolated them from many social environments. The researchers concluded:

> Certainly, some White women on probation and parole contend with negative community conditions. However, the magnifying effects of race on hardship in women offenders' lives is part of a broader picture, in which Black women have been disproportionately affected by growing rates of women on probation, in prison, and on parole.
>
> (p. 22)

Appreciating the intersectionality of boys and men

Although men and boys hold multiple intersecting identities just as women and girls do, overwhelmingly, criminologists overlook how the tenets of intersectionality can aid in making sense out of men's and boys' involvement with and responses to crime. Over a decade ago, feminist criminologist Dana M. Britton (2000:73) criticized that there remained a "screaming silence in criminology around the connection between masculinity and crime." And, more recently, Britton (2011:42) extended her warning: "we are unlikely to be successful in addressing the causes of crime if we fail to understand its intimate relationship with masculinity." An intersectional approach is beginning to be more frequently incorporated to make sense of the experiences of boys and men, as I demonstrate in this section; however, urban sociologist Elijah Anderson's (1978, 1990, 1999, 2011) work serves as a foundational body of intersectional research on boys and men. For more than 40 years, Anderson's field research has thoroughly considered the magnitude of intersecting identities within the social structure. Anderson has investigated the lives of Blacks and Whites, across socioeconomic classes, and all genders, but the bulk of his work and analyses focus on Black men who were working-class, low-income, or in poverty and had been relegated to isolated, disenfranchised communities. Anderson's research has exposed the lived experiences of young Black males who continue to have to work at gaining trust from Whites and social control agents (the police, who are viewed as representatives of the White community) to prove they are *not* criminals, which is generally not a concern for young White males. Even so, as we know, a minority of young Black men (and women) have committed violent and criminal behaviors.

Considering Anderson's array of books, *Code of the Street* (1999) is the one that is most recognized and utilized in criminology. With this work, Anderson introduced the two orientations on which the community (a poor Black neighborhood in Philadelphia) is socially organized: *decent* and *street*. Decent families and community members accepted and strived for "mainstream values more fully than street families, and they attempt to instill them in their children" (p. 38). Decent community members were confronted by the oppositional culture of the streets, whereby decent folks could not easily escape street-oriented individuals, who represented only a small proportion of the community but had come to dominate the public realm, thus forcing every community member, particularly the youth, to be able and ready to fight. The code of the street is a social adaptation to the alienation from general society felt by community members and the uncertainty about police intervention. Consequently, Anderson contended, "the street code thus emerges where the influence of the police ends and where personal responsibility for one's safety is felt to begin" (p. 34).

Respect is the core of the street code, and this is reflected in the maneuvers that young Black men (and women) have to perform on the street. The neighborhood boys and young men must project a self-image that garners respect and communicates that they are not to be "messed with" or "dissed." Manhood must be exhibited by showing "true nerve," which includes not fearing death. "Not to be afraid to die is the quid pro quo of being able to take somebody else's life – for the right reasons, if the situation demands it" (Anderson 1994:92). Finally, a general attitude of fearlessness is expected in self-presentations on the street. With each of these street rituals, decent youth will often code-switch and display more deferential behaviors when in school or at work.

Anderson reasoned that the oppositional culture that manifested in the community represented in *Code of the Street* was not developed in isolation; the street violence is a result of despair and seclusion from the majority White society. However, middle-class outsiders

(Blacks and Whites) feel affirmed in their negative views about the poor inner-city neighborhood, and its residents, where youth perpetuated the violence. These persistent views by outsiders then led young Blacks, including the decent youth, to continue participating in the street orientation: "These decent people are trying hard to be part of the mainstream culture, but the racism, real and perceived, that they encounter helps to legitimate the oppositional culture and, by extension, the code of the street" (Anderson 1999:313).

Criminologist James W. Messerschmidt (1993, 1997, 2013) has also emphasized in his structured action theory the strong effect of intersecting identities, including the role of masculinity, on boys' and men's involvement in crime. Structured action theory avers that crime is best understood through recognition that gender, race, class, and sexual practices are manifested as both a structure and an action. In his consideration of boys who participate in criminal activities, Messerschmidt (1993:87–88) has been mindful that "'[b]oys will be boys' *differently*, depending upon their position in social structures and, therefore, upon their access to power and resources" (emphasis added). He continued, "Collectively, young men experience their daily world from a particular position in society and differentially construct the cultural ideals of hegemonic masculinity." Messerschmidt's applications include the impact of role expectations surrounding masculinity and sexuality for males. He argued that when standard forms of "doing" masculinity or gender are unavailable for boys and men to effectively communicate that they are "manly," crime or violence becomes "a resource for doing masculinity in specific social settings" (p. 85).

Recent contributions to criminology indicate that there may be growing attention to and incorporation of intersectional analyses of boys and men. For example, criminologist Randol Contreras (2013) skillfully weaved masculinity, class, nationality, race, color, and ethnicity into his examination (and personal experience) of Dominican youth in the South Bronx who participated in "drug robberies." The young men highlighted in Contreras's book *The Stickup Kids: Race, Drugs, Violence, and the American Dream* were pressed to do what they could to achieve the "American dream," and their access to the dream eventually evolved into robbing drug dealers of drugs and money in their poverty-stricken neighborhoods. Contreras keenly observed, "With the drugs came unsanctioned masculine violence. Middle-class teens proved toughness on athletic fields and rinks, and if violent enough, received university scholarships; South Bronx youths with drug market exposure proved their courage in other ways" (p. 58). The men whose lives were explored by Contreras started as crack cocaine drug dealers, but during the decline in the crack market in the 1990s, these men were faced with finding a new method for accessing the American dream. Nevertheless, even though "they knew how to manage drug spots, negotiate drug deals, and act around drug dealers," these skills "had little use in a service economy demanding more subservience, less masculinity, more education, less resistance, and more middle-class etiquette," behaviors in which Contreras's friends were ill-equipped and which they did not desire to acquire (p. 112).

As these young men evolved from failed drug dealers into accomplished drug robbers, Contreras demonstrated how the social structure, capitalist principles, and masculinity enabled the stickup kids to commit especially violent and torturous acts against drug dealers. He showed how masculinity can be observed through the role of women in drug robberies, discussing how the male robbers often used a woman to set "a *masculinity trap*, a play on a male's manhood to victimize him" (p. 124; emphases in original text). Contreras (2009, 2013) emphasized that even though the robbers would likely not be able to get the drug dealer in a position to rob him if they did not use "The Girl," the drug robbers exploited and trivialized their female collaborators. Contreras applied an intersectional framework to the role of opportunity that is raised by a number of criminologists, including the research and theories of Gottfredson and Hirschi (1990) and Laub and Sampson (2003) detailed in Chapter 3. Contreras (2013:175) assessed that the stickup kids'

> increasing marginality within both larger society and the drug market raised their chances of being in violent situations. Because not just anyone finds himself castrating a man, or raping a woman, or burning a victim while searching for drugs and cash. Unless, of course, their background and social structural conditions influence them in such directions – unless

the intersection of race, class, gender, history, and biography increases their odds.

O.G. sociologist[3] Victor M. Rios (2011) carried out three years of field research in Oakland, California, to assess the policing and social control of Black and Latino adolescent boys. As detailed in his book *Punished: Policing the Lives of Black and Latino Boys*, Rios interviewed and hung out with 40 boys, ages 14 through 17, in a variety of settings, including in their schools, in court, in their homes, and on street corners. Rios investigated the boys' lived experiences utilizing an intersectional approach in his consideration of how race, gender, class, and age affected the way the boys were responded to by police officers, probation officers, teachers, and community members who executed punitive legal and social policies. Rios delved into the lives of the boys, who were confronted with skepticism and blocked from educational and employment opportunities on a daily basis. Not only did the boys who were officially tagged as criminal or delinquent face these obstacles, *non*-delinquent Black and Latino boys suffered similar fates.

In the course of his field research Rios took care to scrutinize the ways in which manhood was developed among the boys within the larger context of society and within the boys' interactions with school personnel and criminal legal system agents. Rios contended, "One consequence of criminalization and punitive social control for the boys was the development of a specific set of gendered practices" and this contact served as a "production of a *hyper*masculinity" (p. 125; emphasis added). Rios concluded that crime is a method for men and boys to develop, demonstrate, and communicate their manhood. Rios makes evident that Black and Latino boys in particular are challenged with contradictory expectations that demonstrate manhood. Social institutions, including the criminal legal system, "expect a masculine conformity that emphasizes hard work, law abidance, and an acceptance of subordinate social conditions" (p. 133). Sadly, although some of the boys in Rios's study made attempts to follow this expectation, such as securing working-class jobs and accepting "their subordinate status in society," they were faced with the social reality that few work opportunities existed, and many of these opportunities were blocked because of the stereotypical views that labeled the boys as inherently defiant and violent, even though potential employers were unaware of the boys' backgrounds. Meanwhile, "embracing this 'positive' working-class masculinity did not provide the proper resources to survive on the streets, a place to which they constantly returned" (p. 134).

Intersecting criminology

As can be gleaned from the works featured in this chapter, the concept of identity is quite salient in the way individuals respond to certain life events and in the way they are responded to by others, including criminal legal system agents and members of the general public. Recall from Chapter 3 that Peggy Giordano (2010), in her book *Legacies of Crime*, wrote of a woman's *identity* that was void of a gender-racial identity, which we know is very impactful, especially for racially marginalized women (and men). Because persons of Color are often reminded of their dictated place on the racial hierarchy (see Elijah Anderson's "nigger moment" (2011)), overlooking the role of race in the analysis of lived experiences of women involved in crime, the criminal legal system, and social welfare systems makes for incomplete findings. To have, for example, a sample of Black women in a study and to mention their gender and race only in a descriptive manner, and not to critically incorporate the social effects of Black women's identity, is not likely to result in an exhaustive or deep exploration.

In spite of the examples provided in this chapter of the intersectional research and theoretical contributions to criminology regarding boys and men, there remains a vacuity in criminological research on the significance of masculinities, gender, and sexuality in the role of the commission of crime, violence, and other bad acts by boys and men. Two major themes are clear in the research and conceptualization of some exemplars of this research detailed in this chapter. First, just as the women represented in the studies presented throughout this chapter had intertwined identities, marginalization, victimization, and criminalization (oftentimes undeserved), so too were the boys and men confronted with these dispirited realities of a stratified world.

When compared with the girls and women, although they have gender privilege, boys and men of Color still faced significant burdens and obstacles. The second major theme identified in the intersectional criminological research on boys and men is that the research participants engaged in crime or violence, in part, in order to prove, uphold, or defend their *manhood*. Far too many studies within criminology disregard this indisputably important factor of gender formation and presentation in relation to criminality. Research oriented in intersectional criminology, by design, acknowledges that both the man in the 'hood (urban neighborhood) and the man in the hood (a Ku Klux Klan member) do manhood. An intersectional criminology allows for a critical analysis of how each man's identity is formed, is responded to by others, and affects his reactions in the social world.

Several of the investigations outlined in this chapter demonstrate the limits of free will and choice that are seen in colorblind and genderblind criminological theories. Researchers who have employed an intersectional approach have been able to underscore that varying social locations effectively limit the ability for some individuals to *choose* the *non*criminal path. As criminologist Leon E. Pettiway (1997:xiv) tendered, "individual choices are structured by external forces." And in her work on women involved in an illicit street drug market, Lisa Maher (1997:193) concluded, "While they have 'chosen' sexwork, they have not done so under conditions of their own choosing .... [T]hey are choices shaped by a collective consciousness in which gendered and raced meanings of 'crime as work' form an integral part of the habitus."

The increasing number of quantitative studies embracing an intersectional approach serves to support both an intersectional criminology and the theoretical outcomes of the many qualitative studies described in this chapter. Quantitative research has considered the effects of intersectionality in comparing offending rates among young adult boys and girls (Bell 2013), in the variation of school-based victimization of youth by race, ethnicity, and gender and the role of the participation in school activities in this victimization (Peguero and Popp 2012), in the correlation between child abuse and offending among women by race (Makarios 2007), in comparing homicide rates by race and gender (Haynie and Armstrong 2006; Parker and

Hefner 2013), in the sentencing outcomes of offenders by race and gender dependent on the race and gender of judges and prosecutors (Farrell *et al.* 2010), in juvenile court outcomes by race and gender of the youth (Guevara *et al.* 2006), and in the racial differences in recidivism among women released from prison (Huebner *et al.* 2010).

A variety of names have been used to describe an intersectional framework practiced in organizing communities for action and in doing research or building theory, including intersectionality, coined by Kimberlé Crenshaw. This is also the case for criminological research. Although still fairly marginalized in relation to other theoretical observations, the work of criminologists who have incorporated an intersectional perspective into their analyses is becoming more widely disseminated and recognized.

Notes

1 See also sociologist Siobhan Brooks's (2010) research on the experiences of exotic dancers who worked in clubs that catered to queer and heterosexual patrons, and the mechanics of race, racism, sexual stereotyping, and hypersexualization in these environments. Brooks documented the racial and skin color stratifications among women who work/dance in these clubs, wherein White women and lighter women of Color earned more money than darker women. Black women and darker-skinned Latinas faced the greatest amounts of discrimination, racism, and violence.

2 Arnold's and Richie's findings have also been described as feminist pathways theory (Belknap 2015).

3 Rios used the term *O.G. Sociology* to reference that even though he was, at the time of the field research, on track to an elevated social status (a doctorate degree and all that accompanies it), his background is similar to the informants in his study. In gang parlance, O.G. refers to original gangster, a label typically afforded to and reserved for seasoned and respected gang members. Rios utilized the exalted position, and respect, given him by the boys in combination with his academic acumen to allow for the boys' life histories to be responsibly and accurately interpreted, thereby engaging in O.G. Sociology.

5

REVOLUTIONIZING CRIMINOLOGY

The societal impact of intersectional criminology

On May 2, 1973, Assata Shakur was involved in a shootout that resulted in the death of New Jersey state trooper Werner Foerster. At the time, Shakur was a member of the Black Panther Party and the Black Liberation Army. During the shooting, a fellow activist was also killed and Shakur was "shot with both arms held in the air, and then shot again from the back."[1] After her arrest and some medical attention, Shakur was jailed and imprisoned in a number of facilities. While in a New York City jail, Shakur wrote "Women in Prison: How We Are" (1978), published in the academic journal *The Black Scholar*. Shakur summarized, "There are no criminals here at Rikers Island Correctional Institution for Women … only victims. Most of the women (over 95%) are black and Puerto Rican. Many were abused children. Most have been abused by men and all have been abused by 'the system'" (p. 9). Shakur's essay traced the conflict faced by corrections officers who were women of Color in performing authority, and claimed that life inside jail and prison was little different from life on the streets and in the women's neighborhoods. The police state, poverty, alienation, racism, sexism, and drugs existed inside and outside the carceral space, all of which had devastating effects on women of Color. Shakur emphasized the importance of allowing

Black women to speak our own truths and "define our own history" (p. 14), which characterizes a necessary component of emphasizing *voice* and lived experience when incorporating an intersectional perspective in research and theory. Still today, Shakur's essay substantiates the basis and need for an intersectional criminology.

In 1977, Shakur, formerly known as JoAnne (née Byron) Chesimard, was convicted and received a life sentence for killing the police officer. Shakur escaped from a New Jersey prison in 1979 and has been living in exile in Cuba since 1984. On May 2, 2013, the fortieth anniversary of Trooper Foerster's death, the US Federal Bureau of Investigation added Shakur (65 years old at the time) to the Most Wanted Terrorists list, deeming Shakur a "domestic terrorist" and making her the first woman and (only) the second domestic terrorist to be added to the list. The FBI and the New Jersey State Police contributed equally to the two-million-dollar bounty for Shakur's capture. This unique action by the US federal government epitomizes the fear and control of Black women – as well as the fear and control of Black men and other women and men of Color – that is exhibited by certain institutions and individuals. This fear and control is seen in the responses of many members of the general public and in draconian and unjust responses by too many criminal legal systems and system agents. People of Color in the United States had dealt with a devalued status for a long time before Assata Shakur was last seen in the United States and have dealt with it in the four decades since, culminating in the noteworthy national uprisings following the August 9, 2014 shooting death of Michael Brown – an 18-year-old Black man – by police officer Darren Wilson – a 28-year-old White man – in Ferguson, Missouri. The circumstances surrounding Michael Brown's death, and the broader racial–gender–class and justice concerns, mobilized a mass response from members of the Ferguson community as well as local and national activists, politicians, news media agencies and journalists, educators, and scholars. We await the lasting consequences of the responses to this event, but the magnitude of the multidimensional response differed from the organization surrounding similar police/state action and racial conflict in recent years. Issues of race, gender, class, nationalism, citizenship, administration of justice and militarization of police, civil rights, and humanity, and the *intersection* of all these moving parts, are apparent in this case. For *all* criminologists, the calamitous case of Michael Brown and Darren Wilson must be used as the final catalyst to revolutionize our studies in crime.

Intersectional criminology

Variations of intersectionality have been employed in the social sciences for at least the past two decades, particularly in feminist and gender scholarship. Some social science criminologists have also incorporated an intersectional perspective in their research, though not as long and as expansive as other social scientists. However, although some of these scholars claim to be engaging with intersectionality in their research, in their publications they succeed only in alluding to intersectionality. In refereed journal articles presenting these studies,[2] authors insert the term intersectionality, provide a definition for it, and indicate the importance of considering the tenets of intersectionality. This may then be reiterated in the concluding section of the article, but in other situations, intersectionality is abandoned after an article's front matter, never to be seen again. In the former case, even though researchers make the effort to form a relationship with intersectionality, a definitive connection is not made between the findings and intersectionality's tenets. In these cases, the grounding that intersectionality was to provide in order to make sense of the data was somehow circumvented. In some of these cases where in-depth interviews were employed, I question whether the researcher actually conducted a deep analysis of the narratives to determine if patterns emerged that relate to intersectionality. I question whether the researcher inserted the term intersectionality only because of its possible buzzword status (see also Bilge 2013), thus leading me to wonder why peer reviewers failed to recognize there was no actual engagement with an intersectional conceptualization.

While some criminologists at least make attempts to consider intersectionality, another methodological or analytical concern raised by intersectional criminology is the tendency for criminologists to make the identities of their research participants or sample inconspicuous. Researchers typically include the demographics of their research samples in their publications, yet, often the race of Whites is deemed a default and regularly goes unexamined, as though "White" is not a race. When criminologists analyze a study that includes only White individuals, rarely is it discussed how being a White person might have had different effects on their criminality and experiences in the criminal legal system than the experiences of people of Color. Certainly, White is a race. Consequently, criminologists should, at least, contemplate how being White may influence individuals' experiences compared with those of other races. Regardless of the framework or school of thought in which the research is being conducted, intersectional criminology encourages criminologists to go beyond simply providing the study sample's race and gender descriptors. Because identities are still raced, gendered, sexualized, classed, and so on by others and by one's self, I recommend that the social demographics of studies should be specified *and* addressed in write-ups on a social phenomenon such as crime, criminality, and the criminal legal system. If no appraisal or conceptualization is to be offered about the intersectional impact, scholars should simply say that that is their intent. Scholars should also say if they did consider identity and power, but their effect or significance was established to be irrelevant, unfounded, or undetermined. In other research endeavors, scholars make the identities of research respondents conspicuous, which results in thoughtful considerations of social identities in some publications and the perpetuation of stereotypes in others.

Furthermore, in many qualitative research projects, researchers insist on the examination of the role and effect of the researcher in the research setting. Often referred to as positionality and reflexivity, many qualitative scholars consider their roles at the time of research design and through the span of site-immersion, data collection, and post-project analysis. A positivistic-leaning researcher might advocate against this, and would insist researchers appear as "objective" as possible by not identifying how they were affected by or affected the investigation. In feminist and critical race scholarly traditions, however, we believe it important to recognize positionality, and to take advantage of it if it can provide a greater understanding of the informants' experiences. Indeed, this should be the first stage in entering into any research, regardless of the method utilized. Criminologist Leon E. Pettiway (1997) examined the lives of poor, urban women who were faced with multiple burdens with subsequent addictions to drugs, and involvement in sex work to support their addiction. Pettiway not only keenly recognized the need for understanding the effect of the women's life-chances on their experiences, he is also reflexive in recognizing that although he is a gay Black man, his male privilege situates him differently from the women in his study: "I heard how women construct identity even as they are trapped by the interlocking strands of poverty, abuse, drug use, racism, and sexism" (p. xiv). With the placement of research participants at the center and as the experts in their experiences, the role of positionality in the research is certain to be acknowledged – especially in methods based on an intersectional criminological standpoint. Unfortunately, the goal of viewing research participants as experts and of researchers being conscientious is not always practiced in studies on individuals who are socially marginalized by race, gender, socioeconomic status, and other factors. In what criminologist Victor M. Rios (2011) specified as the *jungle-book trope*, certain ethnographers relay a sensationalistic and exotic interpretation of their fieldwork. As an example of this trope, Rios cited sociologist Sudhir Venkatesh's (2008) study of a Chicago street gang composed of Black men. Rios indicates how Venkatesh's tale, described in *Gang Leader for a Day: A Rogue Sociologist Takes to the Street*, and accounts by other researchers not expressly identified by Rios fit the Western "colonial fairy-tale narrative" that conveys, "I got lost in the wild, the wild people took me in and helped me, made me their king, and I lived to tell civilization about it!" (p. 14). Alice Goffman's (2014) investigation of over-policing in a predominantly Black Philadelphia neighborhood in *On the Run: Fugitive Life in an American City* has been offered as another example of the jungle-book trope (Betts 2014). Thus, in raising issues of crime and justice regarding marginalized persons, we must advance a critical analysis for the purposes of effecting progressive change while simultaneously avoid the dramatizing, stereotyping, and exoticizing of lived experiences.

In sum, intersectional criminology is (a) an epistemology for conducting research that better attempts to address the role and impact of identities and power dynamics regarding crime, criminality, and the criminal legal system, (b) a theory to understand the commission of crime and the responses to being criminally victimized,

(c) a theory to understand the formal responses to the commission of crime and to victims of crime, and (d) a perspective for informing communities and the polity about how better to prevent, control, and respond to acts designated as crimes. In strict definition, to *intersect* is to cut across or to overlap, and an *intersection* is the point where at least two things intersect. Feminists of Color have effectively rooted the term "intersect" in the branding of conceptualizations of multiplicative identities operating within conflicting and dominating social structures – namely, intersectionality and intersectional. More precisely, however, the place where we have arrived in conceptualizing the intensity and realness of a person's various social identities in a stratified world is in thinking of these identities as *braided*. That is, social identities are fantastically interwoven, and continually interact with and affect each other, and others respond to individuals based on their social identities. Identities are indivisible; but at different times, spaces, and places, not all facets of an individual's blended identity are visible to others attempting to categorize that person. Naturally, this social manifestation is displayed throughout all social interactions and institutions, including in the commission of crime, the victimization experience, and in the criminal legal system. Thus, a call for an intersectional criminology should be taken seriously and incorporated within the academic field of criminology. I cannot provide a diagram, a model, or step-by-step rules for integrating intersectional criminology into a research project for the purposes of research design or for analysis after data collection or fieldwork is completed. What I hope to have done with this exposition on intersectionality and criminology is to provide a foundation on which individual scholars can construct their research and conceptualization.

Intersectional praxis

Intersectional criminology's foundation in intersectionality, the principles of women of Color feminism, and social-justice-oriented activism makes for a direct path to the formulation of recommendations for policy and for grassroots organizing from research and theory. Specifically, an inherent component of intersectionality is *praxis*: putting theory into action or practice. Criminologists have generally done well in communicating – at least to each other – the mechanisms for and results of racialized, classed, and gendered policies and legal systems and agents steeped in racist, classist, and sexist ideology. Regrettably, women's experiences, particularly those experiences of women of Color, are not often highlighted and widely known. Consequently, many people, including some criminologists, are unaware of the devastating effects of the criminal legal system on women of Color. We know that in many places throughout the world, women of Color have faced the wrath of the criminal legal system alongside their respective male co-ethnics. While some of these interactions involve accessing legal and medical assistance due to being victimized, in other instances, women of Color are faced with being contacted by "crime control" agents for criminal acts they have committed or have been accused of committing. As with their male counterparts, women of Color have also been criminally stereotyped and racially profiled. Furthermore, although to a lesser degree when compared with the experiences of women of Color, many low-income White women are also ensnarled in punitive, unforgiving legal systems.

Criminal legal systems do not operate in an independent universe, unaffected by the mechanisms of a society and its social interactions. Systems of power, hierarchical identities, and interconnected identities traverse all lived experiences and, consequently, power and identity traverse experiences with crime and the criminal legal system, affecting all actors: offender, victim, employee, administrator, policy-maker, lawmaker. Even members of the general public with no direct or significant involvement with criminal activities, offenders, victims, or the criminal legal system can impact how a community deals with crime, crime prevention, and the aftereffects of crime. Residents develop perceptions of "the crime problem" in a community and of offenders and victims from news media reports and representations. Many of these inhabitants vote on crime-related policy and law. If citizens, voting or otherwise, hold unenlightened and uninformed views about crime based on prominent information-disseminators (corporate news outlets, politicians) who share research and crime reports that are not enlightened by an understanding of the effects of societal oppression on crime, we may continue to see no significant shifts in the way communities and greater society think about crime. In my unstandardized and anecdotal reviews of statements made about crime-related issues by commenters in Internet social media forums (Facebook, Twitter, online newspaper article discussions, and the like), I often feel that certain segments of society have not moved far from W.E.B. Du Bois's (1899:241) conclusions based on his research on Blacks and crime in 1890s Philadelphia: "There is a widespread feeling that something is wrong with a race that is responsible for so much crime, and that strong remedies are called for."

In efforts to better control crime in the United States, officials have implemented a series of laws that have ensnared many more individuals under the pretext that such laws would aid in protecting US citizens and communities from violent, predatory offenders and the ravages of illicit (street) drugs. Among US politicians, crime-related policies have tended to have equal support across the mid spectrum of political ideologies, from liberals to moderates to conservatives (though at the extremes – radicals on the Left and some reactionaries on the Right – certain drug and crime policies are not supported). Similarly, many advocates, activists, and constituents pushed lawmakers to enact laws that took violence against women and children more seriously, such as those related to sexual offending and intimate partner abuse. Unfortunately, many laws (and official policies) enacted in the modern era have differentially affected individuals, with the most marginalized offenders and victims having been and still being subject to the least beneficial effects of these laws. Poverty and punishment theorist Loïc Wacquant (2010:209) observed that the source of this persistent punitive position "is not late modernity but neoliberalism, a project that can be indifferently embraced by politicians of the Right or the Left." As a political strategy, this modern "punitive drift" within the most economically and socially powerful countries toward tagging individuals as criminal has been quite successful. However, contrary to reasonable assumptions about such a strategy, "the fast and furious bend toward penalization … is not a response to *criminal* insecurity but to *social* insecurity" (Wacquant 2010:208; emphases in original). Wacquant contended that new controls within the criminal legal system *and* within the social welfare system of the United States and throughout parts of Europe are a result of the significant decrease in industrial and low-wage service jobs and the dismantling of the long-standing racial hierarchy. The ruling class implements and maintains social and penal policies as surveillance and control systems for the lower socioeconomic classes and subordinated racial groups. Wacquant identified *neoliberalism* as going beyond a relation to the economy or political economy in that it is an aim to "remake the nexus of market, state, and citizenship from above" (p. 213). He viewed the role of the inequitable and increasingly punitive criminal legal system as a central precept of neoliberalism.

To better represent the individuals who are overrepresented in the criminal legal system – persons of Color and the economically disadvantaged – criminologists utilizing an intersectional approach in their scholarly work must persevere and press forward, while aware that change will have to be pushed even harder in a society where overt racism and sexism is now rare, but racial, gender, and sexual microaggressions are rampant. Thinking optimistically, the incorporation of intersectionality into criminological work that is broadly disseminated would help to better inform policymakers and lawmakers of the damaging effects of neoliberal policy, which, when rectified, would serve to help all members of society, not only the socially and economically disadvantaged. Regarding the development of intersectionally sound law and policy regarding violence against women of Color, Andrea Smith (2005a) proposed that it is imperative that the women actually subjected to abuse and violence be incorporated into "base-building" efforts in the antiviolence movement as organizers and activists instead of as clients who need to be serviced. As to how criminologists can aid in efforts such as these, and avoid the jungle-book trope when conducting research, one option is to make use of *participatory action research* (PAR), an approach that involves the inclusion of members of the study population as a central component of the research. In PAR, the researcher develops and conducts the research project *with* community members, not *for* them, and the motivation for utilizing PAR is social change and action. Thus, PAR is distinct from other epistemologies because of "its focus on collaboration, political engagement, and an explicit commitment to social justice" (Brydon-Miller *et al.* 2011:388). Participatory action research can utilize any research methods (obviously employing those that would best answer the research question), but an integral component of PAR is the participation of members of the study community. Michelle Fine (2008:215) related that PAR "assumes that those who have been *most* systematically excluded, oppressed, or denied carry specifically revealing wisdom about the history, structure, consequences, and the fracture points in unjust social arrangements," and concluded that the theory of knowledge production in PAR lies in the belief that these individuals hold important knowledge about "the architecture of injustice, in their minds, bodies, and souls; in ways they are conscious and floating; individual and collective" (p. 223).

Using a PAR approach, Black studies and street-life scholar Yasser Payne (2013) sought to determine the relationship between structural opportunity and physical violence in two neighborhoods in Wilmington, Delaware.[3] Payne employed a mixed-methods design of quantitative and ethnographic techniques. The two study neighborhoods primarily consist of low-income Black residents, but middle-class and upper middle-class Blacks also reside in enclaves within these neighborhoods. Fifteen neighborhood members, comprising three women and twelve men ages 20 through 48, were enlisted and trained to serve as *street participatory action researchers*, each of whom had former involvement in "the streets" or the criminal legal system. All street researchers and the 520 research participants were Black. The field observations, in-depth interviews, and completed surveys resulted in a large number of testimonies about exposure to physical violence (interpersonal assaults, knifings, shootings), structural violence (unemployment, poor school opportunities, ineffective or corrupt civic and political leadership), and unnecessarily aggressive law enforcement practices (profiling and frisks, raids). While these results are (sadly) representative of the experiences of many communities of Color across the United States, it was noted that:

> the spirit of community residents remains unusually high, positive, or optimistic .... [W]hile community residents are overwhelmed with physical violence as well as blocked opportunities, the data strongly suggest that study participants love

themselves; they love their families and communities; they want to work; and they want quality educational opportunity.

(p. 5)

Further, the street participatory action researchers directly benefited from their participation in the project. They maintained quality employment as researchers for the duration of the project (though six were unemployed at the time of the 2013 written report on the project), five enrolled in college during or after the project (three in undergraduate programs and two in graduate programs), they gained research experience that improved their educational and professional skill set, and they gave 100 formal presentations to community leaders and residents (39), colleges and universities (40), and the news media (21). The researchers also produced numerous "action" products or events for community members, including a community barbecue, a youth violence forum, a homicide art exhibit, a project documentary video, and public service announcement videos (including one on intimate partner abuse). The incorporation of street researchers in a research project on a multiply-disadvantaged community that distrusts the police, local politicians, and outsiders provides a greater opportunity for action to be implemented at the grassroots level and for the community researchers to motivate their fellow community members to collectively work toward positive community change. This project's approach, method, and analyses unmistakably epitomize the spirit of an intersectionality perspective and praxis.

Policy built from an intersectional perspective is one where great attempts are made to remove stereotypical and inferior views about groups of people from theoretical conceptualization and from policy and practice. Intersectional criminology promotes heavy scrutiny of crime-related policies to assure they are nonracialized, nonsexist, nonsexualized, and, simply, bias-free in all other relevant ways. Intersectional criminology supports raising attention to marginalized individuals in a way that does not sensationalize or demonize them, especially in relation to racialized gender tropes. Intersectional criminology will not support a practice of treating women of Color victims of gendered violence as criminals, while White women victims of gendered violence are treated as true victims. Intersectional criminology will not support a practice that allows police officers to "stop and frisk" and summarily kill male-identified Black and Latino citizens at higher rates than members of other race–gender groups who engage in similar police-observed behaviors. Intersectional criminology will not support policy that allows those with money to be bailed or bonded from jail while individuals with similar crime records ("rap sheets") but without access to funds remain detained, thus possibly leading to an agreement to plead guilty to an offense (even when innocent of it) simply to be freed from the chaos and instability that is the reality in many jails. Intersectional criminology will not support a policy that insists crack cocaine users and dealers receive harsher punishments than powder cocaine users and dealers with similar amounts of drugs and similar crime-activity histories. Intersectional criminology will not support prosecutors' decisions to elevate a murder case to be eligible for a death sentence when the murder victim is a White woman, but does not do the same when the victim is of a different race and gender. Each of these examples is based on policy and law that are race-, gender-, and class-neutral. These examples are not about alignment with a radical, progressive, or liberal ideology; they are grounded in research founded on an intersectionality perspective that brings attention to a society that is based on inequities that relegate people of Color and the lower socioeconomic classes to places where they are unable to access the opportunities afforded to others with elitist social capital.

Revolutionizing criminology

I doubt my musings in this book reflect the definitive statement on intersectionality and its use in criminology. Yet, I believe I have captured the essence of the workings of intersectionality within criminology, whether as a perspective, a theory, an epistemology, or a method. As recognized by its surveyors, intersectionality is a traveling concept that continues to be developed and refined. Although we do not know where intersectionality in criminology is headed next, it is important we take this moment to define it, specify it, and identify it.

Intersectional applications in criminology have homed in on the experiences of women and girls, particularly because of the wider use of intersectionality among feminist criminologists. If they have not yet done so, many feminist, critical, and progressive race criminologists are already in a place to integrate identity and power in their research designs and analyze their findings from an intersectional perspective. Others who see themselves outside of these self-imposed memberships also have the ability to incorporate the perspective in their research analysis and conceptualization. Furthermore, many scholars utilizing intersectionality in their research design and/or theoretical development are solidly embedded in effecting change in communities. Over the previous few decades, the entities overwhelmingly responsible for rerouting the way crime is defined have been grassroots antiracism and feminist activists, as well as critical legal scholars, progressive race criminologists, critical criminologists, feminist criminologists, and feminist scholars of Color.

With the growing interest in critical analysis of constructions of and the commission of crime, we must ponder whether intersectionality is at the forefront of a revolution in the ways we analyze crime-based phenomena in criminological studies. Because paradigm shifts in science (using the broader definition of the concept) are major processes that take significant persuasion, I hope that, at the least, within the next couple of decades we can see a shift *within* the existing paradigm that would be exponentially more inclusive of an intersectional perspective. To shift the paradigm we must start with a shift in ideology and terminology. Instead of using the phrase "mainstream criminology," we should use "orthodox criminology." Doing so opens the discipline to recognizing that there is a dominance of certain criminological schools of thought, and especially that those theories have reached dominance, in part, because of the social status of those disseminating this knowledge (White men). The election of two particular women to the presidency of the American Society of Criminology (ASC) symbolizes that "peripheral" criminological thought is likely at the cusp of driving straight ahead into the core of criminology. Joanne Belknap, who is White and a self- and peer-proclaimed "inconvenient woman,"[4] was elected as ASC president in 2012. Ruth Peterson, who is Black, was elected as ASC president in

2014, and is the first person of Color to serve in this position. It is not only that these two esteemed scholars are women, as six other women have been elected to the ASC presidency since 1989, it is that the areas of study for Belknap and Peterson are solidly within the *critical* and *progressive* framework, and they have each been prolific in fostering critical race and critical feminist theories and research in criminology with their scholarly work and with their substantial mentoring activities.

In qualitative research, particularly the use of in-depth group or individual interviews, we often speak of "giving voice" to research respondents, particularly those respondents who are marginalized. However, individuals whose life-chances have relegated them to a subordinated social position *already* have voice; scholars must make better efforts to *listen* to what these individuals have to say about their lived experiences. Although many progressive race, feminist, and critical criminologists have histories or current statuses as members of marginalized groups, they/we are currently situated as members of a privileged group – college-educated, middle-class to upper-class researchers and professors. Therefore, as criminologists concerned about bringing attention to intersectional matters, progressive race, feminist, and critical criminologists should – if not *must* – serve to use our social capital to provide a conduit between the marginalized and the elite and ruling classes.

In being afforded the opportunity to present intersectional criminology in an extended format, I have been able to provide (1) an explication of intersectionality, (2) examples of the application of intersectional finesse to research in which scholars had purposely or unwittingly neglected the salience of identity politics and social-power disparities, and (3) examples of exemplary research projects that assimilated an intersectional approach. We must utilize intersectionality within criminology because of the salient existence and ferocity of socially structured and stratified identities. To be sure, however, I must repeat a declaration I made in the conclusion of Chapter 2 on the development of intersectionality. Instead of keeping such revered theorizing to ourselves (that is, only women of Color theorizing only about women of Color), and since there has already been some necessary, though still small, movement toward employing intersectionality theory on others' experiences, we should *encourage* its expanded use while simultaneously never forgetting the tremendous challenges faced by women of Color and the many transgressions against women of Color that we have to resist every day.

With the widespread, multidisciplinary attention to and use of intersectionality in conducting research and for theorizing, intersectionality can no longer be viewed as a boutique theory or perspective. Even within criminology, feminist, critical, and progressive race criminologists are forcing intersectionality out of the theoretical margins and into the core of orthodox criminology. A push for intersectional advancement within the discipline of criminology must occur. I believe that continuing on this *tenacious* track to advance an intersectional criminology as a method of examining a problem and producing knowledge is the only way the field of criminology will be revolutionized.

Notes

1 From Shakur's 1998 letter to Pope John Paul II, which can be found at http://www.assatashakur.org/pope.htm (last accessed January 8, 2015).
2 Here, I purposely do not cite the many studies that fit within this category. I applaud these scholars for being inclusive – even if only superficially. My hope is that such scholars interested enough in reading this book will revisit and reflect on their inclusion of intersectionality in their work to determine if the term was invoked simply because it is trending or if they truly conducted and/or analyzed the study findings within the contexts of intersectionality.
3 The report and other information and items related to the Wilmington Street Participatory Action Research Project can be found on the project website: http://www.thepeoplesreport.com/index.html (last accessed January 19, 2015).
4 The Division on Women and Crime of the American Society of Criminology established the CoraMae Richey Mann Inconvenient Woman of the Year Award in 2004 to recognize "the scholar/activist who has participated in publicly promoting the ideals of gender equality and women's rights throughout society, particularly as it relates to gender and crime issues" (http://ascdwc.com/awards/, last accessed January 19, 2015). Belknap was the first recipient of this award.

REFERENCES

Abraham, Margaret. 2000. *Speaking the Unspeakable: Marital Violence Among South Asian Immigrants in the United States*. New Brunswick, NJ: Rutgers University Press.

Adler, Freda. 1975. *Sisters in Crime: The Rise of the New Female Criminal*. New York: McGraw-Hill.

Agnew, Robert. 2011. *Toward a Unified Criminology: Integrating Assumptions about Crime, People, and Society*. New York: New York University Press.

Ahearn, Laura M. 2001. "Language and Agency." *Annual Review of Anthropology* 30: 109–137.

Aikau, Hokulani K., Karla A. Erickson, and Jennifer L. Pierce. 2007. *Feminist Waves, Feminist Generations: Life Stories from the Academy*. Minneapolis, MN: University of Minnesota Press.

Alexander, Karl, Doris Entwisle, and Linda Olson. 2014. *The Long Shadow: Family Background, Disadvantaged Urban Youth, and the Transition to Adulthood*. New York: Russell Sage Foundation.

Alexander-Floyd, Nikol G. 2010. "Critical Race Black Feminism: A 'Jurisprudence of Resistance' and the Transformation of the Academy." *Signs: Journal of Women in Culture and Society* 35(4): 810–820.

Alexander-Floyd, Nikol G. 2012. "Disappearing Acts: Reclaiming Intersectionality in the Social Sciences in a Post-Black Feminist Era." *Signs: Journal of Women in Culture and Society* 24(1): 1–25.

Allan, Kenneth. 2010. *Explorations in Classical Sociological Theory: Seeing the Social World*. Thousand Oaks, CA: Pine Forge Press.

Alvarez-Rivera, Lorna L., and Kathleen A. Fox. 2010. "Institutional Attachments and Self-Control: Understanding Deviance Among Hispanic Adolescents." *Journal of Criminal Justice* 38(4): 666–674.

Andersen, Margaret L., and Dana Hysock. 2011. *Witham Thinking about Women: Sociological Perspectives on Sex and Gender* (9th edn.). Boston, MA: Pearson Education.

Anderson, Elijah. 1978. *A Place on the Corner: A Study of Black Street Corner Men*. Chicago, IL: University of Chicago Press.

Anderson, Elijah. 1990. *Streetwise: Race, Class, and Change in an Urban Community*. Chicago, IL: University of Chicago Press.

Anderson, Elijah. 1994. "The Code of the Street." *The Atlantic Monthly* 273: 80–94.

Anderson, Elijah. 1996. "Introduction to the 1996 Edition of *The Philadelphia Negro*." Pp. ix–xxxvi in *The Philadelphia Negro: A Social Study* by W.E.B. Du Bois (1899). Philadelphia, PA: University of Pennsylvania.

Anderson, Elijah. 1999. *Code of the Street: Decency, Violence, and the Moral Life of the Inner City.* New York: W.W. Norton & Company.

Anderson, Elijah. 2011. *The Cosmopolitan Canopy: Race and Civility in Everyday Life*. New York: W.W. Norton & Company.

Anderson, Kim. 2010. "Affirmations of an Indigenous Feminist." Pp. 81–91 in *Indigenous Women and Feminism: Politics, Activism, Culture* edited by Cheryl Suzack, Shari M. Huhndorf, Jeanne Perreault, and Jean Barman. Vancouver: UBC Press.

Anthias, Floya, and Nira Yuval-Davis. 1983. "Contextualizing Feminism: Gender, Ethnic and Class Divisions." *Feminist Review* 15: 62–75.

Arnold, Regina A. 1990. "Process of Victimization and Criminalization of Black Women." *Social Justice* 17(3): 153–166.

Baca Zinn, Maxine, and Bonnie Thornton Dill. 1996. "Theorizing Difference from Multiracial Feminism." *Feminist Studies* 22(2): 321–331.

Baca Zinn, Maxine, Pierrette Hondagneu-Sotelo, and Michael A. Messner (eds.). 2005. *Gender Through the Prism of Difference* (3rd edn.). New York: Oxford University Press.

Barak, Gregg, Paul Leighton, and Jeanne Flavin. 2010. *Class, Race, Gender, and Crime: The Social Realities of Justice in America* (3rd edn.). Lanham, MD: Rowman & Littlefield.

Battle, Nishaun. 2014. *The Cult of True Womanhood, Punishment, and Black Women: An Intersectionality Examination of 19th Century Punishment in the South*. Ph.D. diss., Howard University.

Baumgardner, Jennifer, and Amy Richards. 2000. *Manifesta: Young Women, Feminism, and the Future*. New York: Farrar, Straus, and Giroux.

Beal, Frances. [1970]1995. "Double Jeopardy: To Be Black and Female." Pp. 145–155 in *Words of Fire: An Anthology of African-American Feminist Thought* edited by Beverly Guy-Sheftall. New York: The New Press.

Beal, Frances. 1975. "Slave of a Slave No More: Black Women in Struggle." *The Black Scholar* 6(6): 2–10.

Beegle, Donna M. 2007. *See Poverty…Be the Difference! Discover the Missing Pieces for Helping People Move Out of Poverty.* Tigard, OH: Communication Across Barriers.

Belknap, Joanne. 2015. *The Invisible Woman: Gender, Crime, and Justice* (4th edn.). Stamford, CT: Cengage Learning.

Belknap, Joanne, and Kristi Holsinger. 2006. "The Gendered Nature of Risk Factors for Delinquency." *Feminist Criminology* 1(1): 48–71.

Bell, Kerryn E. 2013. "Young Adult Offending: Intersectionality of Gender and Race." *Critical Criminology* 21(1): 103–121.

Benda, Brent B. 2005. "The Robustness of Self-Control in Relation to Form of Delinquency." *Youth and Society* 36(4): 418–444.

Betts, Dwayne. 2014. "The Stoop Isn't the Jungle." *Slate.com*, July 10. http://www.slate.com/articles/news_and_politics/jurisprudence/2014/07/alice_goffman_s_on_the_run_she_is_wrong_about_black_urban_life.single.html (last accessed January 7, 2015).

Bilge, Sirma. 2013. "Intersectionality Undone: Saving Intersectionality from Feminist Intersectionality Studies." *Du Bois Review: Social Science Research on Race* 10(2): 405–424.

Blackwell, Brenda S., and Alex R. Piquero. 2005. "On the Relationships Between Gender, Power Control, Self Control, and Crime." *Journal of Criminal Justice* 33(1): 1–17.

Blumstein, Alfred, Jacqueline Cohen, Jeffrey A. Roth, and Christy A. Visher (eds.). 1986. *Criminal Careers and "Career Criminals": Report of the National Academy of Sciences Panel on Research on Criminal Careers.* Washington, DC: National Academy Press.

Bonilla-Silva, Eduardo. 2010. *Racism without Racists: Color-Blind Racism and the Persistence of Racial Inequality in the United States.* Lanham, MD: Rowman & Littlefield.

Bottcher, Jean. 2001. "Social Practices of Gender: How Gender Relates to Delinquency in the Everyday Lives of High-Risk Youths." *Criminology* 39(4): 893–932.

Bouffard, Jeff, Jessica M. Craig, and Alex R. Piquero. 2014. "Comparing Attitudinal and Situational Measures of Self-Control Among Felony Offenders." *Criminal Behaviour and Mental Health.* Online Version of Record published before inclusion in an issue.

Boulware, L. Ebony, Lisa A. Cooper, Lloyd E. Ratner, Thomas A. LaVeist, and Neil R. Powe. 2003. "Race and T in the Health Care System." *Public Health Reports* 118(4): 358.

Bourdieu, Pierre. 1986. "The Forms of Capital." Pp. 46–58 in *Handbook of Theory and Research for the Sociology of Education* edited by J. Richardson. New York: Greenwood Press/ABC-CLIO.

Brah, Avtar, and Ann Phoenix. 2004. "Ain't I a Woman? Revisiting Intersectionality." *Journal of International Women's Studies* 5(3): 75–86.

Braxton, Greg. 2009. "Jackson's Cultural Identity Remains a Sticky Debating Point." *Los Angeles Times*, June 28. http://articles.latimes.com/2009/jun/28/entertainment/et-jackson-race28 (last accessed January 6, 2015).

Britton, Dana M. 2000. "Feminism in Criminology: Engendering the Outlaw." *The ANNALS of the American Academy of Political and Social Science* 571: 57–76.

Britton, Dana M. 2011. *The Gender of Crime*. Lanham, MD: Rowman & Littlefield.

Brooks, Siobhan. 2010. *Unequal Desires: Race and Erotic Capital in the Stripping Industry*. Albany, NY: SUNY Press.

Brown, Elaine. 1992. *A Taste of Power: A Back Woman's Story*. New York: Pantheon Books.

Brown, Ruth Nicole. 2008. *Black Girlhood Celebration: Toward a Hip-Hop Feminism Pedagogy*. New York: Peter Lang.

Brown, Ruth Nicole, and Chamara Jewel Kwakye. 2012. *Wish to Live: The Hip-Hop Feminism Pedagogy Reader*. New York: Peter Lang Publishing.

Brown, Wyatt, and Wesley G. Jennings. 2014. "A Replication and an Honor-Based Extension of Hirschi's Reconceptualization of Self-Control Theory and Crime and Analogous Behaviors." *Deviant Behavior* 35(4): 297–310.

Brydon-Miller, Mary, Michael Kral, Patricia Maguire, Susan Noffke, and Anu Sabhlok. 2011. "Jazz and the Banyan Tree: Roots and Riffs on Participatory Action Research." Pp. 387–400 in *The Sage Handbook of Qualitative Research* (4th edn.) edited by Norman K. Denzin and Yvonna S. Lincoln. Thousand Oaks, CA: Sage.

Bryman, Alan. 2012. *Social Research Methods* (4th edn.). New York: Oxford University Press.

Bui, Hoan N. 2004. *In the Adopted Land: Abused Immigrant Women and the Criminal Justice System*. Westport, CT: Praeger.

Buker, Hasan. 2011. "Formation of Self-Control: Gottfredson and Hirschi's General Theory of Crime and Beyond." *Aggression and Violent Behavior* 16(3): 265–176.

Bump, Philip. 2014. "Attention, Thom Tillis: North Carolina's 'Traditional' Population is Growing, Too." *The Washington Post*, June 15. Available at http://www.washingtonpost.com/blogs/the-fix/wp/2014/06/17/attention-thom-tillis-north-carolinas-traditional-population-is-growing-too/ (last accessed January 6, 2015).

Burton, Velmer S., Jr., Francis T. Cullen, T. David Evans, Leanne Fiftal Alarid, and R. Gregory Dunaway. 1998. "Gender, Self-Control, and Crime." *Journal of Research in Crime and Delinquency* 35(2): 123–147.

Butler, Paul D. 2013. "Black Male Exceptionalism? The Problems and Potential of Black Male-Focused Interventions." *Du Bois Review: Social Science Research on Race* 10(2): 485–511.

Capetillo, Luisa. 1911. *Mi opinión sobre las libertades, derechos y deberes de la mujer: como compañera, madre y ser independiente.* [*My Opinion on the Liberties, Rights, and Duties of the Woman, as Companion, Mother, and Independent Being*]. Times Publishing Company.

Carbado, Devon W. 2013. "Colorblind Intersectionality." *Signs: Journal of Women in Culture and Society* 38(4): 811–845.

Carbado, Devon W., Kimberlé Crenshaw, Vickie M. Mays, and Barbara Tomlinson. 2013. "Intersectionality: Mapping the Movements of a Theory." *Du Bois Review: Social Science Research on Race* 10(2): 303–312.

Carrigan, Tim, Bob Connell, and John Lee. 1985. "Toward a New Sociology of Masculinity." *Theory and Society* 14(5): 551–604.

Castillo, Ana. 1994. *Massacre of the Dreamers: Essays on Xicanisma.* Albuquerque, NM: University of New Mexico Press.

Caudy, Michael S. 2011. *Assessing Racial Differences in Offending Trajectories: A Life-Course View of the Race-Crime Relationship.* Ph.D. diss., University of South Florida. Graduate Theses and Dissertations, http://scholarcommons.usf.edu/etd/3037 (last accessed January 7, 2015).

Centers for Disease Control and Prevention. 2012. "Sexual Experience and Contraceptive Use Among Female Teens – United States, 1995, 2002, and 2006–2010." *Morbidity and Mortality Weekly Report* 61(17): 297–301.

Centers for Disease Control and Prevention. 2013. "Vital Signs: Repeat Births Among Teens – United States, 2007–2010." *Morbidity and Mortality Weekly Report* 62(13): 249–255.

Chapple, Constance L., Jamie Vaske, and Trina L. Hope. 2010. "Sex Differences in the Causes of Self-Control: An Examination of Mediation, Moderation, and Gendered Etiologies." *Journal of Criminal Justice* 38(6): 1122–1131.

Chesney-Lind, Meda. 2006. "Patriarchy, Crime, and Justice: Feminist Criminology in an Era of Backlash." *Feminist Criminology* 1(1): 6–26.

Chesney-Lind, Meda, and Merry Morash. 2013. "Transformative Feminist Criminology: A Critical Re-thinking of a Discipline." *Critical Criminology* 21(3): 287–304.

Chesney-Lind, Meda, and Noelie Rodriguez. 1983. "Women Under Lock and Key: A View from the Inside." *The Prison Journal* 63(2): 47–65.

Cho, Sumi. 2013. "Post-Intersectionality: The Curious Reception of Intersectionality in Legal Scholarship." *Du Bois Review: Social Science Research on Race* 10(2): 385–404.

Cho, Sumi, Kimberlé Crenshaw, and Leslie McCall. 2013. "Toward a Field of Intersectionality Studies: Theory, Applications, and Praxis." *Signs: Journal of Women in Culture and Society* 38(4): 785–810.

Choo, Hae Yeon, and Myra Marx Ferree. 2010. "Practicing Intersectionality in Sociological Research: A Critical Analysis of Inclusions, Interactions, and Institutions in the Study of Inequalities." *Sociological Theory* 28(2): 129–149.

Chow, Esther Ngan-Ling. 1987. "The Development of Feminist Consciousness among Asian American Women." *Gender & Society* 1(3): 284–299.

Clay, Andreana. 2008. "'Like an Old Soul Record': Black Feminism, Queer Sexuality, and the Hip-Hop Generation." *Meridians* 8(1): 53–73.

Clay, Andreana. 2012. *The Hip-Hop Generation Fights Back: Youth Activism and Post-Civil Rights Politics*. New York: New York University Press.

Clear, Todd R. 2001. "Has Academic Criminal Justice Come of Age? ACJS Presidential Address Washington, DC, April 2001." *Justice Quarterly* 18(4): 709–726.

Cleaver, Kathleen N. 1997. "Racism, Civil Rights, and Feminism." Pp. 35–43 in *Critical Race Feminism: A Reader* edited by Adrien K. Wing. New York: New York University Press.

Cobbina, Jennifer E., Merry Morash, Deborah A. Kashy, and Sandi W. Smith. 2014. "Race, Neighborhood Danger, and Coping Strategies Among Female Probationers and Parolees." *Race and Justice* 4(1): 3–28.

Cochran, John K., Peter B. Wood, Christine S. Sellers, Wendy Wilkerson, and Michelle B. Chamlin. 1998. "Academic Dishonesty and Low Self-Control: An Empirical Test of General Theory of Crime." *Deviant Behavior* 19(3): 227–255.

Cole, Johnetta B. 1995. "Epilogue." Pp. 549–551 in *Words of Fire: An Anthology of African-American Feminist Thought* edited by Beverly Guy-Sheftall. New York: The New Press.

Cole, Johnetta B, and Beverly Guy-Sheftall. 2003. *Gender Talk: The Struggle for Women's Equality in African American Communities*. New York: Ballantine.

Collins, Patricia Hill. 1996. "What's In a Name? Womanism, Black Feminism and Beyond." *The Black Scholar* 26(1): 9–17.

Collins, Patricia Hill. 2000a. *Black Feminist Thought: Knowledge, Consciousness, and the Politics of Empowerment* (2nd edn.). New York: Routledge.

Collins, Patricia Hill. 2000b. "What's Going On? Black Feminist Thought and the Politics of Postmodernism." Pp. 41–73 in *Working the Ruins: Feminist Poststructural Theory and Methods in Education* edited by Elizabeth A. St. Pierre and Wanda S. Pillow. New York: Routledge.

Collins, Patricia Hill. 2005. *Black Sexual Politics: African Americans, Gender, and the New Racism*. New York: Routledge.

Collins, Patricia Hill. 2006. *From Black Power to Hip Hop: Racism, Nationalism, and Feminism*. Philadelphia, PA: Temple University Press.

Comaroff, John L., and Jean Comaroff. 1997. *Of Revelation and Revolution: The Dialectics of Modernity on a South African Frontier*. Chicago, IL: University of Chicago Press.

Comas-Díaz, Lillian. 2001. "Hispanics, Latinos, or Americanos: The Evolution of Identity." *Cultural Diversity and Ethnic Minority Psychology* 7(2): 115–120.

Combahee River Collective. 2000[1983]. "The Combahee River Collective Statement." Pp. 264–274 in *Home Girls: A Black Feminist Anthology* edited by Barbara Smith. New Brunswick, NJ: Rutgers University Press.

Connell, R.W. 1983. *Which Way Is Up? Essays on Sex, Class and Culture*. Sydney, Australia: Allen & Unwin.

Connell, R.W. 1987. *Gender and Power: Society, the Person, and Sexual Politics*. Sydney, Australia: Allen & Unwin.

Connell, R.W., and James W. Messerschmidt. 2005. "Hegemonic Masculinity: Rethinking the Concept." *Gender & Society* 19(6): 829–859.

Contreras, Randol. 2009. "'Damn, Yo – Who's That Girl?' An Ethnographic Analysis of Masculinity in Drug Robberies." *Journal of Contemporary Ethnography* 38(4): 465–492.

Contreras, Randol. 2013. *The Stickup Kids: Race, Drugs, Violence, and the American Dream*. Berkeley, CA: University of California Press.

Cooper, Anna Julia. 1892. *A Voice from the South*. Xenia, OH: The Aldine Printing House.

Cooper, Jonathon A., Anthony Walsh, and Lee Ellis. 2010. "Is Criminology Moving Toward a Paradigm Shift? Evidence from a Survey of the American Society of Criminology." *Journal of Criminal Justice Education* 21(3): 332–347.

Cotera, Marta. [1980]1997. "Feminism: The Chicano and Anglo Versions – A Historical Analysis." Pp. 223–231 in *Chicana Feminist Thought: The Basic Historical Writings* edited by Alma M. García. New York: Routledge.

Craig, Jessica M. "The Effects of Marriage and Parenthood on Offending Levels Over Time Among Juvenile Offenders Across Race and Ethnicity." *Journal of Crime and Justice* ahead-of-print (2014): 1–20.

Crenshaw, Kimberlé. 1989. "Demarginalizing the Intersection of Race and Sex: A Black Feminist Critique of Antidiscrimination Doctrine, Feminist Theory and Antiracist Politics." *University of Chicago Legal Forum* 139–167.

Crenshaw, Kimberlé. 1991. "Mapping the Margins: Intersectionality, Identity, Politics, and Violence Against Women of Color." *Stanford Law Review* 43(6): 1241–1299.

Crenshaw, Kimberlé. 2011. "Postcript." Pp. 221–233 in *Framing Intersectionality: Debates on a Multifaceted Concept in Gender Studies* edited by Helma Lutz, Maria Teresa Herrera Vivar, and Linda Supik. Surrey, England: Ashgate.

Daly, Kathleen. 1992. "Women's Pathways to Felony Court: Feminist Theories of Lawbreaking and Problems of Representation." *Southern California Review of Law and Women's Studies* 2: 11–52.

Daly, Kathleen. 1993. "Class-Race-Gender: Sloganeering in Search of Meaning." *Social Justice* 20(1/2): 56–71.

Daly, Kathleen, and Lisa Maher (eds.). 1998. *Criminology at the Crossroads: Feminist Readings in Crime and Justice*. New York: Oxford University Press.

Daly, Kathleen, and Meda Chesney-Lind. 1988. Feminism and Criminology." *Justice Quarterly* 5(4): 497–538.

Davis, Angela Y. 1971. "Reflections on the Black Woman's Role in the Community of Slaves." *The Black Scholar* 3(4): 2–15.

Davis, Angela Y. 1983. *Women, Race and Class*. New York: Vintage Books.

Davis, F. James. 1991. *Who Is Black? One Nation's Definition*. University Park, PA: Pennsylvania State University Press.

Davis, Kathy. 2008. "Intersectionality as Buzzword: A Sociology of Science Perspective on What Makes a Feminist Theory Successful." *Feminist Theory* 9(1): 67–85.

Deane, Glenn, David P. Armstrong, and Richard B. Felson. 2005. "An Examination of Offense Specialization Using Marginal Logit Models." *Criminology* 43(4): 955–988.

DeHart, Dana, and Shannon M. Lynch. 2013. "The Relationship Between Victimization and Offending." Pp. 120–137 in *Routledge International Handbook of Crime and Gender Studies* edited by Claire M. Renzetti, Susan L. Miller, and Angela R. Gover. New York: Routledge.

DeKeseredy, Walter S. 2011. *Contemporary Critical Criminology*. New York: Routledge.

Del Castillo, Adelaida R. 2005. "La Liga Femenil Mexicanista." In *The Oxford Encyclopedia of Latinos and Latinas in the United States* edited by Suzanne Oboler and Deena J. González. New York: Oxford University Press.

Delgado, Richard, and Jean Stefancic. 2012. *Critical Race Theory: An Introduction*. New York: New York University Press.

Delgado Bernal, Dolores, C. Alejandra Elenes, Francisca E. Godinez, and Sofia Villenas (eds.). 2006. *Chicana/Latina Education in Everyday Life*. Albany, NY: State University of New York Press.

De Lisi, Matt, Kevin M. Beaver, Kevin A. Wright, John Paul Wright, Michael G. Vaughn, and Chad R. Trulson. 2011. "Criminal Specialization Revisited: A Simultaneous Quantile Regression Approach." *American Journal of Criminal Justice* 36(2): 73–92.

DeNavas-Walt, Carmen, Robert Cleveland, and Bruce H. Webster, Jr. 2003. *Income in the United States: 2002*. Washington, DC: US Government Printing Office.

Dillon, Michele. 2010. *Introduction to Sociological Theory: Theorists, Concepts, and their Applicability to the Twenty-First Century*. West Sussex, UK: Wiley-Blackwell.

Dogan, Mattei. 1996. "The Hybridization of Social Science Knowledge." *Library Trends* 45(2): 296–314.

Doherty, Elaine Eggleston, and Margaret E. Ensminger. 2013. "Marriage and Offending among a Cohort of Disadvantaged African Americans." *Journal of Research in Crime and Delinquency* 50(1): 104–131.

Dovidio, John F. 2001. "On the Nature of Contemporary Prejudice: The Third Wave." *Journal of Social Issues* 57(4): 829–849.

Dreger, Alice D., and April M. Herndon. 2009. "Progress and Politics in the Intersex Rights Movement: Feminist Theory in Action." *GLQ: A Journal of Lesbian and Gay Studies* 15(2): 199–224.

Du Bois, William E. Burghardt (W.E.B.). 1892. "The Enforcement of the Slave-Trade Laws." Pp. 149–174 in *Annual Report of the American Historical Association for the Year 1891*. Washington, DC: Government Printing Office.

Du Bois, William E. Burghardt 1899. *The Philadelphia Negro: A Social Study*. Philadelphia, PA: University of Pennsylvania.

Du Bois, William E. Burghardt 1903. *The Souls of Black Folk*. Chicago, IL: A.C. McClurg & Co.

Duneier, Mitchell. 1999. *Sidewalk*. New York: Farrar, Straus and Giroux.

Eckberg, Douglas Lee, and Lester Hill, Jr. 1979. "The Paradigm Concept and Sociology: A Critical Review." *American Sociological Review* 44(6): 925–937.

Edin, Kathryn, and Maria Kefalas. 2005. *Promises I Can Keep: Why Poor Women Put Motherhood Before Marriage*. Berkeley, CA: University of California Press.

Ellis, Lee, Jonathon A. Cooper, and Anthony Walsh. 2008. "Criminologists' Opinions About Causes and Theories of Crime and Delinquency: A Follow-Up." *The Criminologist* 33(3): 23–26.

Emirbayer, Mustafa, and Ann Mische. 1998. "What Is Agency?" *American Journal of Sociology* 103(4): 962–1023.

Enck-Wanzer, Darrel (ed.). 2010. *The Young Lords Party: A Reader*. New York: New York University Press.

Erez, Edna, Madelaine Adelman, and Carol Gregory. 2009. "Intersections of Immigration and Domestic Violence: Voices of Battered Immigrant Women." *Feminist Criminology* 4(1): 32–56.

Farley, John E. 2012. *Majority/Minority Relations* (6th edn.). Upper Saddle River, NJ: Prentice Hall.

Farrell, Amy, Geoff Ward, and Danielle Rousseau. 2010. "Intersections of Gender and Race in Federal Sentencing: Examining Court Contexts and Effects of Representative Court Authorities." *Journal of Gender, Race and Justice* 14: 85–125.

Fausto-Sterling, Anne. 1995. "Gender, Race, and Nation: The Comparative Anatomy of 'Hottentot' Women in Europe, 1815–1817." Pp. 19–48 in *Deviant Bodies: Critical Perspectives on Difference in Science and Popular Culture* edited by Jennifer Terry and Jacqueline Urla. Bloomington, IN: Indiana University Press.

Fausto-Sterling, Anne. 2012. *Sex/Gender: Biology in a Social World*. New York: Routledge.

Feagin, Joe R. 2010. *Racist America: Roots, Current Realities, and Future Reparations* (2nd edn.). New York: Routledge.

Fields, Jessica. 2008. *Risky Lessons: Sex Education and Social Inequality*. Piscataway, NJ: Rutgers University Press.

Finchilescu, Gillian, and Colin Tredoux. 2010. "The Changing Landscape of Intergroup Relations in South Africa." *Journal of Social Issues* 66(2): 223–236.

Fine, Michelle. 2008. "An Epilogue, of Sorts." Pp. 213–234 in *Revolutionizing Education: Youth Participatory Action Research in Motion* edited by Julio Cammarota and Michelle Fine. New York: Routledge.

Fine, Michelle, and Lois Weis. 1998. *The Unknown City: The Lives of Poor and Working-Class Young Adults*. Boston, MA: Beacon Press.

Flavin, Jeanne. 2001. "Feminism for the Mainstream Criminologist: An Invitation." *Journal of Criminal Justice* 29(4): 271–285.

Freedman, Estelle B. 2002. *No Turning Back: The History of Feminism and the Future of Women*. New York: Ballantine.

Friedan, Betty. 1963. *The Feminine Mystique*. New York: Norton.

Friedrichs, David O., and Martin D. Schwartz. 2008. "Low Self-Control and High Organizational Control: The Paradoxes of White-Collar Crime." Pp. 145–159 in *Out of Control: Assessing the General Theory of Crime* edited by Erich Goode. Stanford, CA: Stanford Social Sciences.

Gabbidon, Shaun L. 2007. *W.E.B. Du Bois on Crime and Justice: Laying the Foundations of Sociological Criminology*. Burlington, VT: Ashgate.

Gabbidon, Shaun L. 2010. *Criminological Perspectives on Race and Crime* (2nd edn.). New York: Routledge.

Gallagher, Charles A. 2009. *Rethinking the Color Line: Readings in Race and Ethnicity* (4th edn.). New York: McGraw-Hill.

García, Alma M. (ed.). 1997. *Chicana Feminist Thought: The Basic Historical Writings*. New York: Routledge.

Garcia, Lorena. 2012. *Respect Yourself, Protect Yourself: Latina Girls and Sexual Identity*. New York: New York University Press.

Geis, Gilbert. 2008. "Self-Control: A Hypercritical Assessment." Pp. 203–216 in *Out of Control: Assessing the General Theory of Crime* edited by Erich Goode. Stanford, CA: Stanford Social Sciences.

Gibson, Chris L., Jeffrey T. Ward, John Paul Wright, Kevin M. Beaver, and Matt Delisi. 2010. "Where Does Gender Fit in the Measurement of Self-Control?" *Criminal Justice and Behavior* 37(8): 883–903.

Giddings, Paula. 1984. *When and Where I Enter: The Impact of Black Women on Race and Sex in America*. New York: William Morrow & Co.

Gilbert, Oliver. 1998[1850]. *Narrative of Sojourner Truth*. New York: Penguin.

Gilfus, Mary E. 1992. "From Victims to Survivors to Offenders: Women's Routes Of Entry and Immersion into Street Crime." *Women & Criminal Justice* 4(1): 63–89.

Giordano, Peggy C. 2010. *Legacies of Crime: A Follow-Up of the Children of Highly Delinquent Girls and Boys*. New York: Cambridge University Press.

Glenn, Evelyn Nakano. 2008. "Yearning for Lightness: Transnational Circuits in the Marketing and Consumption of Skin Lighteners." *Gender & Society* 22(3): 281–302.

Glueck, Sheldon, and Eleanor Glueck. 1950. *Unraveling Juvenile Delinquency*. New York: Commonwealth Fund.

Glueck, Sheldon, and Eleanor Glueck. 1968. *Delinquents and Nondelinquents in Perspective*. Cambridge, MA: Harvard University Press.

Goffman, Alice. 2014. *On the Run: Fugitive Life in an American City*. Chicago, IL: University of Chicago Press.

Goldsmith, Arthur H., Darrick Hamilton, and William Darity. 2007. "From Dark to Light: Skin Color and Wages Among African-Americans." *Journal of Human Resources* 42(4): 701–738.

González, Gabriela. 2006. "Jovita Idar Juárez." Pp. 336–337 in *Latinas in the United States: A Historical Encyclopedia* edited by Vicki L. Ruiz, and Virginia Sánchez Korrol. Bloomington, IN: Indiana University Press.

Goode, Erich. 2008. "Out of Control? An Introduction to the General Theory of Crime." Pp. 3–25 in *Out of Control: Assessing the General Theory of Crime* edited by Erich Goode. Stanford, CA: Stanford Social Sciences.

Gordon, Vivian V. 1987. *Black Women, Feminism and Black Liberation: Which Way?* Chicago, IL: Third World Press.

Gottfredson, Michael R. 2006. "The Empirical Status of Control Theory in Criminology." Pp. 77–100 in *Taking Stock: The Status of Criminological Theory* edited by Francis T. Cullen, John P. Wright, and Kristie R. Blevins. New Brunswick, NJ: Transaction.

Gottfredson, Michael R. 2011. "Some Advantages of a Crime-Free Criminology." Pp. 35–48 in *What Is Criminology?* edited by Mary Bosworth, and Carolyn Hoyle. New York: Oxford University Press.

Gottfredson, Michael R., and Travis Hirschi. 1990. *A General Theory of Crime*. Stanford, CA: Stanford University Press.

Gottfredson, Michael R., and Travis Hirschi. 2003. "Self-Control and Opportunity." Pp. 5–20 in *Control Theories of Crime and Delinquency* edited by Chester L. Britt, and Michael R. Gottfredson. New Brunswick, NJ: Transaction.

Grasmick, Harold G., Charles R. Tittle, Robert J. Bursik, and Bruce J. Arneklev. 1993. "Testing the Core Empirical Implications of Gottfredson and Hirschi's General Theory of Crime." *Journal of Research in Crime and Delinquency* 30(1): 5–29.

Green, Joyce (ed.). 2007. *Making Space for Indigenous Feminism*. Black Point, Nova Scotia: Fernwood Publishing.

Greenberg, David F. 2008. "Age, Sex, and Racial Distributions of Crime." Pp. 38–48 in *Out of Control: Assessing the General Theory of Crime* edited by Erich Goode. Stanford, CA: Stanford Social Sciences.

Guevara, Lori, Denise Herz, and Cassia Spohn. 2006. "Gender and Juvenile Justice Decision Making: What Role Does Race Play?" *Feminist Criminology* 1(4): 258–282.

Gutierrez y Muhs, Gabriella, Yolanda Flores Niemann, Carmen G. González, and Angela P. Harris (eds.). 2012. *Presumed Incompetent: The Intersections of Race and Class for Women in Academia*. Boulder, CO: University of Colorado Press.

Guy-Sheftall, Beverly (ed.). 1995. *Words of Fire: An Anthology of African-American Feminist Thought*. New York: The New Press.

Gyimah-Brempong, Kwabena, and Gregory N. Price. 2006. "Crime and Punishment: And Skin Hue Too?" *The American Economic Review* 96(2): 246–250.

Habecker, Shelly. 2012. "Not Black, but Habasha: Ethiopian and Eritrean Immigrants in American Society." *Ethnic and Racial Studies* 35(7): 1200–1219.

Hamilton, Brady E., Joyce A. Martin, and Stephanie J. Ventura. 2012. "Births: Preliminary Data for 2011." *National Vital Statistics Reports* 61(5): 1–18.

Haney López, Ian. 2006. *White by Law: The Legal Construction of Race* (revised and updated edn.). New York: New York University Press.

Hannon, Lance, Robert DeFina, and Sarah Bruch. 2013. "The Relationship Between Skin Tone and School Suspension for African Americans." *Race and Social Problems* 5(4): 281–295.

Hanson, Laura J. 2010. "W.E.B. Du Bois." Pp. 53–58 in *Fifty Key Thinkers in Criminology* edited by Keith Hayward, Shadd Maruna, and Jayne Mooney. New York: Routledge.

Harding, Sandra G. 1987. "Introduction: Is There a Feminist Method?" Pp. 1–14 in *Feminism and Methodology: Social Science Issues* edited by Sandra G. Harding. Bloomington, IN: Indiana University Press.

Harnois, Catherine E., and Mosi Ifatunji. 2011. "Gendered Measures, Gendered Models: Toward an Intersectional Analysis of Interpersonal Racial Discrimination." *Ethnic and Racial Studies* 34(6): 1006–1028.

Harris, Angela P. 1990. "Race and Essentialism in Feminist Legal Theory." *Stanford Law Review* 42(3): 581–616.

Harris, Cheryl I. 1993. "Whiteness as Property." *Harvard Law Review* 106(8): 1707–1791.

Harris, Duchess. 2009. *Black Feminist Politics from Kennedy to Clinton*. New York: Palgrave Macmillan.

Haynie, Dana L., and David P. Armstrong. 2006. "Race- and Gender-Disaggregated Homicide Offending Rates: Differences and Similarities by Victim-Offender Relations Across Cities." *Homicide Studies* 10(1): 3–32.

Henning, Denise K. 2007. "Yes, My Daughters, We Are Cherokee Women." Pp. 187–198 in *Making Space for Indigenous Feminism* edited by Joyce Green. Black Point, Nova Scotia: Fernwood Publishing.

Hernández, Daisy, and Bushra Rehman. 2002. *Colonize This! Young Women of Color on Today's Feminism*. Berkeley, CA: Seal Press.

Hewitt, Nancy A. 2005. "Luisa Capetillo: Feminist of the Working Class." Pp. 120–134 in *Latina Legacies: Identity, Biography, and Community* edited by Vicki L. Ruiz, and Virginia Sánchez Korrol. New York: Oxford University Press.

Higgins, George E. 2004. "Gender and Self-Control Theory: Are There Differences in the Measures and the Theory's Causal Model?" *Criminal Justice Studies: A Critical Journal of Crime, Law and Society* 17(1): 33–55.

Higgins, George E., and Melissa L. Ricketts. 2005. "Self-Control Theory, Race, and Delinquency." *Journal of Ethnicity in Criminal Justice* 3(3): 5–22.

Higgins, George E., Scott E. Wolfe, and Catherine D. Marcum. 2008. "Digital Piracy: An Examination of Three Measurements of Self-Control." *Deviant Behavior* 29(5): 440–460.

Hill, Mark E. 2002. "Skin Color and the Perception of Attractiveness among African Americans: Does Gender Make a Difference?" *Social Psychology Quarterly* 65(1): 77–91.

Hirschi, Travis. 1969. *Causes of Delinquency*. Berkeley, CA: University of California Press.

Hirschi, Travis. 2004. "Self-Control and Crime." Pp. 537–552 in *Handbook of Self-Regulation: Research, Theory, and Applications* edited by Roy F. Baumeister, and Kathleen D. Vohs. New York: Guilford.

Hirschi, Travis, and Michael R. Gottfredson. 1995. "Control Theory and the Life-Course Perspective." *Studies on Crime & Crime Prevention* 4(2): 131–142.

Hirschi, Travis, and Michael R. Gottfredson. 2001. "Self-Control Theory." Pp. 81–96 in *Explaining Criminals and Crime: Essays in Contemporary Criminological Theory*. Los Angeles: Roxbury.

Hirschi, Travis, and Michael R. Gottfredson. 2008. "Critiquing the Critics: The Authors Respond." Pp. 217–231 in *Out of Control: Assessing the General Theory of Crime* edited by Erich Goode. Stanford, CA: Stanford Social Sciences.

Hooks, Bell. 2000. *Feminist Theory: From Margin to Center* (2nd edn.). Cambridge, MA: South End Press.

Hooper, Cindy. 2012. *Conflict: African American Women and the New Dilemma of Race and Gender Politics*. Santa Barbara, CA: Praeger.

Horne, Gerald. 2010. *W.E.B. Du Bois: A Biography*. Santa Barbara, CA: Greenwood Press/ABC-CLIO.

Howell, Joseph T. 1972. *Hard Living on Clay Street: Portraits of Blue Collar Families*. New York: Anchor Books/Doubleday.

Huebner, Beth M., Christina DeJong, and Jennifer Cobbina. 2010. "Women Coming Home: Long-Term Patterns of Recidivism." *Justice Quarterly* 27(2): 225–254.

Huhndorf, Shari M., and Cheryl Suzack. 2010. "Indigenous Feminism: Theorizing the Issues." Pp. 1–17 in *Indigenous Women and Feminism: Politics, Activism, Culture* edited by Cheryl Suzack, Shari M. Huhndorf, Jeanne Perreault, and Jean Barman. Vancouver: UBC Press.

Hunter, Margaret L. 2005. *Race, Gender, and the Politics of Skin Tone*. New York: Routledge.

Hunter, Margaret L. 2013. "The Consequences of Colorism." Pp. 247–256 in *The Melanin Millennium: Skin Color and 21st Century International Discourse* edited by Ronald E. Hall. Dordrecht: Springer.

INCITE! Women of Color Against Violence. 2006. *Color of Violence: The INCITE! Anthology*. Cambridge, MA: South End Press.

INCITE! 2014. "Community Accountability." Available at http://incite-national.org/page/community-accountability (last accessed January 8, 2015).

International Labour Office. 2011. *Equality at Work: The Continuing Challenge*. Geneva: International Labour Office.

Iovanni, LeeAnn, and Susan L. Miller. 2008. "A Feminist Consideration of Gender and Crime." Pp. 127–141 in *Out of Control: Assessing the General Theory of Crime* edited by Erich Goode. Stanford, CA: Stanford Social Sciences.

Jarmakani, Amira. 2011. "Arab American Feminisms: Mobilizing the Politics of Invisibility." Pp. 227–241 in *Arab and Arab American Feminisms: Gender, Violence, and Belonging* edited by Rabab Abdulhadi, Evelyn Alsultany, and Nadine Naber. Syracuse, NY: Syracuse University Press.

Jennings, Wesley G., Alex R. Piquero, and Jennifer M. Reingle. 2012. "On the Overlap Between Victimization and Offending: A Review of the Literature." *Aggression and Violent Behavior* 17(1): 16–26.

Jones, Nikki. 2009. "W.E.B. Du Bois." Pp. 242–246 in *The Encyclopedia of Race and Crime* edited by Helen Taylor Greene and Shaun L. Gabbidon. Thousand Oaks, CA: Sage.

Jones, Nikki. 2010. *Between Good and Ghetto: African American Girls and Inner-City Violence*. New Brunswick, NJ: Rutgers University Press.

Joseph, Janice (2006). "Intersectionality of Race/Ethnicity, Class, and Justice: Women of Color." Pp. 292–312 in *Women, Law, and Social Control* (2nd edn.), edited by A.V. Merlo, and J.M. Pollock. Boston, MA: Allyn & Bacon.

Kessler, Suzanne J., and Wendy McKenna. 1978. *Gender: An Ethnomethodological Approach*. New York: Wiley Interscience.

King, Deborah K. 1988. "Multiple Jeopardy, Multiple Consciousness: The Context of Black Feminist Ideology. *Signs: Journal of Women in Culture and Society* 14: 42–72.

King, Ryan D., and Scott J. South. 2011. "Crime, Race, and the Transition to Marriage." *Journal of Family Issues* 32(1): 99–126.

Kitwana, Bakari. 2002. *The Hip-Hop Generation: Young Blacks and the Crisis in American Culture*. New York: Basic Civitas.

Krogstad, Jens Manuel. 2014. "Census Bureau Explores New Middle East/North Africa Ethnic Category." *Pew Hispanic Center, Pew Research Center*, March 24. Available at http://www.pewresearch.org/fact-tank/2014/03/24/census-bureau-explores-new-middle-eastnorth-africa-ethnic-category/ (last accessed January 6, 2015).

Kuhn, Thomas. 1962/1970. *The Structure of Scientific Revolutions*. Chicago, IL: University of Chicago Press.

Kuper, Laura E., Laurel Wright, and Brian Mustanski. 2014. "Stud Identity Among Female-Born Youth of Color: Joint Conceptualizations of Gender Variance and Same- Sex Sexuality." *Journal of Homosexuality* 61(5): 714–731.

Kuper, Laura E., Robin Nussbaum, and Brian Mustanski. 2012. "Exploring the Diversity of Gender and Sexual Orientation Identities in an Online Sample of Transgender Individuals." *Journal of Sex Research* 49(2–3): 244–254.

LaFree, Gary. 1989. *Rape and Criminal Justice: The Social Construction of Sexual Assault*. Belmont, CA: Wadsworth.

LaFree, Gary. 2007. "Expanding Criminology's Domain: The American Society of Criminology 2006 Presidential Address." *Criminology* 45(1): 1–31.

LaGrange, Teresa C., and Robert A. Silverman. 1999. "Low Self-Control and Opportunity: Testing the General Theory of Crime as an Explanation for Gender Differences in Delinquency." *Criminology* 37(1): 41–72.

Lamont, Michèle. 2000. *The Dignity of Working Men: Morality and the Boundaries of Race, Class, and Immigration*. New York: Russell Sage.

Lareau, Annette. 2003. *Unequal Childhoods: Class, Race, and Family Life*. Berkeley, CA: University of California Press.

LaRocque, Emma. 2007. "Métis and Feminist: Ethical Reflections on Feminism, Human Rights and Decolonization." Pp. 53–71 in *Making Space for Indigenous Feminism* edited by Joyce Green. Black Point, Nova Scotia: Fernwood Publishing.

Latour, Francie. 2012. "The Myth of Native American Blood." *Boston.com*, June 1. http://www.boston.com/community/blogs/hyphenated_life/2012/06/the_myth_of_native_american_bl.html (last accessed January 6, 2015).

Laub, John H., and Robert J. Sampson. 1993. "Turning Points in the Life Course: Why Change Matters to the Study of Crime." *Criminology* 31(3): 301–325.

Laub, John H., and Robert J. Sampson. 2003. *Shared Beginnings, Divergent Lives: Delinquent Boys to Age 70*. Cambridge, MA: Harvard University Press.

Laughlin, Kathleen A., Julie Gallagher, Dorothy Sue Cobble, Eileen Boris, Premilla Nadasen, Stephanie Gilmore, and Leandra Zarnow. 2010. "Is it Time to Jump Ship: Historians Rethink the Waves Metaphor." *Feminist Formations* 22(1): 76–135.

Lewis, Diane K. 1977. "A Response to Inequality: Black Women, Racism, and Sexism." *Signs: Journal of Women in Culture and Society* 3(2): 339–361.

Lewis, Gail. 2013. "Unsafe Travel: Experiencing Intersectionality and Feminist Displacements." *Signs: Journal of Women in Culture and Society* 38(4): 869–892.

Lombroso, Cesare. 1876. *L'uomo delinquente studiato in rapporto alla antropologia, alla medicina legale ed alle discipline carcerarie* [*The criminal man studied in relationship to anthropology, forensic medicine and prison doctrines*]. Milan: Ulrico Hoepli.

Lopez, Mark Hugo, and Jens Manuel Krogstad. 2014. "'Mexican,' 'Hispanic,' 'Latin American' Top List of Race Write-Ins on the 2010 Census." *Pew Hispanic Center, Pew Research Center*, April 4. http://www.pewresearch.org/fact-tank/2014/04/04/mexican-hispanic-and-latin-american-top-list-of-race-write-ins-on-the-2010-census/ (last accessed January 6, 2015).

Luker, Kristin. 1996. *Dubious Conceptions: The Politics of Teenage Pregnancy*. Cambridge, MA: Harvard University Press.

Lutz, Helma, Maria Teresa Herrera Vivar, and Linda Supik. 2011. "Framing Intersectionality: An Introduction." Pp. 1–23 in *Framing Intersectionality: Debates on a Multifaceted Concept in Gender Studies* edited by Helma Lutz, Maria Teresa Herrera Vivar, and Linda Supik. Surrey, England: Ashgate.

Lykke, Nina. 2003. "Intersektionalitet – ett användbart begrepp för genusforskningen" ["Intersectionality: A Useful Concept for Gender Research"]. *Kvinnovetenskaplig tidskrift* 23(1): 47–57.

McCall, Leslie. 2005. "The Complexity of Intersectionality." *Signs: Journal of Women in Culture and Society* 30(3): 1771–1800.

McConahay, John B. 1986. "Modern Racism, Ambivalence, and the Modern Racism Scale." Pp. 91–125 in *Prejudice, Discrimination, and Racism* edited by John F. Dovidio, and Samuel L. Gaertner. San Diego, CA: Academic Press.

McCorkel, Jill A. 2013. *Breaking Women: Gender, Race, and the New Politics of Imprisonment*. New York: New York University Press.

McGloin, Jean Marie, Christopher J. Sullivan, Alex R. Piquero, and Travis C. Pratt. 2007. "Local Life Circumstances and Offending Specialization/Versatility Comparing Opportunity and Propensity Models." *Journal of Research in Crime and Delinquency* 44(3): 321–346.

McKay, Nellie Y. 1993. "Acknowledging Differences: Can Women Find Unity Through Diversity?" Pp. 267–282 in *Theorizing Black Feminisms: The Visionary Pragmatism of Black Women* edited by Stanlie M. James, and Abena P.A. Busia. New York: Routledge.

MacKinnon, Catherine A. 1982. "Feminism, Marxism, Method, and the State: An Agenda for Theory." *Signs: Journal of Women in Culture and Society* 7(3): 515–544.

MacKinnon, Catherine A. 2002. "Keeping It Real: On Anti-'Essentialism.'" Pp. 71–83 in *Crossroads, Directions, and a New Critical Race Theory* edited by Francisco Valdes, James McCristal Culp, and Angela P. Harris. Philadelphia, PA: Temple University Press.

Maher, Lisa. 1997. *Sexed Work: Gender, Race, and Resistance in a Brooklyn Drug Market*. Oxford: Oxford University Press.

Makarios, Matthew D. 2007. "Race, Abuse, and Female Criminal Violence." *Feminist Criminology* 2(2): 100–116.

Maloy, Simon. 2014. "GOP Candidate's Racial Confusion: How Thom Tillis Defines a 'Traditional population.'" *Salon*, June 17. http://www.salon.com/2014/06/17/gop_candidates_racial_confusion_how_thom_tillis_defines_a_traditional_population/ (last accessed January 6, 2015).

Marable, Manning. 1983. "Groundings with My Sisters: Patriarchy and the Exploitation of Black Women." *Journal of Ethnic Studies* 11(2): 1–39.

Marable, Manning. 2000. *How Capitalism Underdeveloped Black America: Problems in Race, Political Economy, and Society* (updated edn.). Cambridge, MA: South End.

Marenin, Otwin, and Michael D. Reisig. 1995. "'A General Theory of Crime' and Patterns of Crime in Nigeria: An Exploration of Methodological Assumptions." *Journal of Criminal Justice* 23(6): 501–518.

Messerschmidt, James W. 1993. *Masculinities and Crime: Critique and Reconceptualization of Theory*. Lanham, MD: Rowman & Littlefield.

Messerschmidt, James W. 1997. *Crime as Structured Action: Gender, Race, Class, and Crime in the Making*. Thousand Oaks, CA: Sage.

Messerschmidt, James W. 2013. *Crime as Structured Action: On the Intersection of Masculinities, Race, Class, Sexuality, and Crime*. Lanham, MD: Rowman & Littlefield.

Miller, Holly Ventura, Wesley G. Jennings, Lorna L. Alvarez-Rivera, and Lonn Lanza-Kaduce. 2009. "Self-Control, Attachment, and Deviance Among Hispanic Adolescents." *Journal of Criminal Justice* 37(1): 77–84.

Miller, Jody. 1996. "An Examination of Disposition Decision-Making for Delinquent Girls." Pp. 219–245 in *Race, Gender, and Class in Criminology: The Intersection* edited by Martin D. Schwartz, and Dragan Milovanovic. New York: Garland.

Miller, Jody. 2008. *Getting Played: African American Girls, Urban Inequality, and Gendered Violence*. New York: New York University Press.

Miller, Susan L., and Cynthia Burack. 1993. "A Critique of Gottfredson and Hirschi's General Theory of Crime: Selective (In)Attention to Gender and Power Positions." *Women & Criminal Justice* 4(2): 115–134.

Modell, John. 1994. "Review of *Crime in the Making: Pathways and Turning Points Through Life* by Robert J. Sampson and John H. Laub." *American Journal of Sociology* 99(5): 1389–1391.

Moffitt, Terrie E., Robert F. Krueger, Avshalom Caspi, and Jeff Fagan. 2000. "Partner Abuse and General Crime: How Are They the Same? How Are They Different?" *Criminology* 38: 199–232.

Monk, Ellis P. 2014. "Skin Tone Stratification among Black Americans, 2001–2003." *Social Forces*. Online Version of Record published before inclusion in an issue.

Moore, Dawn. 2008. "Feminist Criminology: Gain, Loss and Backlash." *Sociology Compass* 2(1): 48–61.

Morgan, Joan. 1999. *When Chickenheads Come Home to Roost: My Life as a Hip-Hop Feminist*. New York: Simon & Schuster.

Morris, Gregory D., Peter B. Wood, and R. Gregory Dunaway. 2006. "Self-Control, Native Traditionalism, and Native American Substance Use: Testing the Cultural Invariance of a General Theory of Crime." *Crime & Delinquency* 52(4): 572–598.

Morris, Robert G., Jurg Gerber, and Scott Menard. 2011. "Social Bonds, Self-Control, and Adult Criminality A Nationally Representative Assessment of Hirschi's Revised Self-Control Theory." *Criminal Justice and Behavior* 38(6): 584–599.

Moynihan, Daniel P. 1965. *The Negro Family: The Case for National Action*. Washington, DC: US Government Printing Office.

Naber, Nadine. 2006. "Arab American Femininities: Beyond Arab Virgin/American(ized) Whore." *Feminist Studies* 32(1): 87–111.

Nash, Jennifer C. 2008. "Re-Thinking Intersectionality." *Feminist Review* 89(1): 1–15.

Ness, Cindy D. 2010. *Why Girls Fight: Female Youth Violence in the Inner City*. New York: New York University Press.

Nielsen, Amie L. 1999. "Testing Sampson and Laub's Life Course Theory: Age, Race/Ethnicity, and Drunkenness." *Deviant Behavior* 20(2): 129–151.

Nofziger, Stacey. 2010. "A Gendered Perspective on the Relationship Between Self-Control and Deviance." *Feminist Criminology* 5(1): 29–50.

Oboler, Suzanne. 1995. *Ethnic Labels, Latino Lives: Identity and the Politics of (Re)Presentation in the United States*. Minneapolis, MN: University of Minnesota Press.

Oliver, Melvin L., and Thomas M. Shapiro. 2006. *Black Wealth/White Wealth: A New Perspective on Racial Inequality* (2nd edn.). New York: Routledge.

Omi, Michael, and Howard Winant. 1994. *Racial Formation in the United States: From the 1960s to the 1990s.* New York: Routledge.

Osgood, D. Wayne, and Christopher J. Schreck. 2007. "A New Method for Studying the Extent, Stability, and Predictors of Individual Specialization in Violence." *Criminology* 45(2): 273–312.

Pager, Devah. 2007. *Marked: Race, Crime, and Finding Work in an Era of Mass Incarceration.* Chicago, IL: University of Chicago Press.

Painter, Nell I. 1996. *Sojourner Truth: A Life, a Symbol.* New York: W.W. Norton.

Parker, Karen F., and M. Kristen Hefner. 2013. "Intersections of Race, Gender, Disadvantage, and Violence: Applying Intersectionality to the Macro-Level Study of Female Homicide." *Justice Quarterly.* Published online: http://www.tandfonline.com/doi/abs/10.1080/07418825.2012.761719#.VK1L-nvpUXE (last accessed January 7, 2015).

Parry, Manon. 2010. "Betty Friedan." Pp. 198–199 in *Culture Wars: An Encyclopedia of Issues, Viewpoints, and Voices* edited by Roger Chapman. Armonk, NY: M.E. Sharpe.

Payne, Yasser Arafat. 2013. *The People's Report: The Link Between Structural Violence and Crime in Wilmington, Delaware.* Available at http://www.thepeoplesreport.com/images/pdf/The_Peoples_Report_final_draft_9-12-13.pdf (last accessed January 7, 2015).

Peguero, Anthony A., and Ann Marie Popp. 2012. "Youth Violence at School and the Intersection of Gender, Race, and Ethnicity." *Journal of Criminal Justice* 40(1): 1–9.

Peoples, Whitney A. 2008. "'Under Construction': Identifying Foundations of Hip-Hop Feminism and Exploring Bridges between Black Second-Wave and Hip-Hop Feminisms." *Meridians* 8(1): 19–52.

Peterson, Ruth D. 2012. "The Central Place of Race in Crime and Justice – The American Society of Criminology's 2011 Sutherland Address." *Criminology* 50(2): 303–327.

Pettiway, Leon E. 1997. *Workin' It: Women Living Through Drugs and Crime.* Philadelphia, PA: Temple University Press.

Pierce, Chester. 1974. "Psychiatric Problems of the Black Minority." Pp. 512–523 in *American Handbook of Psychiatry* edited by Silvano Arieti. New York: Basic Books.

Piquero, Alex R. 2009. "Self-Control Theory: Research Issues." Pp. 153–168 in *Handbook on Crime and Deviance* edited by Marvin D. Krohn, Alan J. Lizotte, and Gina Penly Hall. New York: Springer.

Piquero, Alex R., and Jeff A. Bouffard. 2007. "Something Old, Something New: A Preliminary Investigation of Hirschi's Redefined Self-Control." *Justice Quarterly* 24(1): 1–27.

Piquero, Alex R., John M. MacDonald, and Karen F. Parker. 2002. "Race, Local Life Circumstances, and Criminal Activity." *Social Science Quarterly* 83(3): 654–670.

Piquero, Alex R., David P. Farrington, and Alfred Blumstein. 2007. *Key Issues in Criminal Career Research: New Analyses of the Cambridge Study In Delinquent Development*. New York: Cambridge University Press.

Pollock, Joycelyn M. 2014. *Women's Crimes, Criminology, and Corrections*. Long Grove, IL: Waveland Press.

Potter, Hillary. 2006. "An Argument for Black Feminist Criminology: Understanding African American Women's Experiences With Intimate Partner Abuse Using an Integrated Approach." *Feminist Criminology* 1(2): 106–124.

Potter, Hillary. 2008. *Battle Cries: Black Women and Intimate Partner Abuse*. New York: New York University Press.

Pough, Gwendolyn D., Elaine Richardson, Aisha Durham, and Rachel Raimist. 2007. *Home Girls Make Some Noise! Hip Hop Feminism Anthology*. Mira Loma, CA: Parker Publishing.

Pratt, Travis C., and Francis T. Cullen. 2000. "The Empirical Status of Gottfredson and Hirschi's General Theory of Crime: A Meta-Analysis." *Criminology* 38(3): 931–964.

Pratt, Travis C., M. G. Turner, and Alex R. Piquero. 2004. "Parental Socialization And Community Context: A Longitudinal Analysis of the Structural Sources of Low Self-Control." *Journal of Research in Crime and Delinquency* 41(3): 219–243.

Quinney, Richard. 1970. *The Social Reality of Crime*. Boston, MA: Little, Brown and Company.

Rafter, Nicole (ed.). 2009. *The Origins of Criminology: A Reader*. New York: Routledge.

Renzetti, Claire M. 2013. *Feminist Criminology*. New York: Routledge.

Richie, Beth E. 1996. *Compelled to Crime: The Gender Entrapment of Battered Black Women*. New York: Routledge.

Richie, Beth E. 2012. *Arrested Justice: Black Women, Violence, and America's Prison Nation*. New York: New York University Press.

Rios, Victor M. (2011). *Punished: Policing the Lives of Black and Latino Boys*. New York: New York University Press.

Roberts, Dorothy. 1997. *Killing the Black Body: Race, Reproduction, and the Meaning of Liberty*. New York: Vintage Books.

Rose, Margaret. 1990. "Traditional and Nontraditional Patterns of Female Activism in the United Farm Workers of America, 1962 to 1980." *Frontiers: A Journal of Women's Studies* 11(1): 26–32.

Roth, Benita. 2004. *Separate Roads to Feminism: Black, Chicana, and White Feminist Movements in America's Second Wave*. New York: Cambridge University Press.

Ruiz, Vicki L., and Virginia Sánchez Korrol (eds.). 2006. *Latinas in the United States: A Historical Encyclopedia*. Indiana University Press.

Russell-Brown, Katheryn. 2004. *Underground Codes: Race, Crime, and Related Fires*. New York: New York University Press.

Russell-Brown, Katheryn. 2009. *The Color of Crime* (2nd edn.). New York: New York University Press.

Sáenz, Rogelio, and Aurelia Lorena Murga. 2011. *Latino Issues: A Reference Handbook*. Santa Barbara, CA: ABC-CLIO.

Salisbury, Emily J., and Patricia Van Voorhis. 2009. "Gendered Pathways A Quantitative Investigation of Women Probationers' Paths to Incarceration." *Criminal Justice and Behavior* 36(6): 541–566.

Sampson, Robert J., and John H. Laub. 1993. *Crime in the Making: Pathways and Turning Points through Life*. Cambridge, MA: Harvard University Press.

Sampson, Robert J., and John H. Laub. 1997. "A Life-Course Theory of Cumulative Disadvantage and the Stability of Delinquency." Pp. 133–161 in *Developmental Theories of Crime and Delinquency*. (*Advances in Criminological Theory*, Volume 7), edited by Terence P. Thornberry. New Brunswick, NJ: Transaction.

Sampson, Robert J., and John H. Laub. 2005. "A Life-Course View of the Development of Crime." *The ANNALS of the American Academy of Political and Social Science* 602: 12–45.

Sampson, Robert J., John H. Laub, and Christopher Wimer. 2006. "Does Marriage Reduce Crime? A Counterfactual Approach to Within-Individual Causal Effects." *Criminology* 44(3): 465–508.

Sanchez-Hucles, Janis, Alex E. Dryden, and Barbara Winstead. 2012. "The Multiple Identities of Feminist Women of Color: Creating a New Feminism?" Pp. 91–112 in *Navigating Multiple Identities: Race, Gender, Culture, Nationality, and Roles*, edited by Ruthellen Josselson, and Michele Harway. New York: Oxford University Press.

Santelli, John S., Richard Lowry, Nancy D. Brener, and Leah Robin. 2000. "The Association of Sexual Behaviors With Socioeconomic Status, Family Structure, and Race/Ethnicity Among US Adolescents." *American Journal of Public Health* 90(10): 1582–1588.

Schilt, Kristen, and Laurel Westbrook. 2009. "Doing Gender, Doing Heteronormativity 'Gender Normals,' Transgender People, and the Social Maintenance of Heterosexuality." *Gender & Society* 23(4): 440–464.

Schmalleger, Frank. 2014. *Criminology*. Boston, MA: Prentice Hall.

Schwartz, Martin D., and Dragan Milovanovic (eds.). 1996. *Race, Gender, and Class in Criminology: The Intersection*. New York: Garland.

Segura, Denise A., and Elisa Facio. 2008. "Adelante Mujer: Latina Activism, Feminism, and Empowerment." Pp. 294–307 in *Latinas/os in the United States: Changing the Face of América* edited by Havidán Rodríguez, Rogelio Sáenz, and Cecilia Menjívar. New York: Springer.

Seidman, Steven, Nancy Fischer, and Chet Meeks (eds.). 2011. *Introducing the New Sexuality Studies* (2nd edn.). New York: Routledge.

Shakur, Assata (JoAnne Chesimard). 1978. "Women in Prison: How We Are." *The Black Scholar* 9(7): 8–15.

Shaw, Clifford R., and Henry D. McKay. 1931. *Social Factors in Juvenile Delinquency: A Study of the Community, the Family, and the Gang in Relation to Delinquent Behavior, for the National Commission on Law Observance and Enforcement*. Washington, DC: US Government Printing Office.

Shaw, Clifford R., and Henry D. McKay. 1942. *Juvenile Delinquency and Urban Areas: A Study of Rates of Delinquents in Relation to Differential Characteristics of Local Communities in American Cities*. Chicago, IL: University of Chicago Press.

Shekarkhar, Zahra, and Chris L. Gibson. 2011. "Gender, Self-Control, and Offending Behaviors Among Latino Youth." *Journal of Contemporary Criminal Justice* 27(1): 63–80.

Simpson, Sally S., and Nicole Leeper Piquero. 2002. "Low Self-Control, Organizational Theory, and Corporate Crime." *Law and Society Review* 36(3): 509–547.

Smedley, Brian D., Adrienne Y. Stith, and Alan R. Nelson. 2009. *Unequal Treatment: Confronting Racial and Ethnic Disparities in Healthcare*. Washington, DC: The National Academies Press.

Smith, Andrea. 2005a. *Conquest: Sexual Violence and American Indian Genocide*. Cambridge, MA: South End Press.

Smith, Andrea. 2005b. "Native American Feminism, Sovereignty, and Social Change." *Feminist Studies* 31(1): 116–132.

Smith, Barbara (ed.). 1983. *Home Girls: A Black Feminist Anthology*. New York: Kitchen Table: Women of Color Press.

Smith, Robert Courtney. 2014. "Black Mexicans, Conjunctural Ethnicity, and Operating Identities: Long-Term Ethnographic Analysis." *American Sociological Review* 79(3): 517–548.

Sokoloff, Natalie J. (ed.). 2005. *Domestic Violence at the Margins: Readings on Race, Class, Gender, and Culture*. New Brunswick, NJ: Rutgers University Press.

Spence, Janet T., and Camille Buckner. 1995. "Masculinity and Femininity: Defining the Undefinable." Pp. 105–138 in *Gender, Power, and*

Communication in Human Relationships edited by Pamela J. Kalbfleisch, and Michael J. Cody. Hillsdale, NJ: Lawrence Erlbaum Associates.

Springer, Kimberly. 2002. "Third Wave Black Feminism?" *Signs: Journal of Women in Culture and Society* 27(4): 1059–1082.

Springer, Kimberly. 2005. *Living for the Revolution: Black Feminist Organizations, 1968–1980.* Durham, NC: Duke University Press.

Sue, Christina A. 2009. "An Assessment of the Latin Americanization Thesis." *Ethnic and Racial Studies* 32(6): 1058–1070.

Sue, Christina A. 2013. *Land of the Cosmic Race: Racism, Race Mixture, and Blackness in Mexico.* New York: Oxford University Press.

Sue, Derald Wing. 2010. *Microaggressions in Everyday Life: Race, Gender, and Sexual Orientation.* Hoboken, NJ: John Wiley & Sons.

Sullivan, Christopher J., Jean McGloin, Travis C. Pratt, and Alex R. Piquero. 2006. "Rethinking the 'Norm' of Offender Generality: Investigating Specialization in the Short-Term." *Criminology* 44(1): 199–233.

Taylor, Paul, Mark Hugo Lopez, Jessica Hamar Martínez, and Gabriel Velasco. 2012. *When Labels Don't Fit: Hispanics and Their Views of Identity.* Washington, DC: Pew Hispanic Center, Pew Research Center.

Telles, Edward E. 2004. *Race in Another America: The Significance of Skin Color in Brazil.* Princeton, NJ: Princeton University Press.

Tijerina-Revilla, Anita. 2009. "Are All Raza Womyn Queer? An Exploration of Sexual Identities in a Chicana/Latina Student Organization." *NWSA Journal* 21(3): 46–62.

Tittle, Charles R., and Ekaterina V. Botchkovar. 2005. "The Generality and Hegemony of Self-Control Theory: A Comparison of Russian and US Adults." *Social Science Research* 34(4): 703–731.

Tittle, Charles R., David A. Ward, and Harold G. Grasmick. 2003. "Gender, Age, and Crime/Deviance: A Challenge to Self-Control Theory." *Journal of Research in Crime and Delinquency* 40(4): 426–453.

Tonry, Michael, Lloyd E. Ohlin, and David P. Farrington. 1991. *Human Development and Criminal Behavior: New Ways of Advancing Knowledge.* New York: Springer-Verlag.

Townshend, Charles. 2011. *Terrorism: A Very Short Introduction.* Oxford: Oxford University Press.

Tracy, Paul E., and Kimberly Kempf-Leonard. 1996. *Continuity and Discontinuity in Criminal Careers.* New York: Plenum Press.

Unnever, James D., and Shaun L. Gabbidon. 2011. *A Theory of African American Offending: Race, Racism, and Crime.* New York: Routledge.

Unnever, James D., Francis T. Cullen, and Travis C. Pratt. 2003. "Parental Management, ADHD, and Delinquent Involvement: Reassessing Gottfredson and Hirschi's General Theory." *Justice Quarterly* 20(3): 471–500.

US Census Bureau. 2004. *Global Population Profile: 2002*. Washington, DC: US Government Printing Office.

US Census Bureau. 2012. "US Census Bureau Projections Show a Slower Growing, Older, More Diverse Nation a Half Century from Now." *US Census Bureau*, December 12. http://www.census.gov/newsroom/releases/archives/population/cb12-243.html (last accessed January 6, 2015).

Valentine, David. 2007. *Imagining Transgender: An Ethnography of a Category*. Durham, NC: Duke University Press.

Vasquez, Jessica M. 2010. "Blurred Borders for Some but not 'Others': Racialization, 'Flexible Ethnicity,' Gender, and Third-Generation Mexican American Identity." *Sociological Perspectives* 53(1): 45–72.

Vazsonyi, Alexander T., and Jennifer M. Crosswhite. 2004. "A Test of Gottfredson and Hirschi's General Theory of Crime in African American Adolescents." *Journal of Research in Crime and Delinquency* 41(4): 407–432.

Venkatesh, Sudhir. 2008. *Gang Leader for a Day: A Rogue Sociologist Takes to the Streets*. New York: Penguin Group.

Vigil, Ernesto B. 1999. *The Crusade for Justice: Chicano Militancy and the Government's War on Dissent*. Madison, WI: University of Wisconsin Press.

Viglione, Jill, Lance Hannon, and Robert DeFina. 2011. "The Impact of Light Skin on Prison Time for Black Female Offenders." *The Social Science Journal* 48(1): 250–258.

Villalón, Roberta. 2010. *Violence Against Latina Immigrants: Citizenship, Inequality, and Community*. New York: New York University Press.

Visher, Christy A. 1983. "Gender, Police Arrest Decisions, and Notions of Chivalry." *Criminology* 21(1): 5–28.

Vogt Yuan, Anastasia S. 2010. "Black–White Differences in Aging Out of Substance Use and Abuse." *Sociological Spectrum* 31(1): 3–31.

Wacquant, Loïc. 2010. "Crafting the Neoliberal State: Workfare, Prisonfare, and Social Insecurity." *Sociological Forum* 25(2): 197–220.

Walker, Alice. 1983. *In Search of Our Mothers' Gardens: Womanist Prose*. Orlando, FL: Harcourt.

Wang, Gabe T., Hengrui Qiao, Shaowei Hong, and Jie Zhang. 2002. "Adolescent Social Bond, Self-Control, and Deviant Behavior in China." *International Journal of Contemporary Sociology* 39(1): 52–68.

Ward, Jeffrey T., John H. Boman, and Shayne Jones. 2012. "Hirschi's Redefined Self-Control: Assessing the Implications of the Merger Between Social- and Self-Control Theories." *Crime & Delinquency*. Online Version of Record published before inclusion in an issue.

Warren, Carol A.B., and Tracy Xavia Karner. 2010. *Discovering Qualitative Methods: Field Research, Interviews, and Analysis* (2nd edn.). New York: Oxford University Press.

Weber, Jennifer Beggs. 2012. "Becoming Teen Fathers: Stories of Teen Pregnancy, Responsibility and Masculinity." *Gender & Society* 26(6): 900–921.

Weeks, Jeffrey. 2010. *Sexuality* (3rd edn.). Oxford: Routledge.

Weis, Lois, Michelle Fine, Amira Proweller, Corrine Bertram, and Julia Marusza. 1998. "'I've Slept in My Clothes Long Enough': Excavating the Sounds of Domestic Violence Among Women in the White Working Class." *The Urban Review* 30(1): 1–27.

West, Candace, and Sarah Fenstermaker. 1995. "Doing Difference." *Gender & Society* 9(1): 8–37.

West, Candace, and Don H. Zimmerman. 1987. "Doing Gender." *Gender & Society* 1(2): 125–151.

White, Deborah Gray. 1999. *Too Heavy a Load: Black Women in Defense of Themselves, 1894–1994*. New York: W.W. Norton.

Williams, Rhonda Y. 2008. "Black Women and Black Power." *Organization of American Historians Magazine of History* 22(3): 22–26.

Wing, Adrien K. (ed.). 1997. *Critical Race Feminism: A Reader*. New York: New York University Press.

Wing, Adrien K. 2003. *Critical Race Feminism: A Reader* (2nd edn.). New York: New York University Press.

Woods, Jordan Blair. 2014. "'Queering Criminology': Overview of the State of the Field." Pp. 15–41 in *Handbook of LGBT Communities, Crime, and Justice* edited by Dana Peterson, and Vanessa R. Panfil. New York: Springer.

Wright, John Paul, Stephen G. Tibbetts, and Leah E. Daigle. 2015. *Criminals in the Making* (2nd edn.). Thousand Oaks, CA: Sage.

Wright, Richard, Robert H. Logie, and Scott Decker. 1995. "Criminal Expertise and Offender Decision Making: An Experimental Study of the Target Selection Process in Residential Burglary." *Journal of Research in Crime and Delinquency* 32(1): 39–53.

Yamada, Mitsuye. 1981[2001]. "Invisibility Is an Unnatural Disaster." Pp. 34–40 in *This Bridge Called My Back: Writings by Radical Women of Color* edited by Cherríe L. Moraga, and Gloria E. Anzaldúa. Berkeley, CA: Third Women Press.

Young Lords Party Central Committee. 25 September 1970. "The Young Lords Party Position Paper on Women." *Palante* 2(12): 11–14.

Zahn, Margaret A., Robert Agnew, Diana Fishbein, Shari Miller, Donna-Marie Winn, Gayle Dakoff, Candace Kruttschnitt, Peggy Giordano, Denise

C. Gottfredson, Allison A. Payne, Barry C. Feld, and Meda Chesney-Lind. 2010. *Causes and Correlates of Girls' Delinquency*. Washington, DC: Office of Juvenile Justice and Delinquency Prevention, US Department of Justice. Available at https://www.ncjrs.gov/pdffiles1/ojjdp/226358.pdf (last accessed January 7, 2015).

Zuberi, Tukufu. 2001. *Thicker Than Blood: How Racial Statistics Lie*. Minneapolis, MN: University of Minnesota Press.

INDEX